COUNTERINSURGENCY AND THE GLOBAL WAR ON TERROR

COUNTERINSURGENCY AND THE GLOBAL WAR ON TERROR

Military Culture and Irregular War

ROBERT M. CASSIDY

PRAEGER SECURITY INTERNATIONAL
Westport, Connecticut • London

Library of Congress Cataloging-in-Publication Data

Cassidy, Robert M., Ph.D.
  Counterinsurgency and the Global War on Terror : military culture and irregular war /
Robert M. Cassidy.
      p. cm.
  Includes bibliographical references and index.
  ISBN 0-275-98990-9 (alk. paper)
      1. Counterinsurgency.   2. War on Terrorism, 2001–   3. Insurgency.   4. World politics—
21st century.   I. Title.
  U241.C37   2006
  355.02'18—dc22   2006001236

British Library Cataloguing in Publication Data is available.

Library of Congress Catalog Card Number: 2006001236
ISBN: 0-275-98990-9

First published in 2006

Praeger Security International, 88 Post Road West, Westport, CT 06881
An imprint of Greenwood Publishing Group, Inc.
www.praeger.com

Printed in the United States of America

The paper used in this book complies with the
Permanent Paper Standard issued by the National
Information Standards Organization (Z39.48-1984).

10   9   8   7   6   5   4   3   2   1

Contents

Preface

THIS STUDY BEGINS with a quick examination of the war that the United States has waged since September 2001, examining it not as a "Global War on Terror" (GWOT), but as a global insurgency and counterinsurgency. al Qaeda and its affiliates comprise a novel and evolving form of networked insurgents who operate globally. They have harnessed the advantages of globalization. They employ terrorism as tactics, subsuming this terror within their overarching aims to undermine the Western system of states. Placing the war against al Qaeda and its allied groups and organizations in the context of a global insurgency also presents implications for doctrine, interagency coordination, and military cultural change. Military cultural change is a precondition to military transformation. This book views the current war as an evolving insurgency of a new kind. While it has some similarities to twentieth-century revolutionary guerrilla war, it also engenders differences. Two things are certain—this evolving hybrid form of insurgency remains the strategy of the weak, and it embraces the hit-and-run tactics associated with guerrillas.

The book combines the foremost maxims of the most prominent Western philosopher of war and the most renowned Eastern philosopher of war to arrive at this threefold overarching theme: know the enemy, know yourself, and know what kind of war you are embarking upon. Thus, the first chapter offers a distilled analysis of al Qaeda and its associated networks, with a particular focus on ideology and culture. The second chapter offers some generalizations about the challenges that big powers face when they prosecute counterinsurgencies. The subsequent three chapters each examine the Russian, American, and British military cultures in the context of their capacity or propensity for counterinsurgency. The concluding chapter focuses on historical examples of American, British, and French examples of successful and effective approaches during some of their many counterinsurgent wars during and before the twentieth century. This chapter also offers some value in that it refines and distills some ideas about measuring the effectiveness and the success of counterinsurgent efforts.

This study is germane because it provides a different perspective on an evolving approach to prosecuting the war. The conclusion offers implications for the U.S. military because it did for a very long time almost exclusively embrace a conventional, big-war, paradigm, to the detriment of a capacity to prosecute counterinsurgency. The insights in this book offer value in that they look at both the cultural impediments and successful techniques for waging counterinsurgency, incorporating over a century's worth of survey examples from several different military traditions.

Acknowledgments

I THANK Colonel Dean Nowowiejski for initiating some of the research that ultimately found its way into this book; it appears in the concluding chapter, which examines the lessons that the U.S. Army should have learned from Vietnam and earlier. I am also grateful to Dr. Kevin Stringer for his excellent contribution of the section on the British experience with indigenous forces in Chapter 6. I also thank Fred Wham at the Center for Army Lessons Learned and Meg Tulloch at the USAREUR Research Library. I add a very special thanks to my wife, Chris; my son, Robert; and my daughter, Hailey, for supporting my writing hobby. Finally, we should continue to acknowledge, offer our gratitude to, and show our respect for those soldiers serving in our legions who are defending the rights of our citizens at home and abroad, who, by their presence bring benefits to the populations in forsaken nether regions that genuinely seek liberty and basic rights. Our citizens also need to understand, support, and protect the obligations we made to our soldiers and their families, as they themselves are protecting America's overseas enterprises with their sacrifices.

World War X

The Revolution in Global Insurgency[1]

> Tomorrow's guerrilla armies, in Africa, in Asia, in Latin America, will be drawn from the ranks of the world's have-nots, the hungry peasants and urban slum dwellers who meet the first requirement of the guerrilla, having nothing to lose but their lives.—*The War of the Flea*[2]

> This is a guerrilla war. Not one waged within a state, but one waged across states. Each guerrilla action is designed to elicit an overreaction that will, in turn, increase the guerrilla's support within Islam. The aggressor has a discernible organization. It has forces organized into combat formations, dispersed individuals with varying degrees of training, field commanders, and senior leadership.—*Waging Ancient War*[3]

THE FIRST QUOTE, from a book published in 1965, is prescient, and the second quote is percipient. On the one hand, many of today's guerrillas and terrorists do in fact come from Asia, Africa, and South America while others also come from the Caucasus, the Balkans, and other fringes of Eurasia. The terrorists and global guerrillas of the twenty-first century are incubating in Asia, Africa, South America, and the periphery of Europe. They also hail from amid the populations of the West as alienated expatriates galvanize in and around mosques where they become proselytes to a radicalized version of Islam, preached by mullahs linked to al Qaeda–affiliated groups. On the other hand, America's enemies in this global conflict, especially those affiliated with or allied with "the base" (al Qaeda), are fighting a guerrilla war of global scale and scope in Iraq, Afghanistan, the Philippines, the Horn of Africa, and Europe. Employing terror to attack the United States and its allies at home and abroad, from the sea, the air, and the ground, they aim to erode the will of the coalition and its indigenous partners using guerrilla tactics and suicide bombers to shed blood and *to protract* the war. However, the "Global War on Terrorism" (GWOT) is a misnomer and is not very helpful in describing and circumscribing our enemy and the kind of war we are prosecuting. From November 2005 through March of 2006, moreover, the leadership in the American defense establishment began to alter its vernacular to somewhat supplant the awkward misnomer of GWOT with the term the "Long War." National security documents that emerged during this period, in fact, began to describe this "Long War" as the defining struggle of this generation and as one that shifts emphasis from large-scale conventional military operations to small-scale counterinsurgency operations. The Long War will be unlimited in time and in space and it may last for decades, as it will be a protracted, or perennial, war to defeat a movement animated by takfir ideologues with a global following. The war against al Qaeda, its associate groups, and other groups that rally behind the ideological banner of radical Islamic fundamentalism is better viewed as a global counterinsurgency in which the United States and its coalition partners endeavor to isolate and eradicate an overlapping network of nasty nihilists who seek sanctuary, support, and recruits in the ungoverned periphery and in failing states.

The paradox is that these same groups have harvested the benefits of globalization and the information age to bring about a revolution in insurgent warfare. In a 1997 interview, bin Laden himself characterized his organization as both a result of and a reaction to globalization. al Qaeda and others have adopted networked and dispersed organizational approaches, employing information age technology and exploiting the freedom of transnational movement introduced by globalization, to attack strategic targets asymmetrically in some of the most powerful states. It is also clear that al Qaeda and similar groups are harvesting the benefits of this revolution in unorthodox warfare to help wage and to supply some of the manpower for the insurgencies in Afghanistan and Iraq. The vehicle for this transformation is the non-state armed group and al Qaeda was the first such group to achieve genuinely revolutionary changes "in terms of its capacity to use violence in new ways to level direct strategic blows against the United States with strategic consequences." Moreover, the escalated insurgent violence and the concomitant bloodshed in Iraq is a potential harbinger for grave strategic consequences because if a "peace with dishonor" approach compels the United States and its coalition partners to withdraw before reconstruction and democratization objectives are genuinely met, this may be perceived as a strategic defeat for the United States and the West. Indicators of the global nature of this insurgency are manifold: For instance, Abu Masab Zarqawi, a Jordanian, is leading one very lethal faction of the insurgency in Iraq—al Qaeda Committee for the Land of Two Rivers—that is nominally linked to al Qaeda and that employs a potpourri of international suicide *mujahideen* from Saudi Arabia, Sudan, Yemen, Chechnya, and elsewhere. Second, although not in alliance, both al Qaeda and Hezbollah and their affiliated surrogates have employed guerrilla and terrorist tactics to attack Western and Israeli targets globally and within regional contexts—evidence of this is the fact that Hezbollah and elements of the Iranian Guards Corps have been purportedly importing highly lethal shape-charge technology developed in Lebanon into Iraq for use by Iranian bomb squads; and third, both Sunni-derived and Shiite-derived radical fundamentalist ideologies, using similar militantly anti-Western rationale, are being instrumentalized to mobilize and animate jihadists from all around the globe.[4]

The bad news is that counterinsurgency is more difficult than fighting against enemies who fight according to the West's preferred paradigm of war. Modern military history shows that the West and its military forces have generally dominated and monopolized the conventional paradigm of war, usually winning when the East or the South decided to fight them according to this paradigm. The philosophies of Jomini, Clausewitz, and Svechin are embedded in the cultures of Western militaries, and some of them have exhibited an almost exclusive preference for a big, conventional-war, paradigm. One characteristic of this preferred way of war has been an embracement of the direct use of military force, combining maneuver and firepower to mass combat power at the decisive point in order bring about the *destruction* or *annihilation* of some enemy force or army. Conversely, the U.S. Army has historically marginalized counterinsurgency as an ephemeral anomaly. Unfortunately, this military cultural propensity has prevented the U.S. Army and some other Western armies from seriously studying and learning the theory and practice of counterinsurgency warfare and from embedding it in their institutional memories. This is despite having an institutional history with many examples of success, or at least qualified success, in counterinsurgency.

A mutating and ideologically driven global insurgency engendered by a stateless, adaptive, complex, and polycephalous host, moreover, is even more challenging than traditional insurgencies. Another challenge is that the type of enemy that we are most likely to fight for the foreseeable future is one who has for many more centuries embraced a different philosophy of war. Potential adversaries are from Asia and the East, from cultures that have generally espoused an Eastern tradition of war. The Eastern way of war stems from the philosophies of Sun Tzu and Mao Tse-Tung, and it is distinguishable from the Western way by its reliance on indirectness, perfidy, attrition, and protraction. In other words, the Eastern way of war is inherently more irregular, unorthodox, and asymmetric than our traditional conception of war. According to one distinguished British historian, the history of culture's development in Asia clearly demonstrates that is a major determinant of the character of warfare. If there is such a thing as an Oriental way of war as something that is discernible and distinct from a European way of warfare, it is characterized by behavior unique to it. John Keegan has posited that delay, evasion, and indirectness are three distinguishable behavioral traits of an Eastern way of war. Furthermore, as a result of the U.S. coalitions' two victories against Iraq during the two principally conventional wars in the Persian Gulf in 1991 and 2003, it is unlikely that another second-tier power will be so injudicious as to fight the United States and its allies according to this Western warfare paradigm again.[5]

Otto von Bismarck was once reported to have stated: "Fools say they learn from experience; I prefer to learn from the experience of others." The fact that a significant number of American and coalition troops have been fighting to counter insurgencies in Afghanistan, Iraq, the Philippines, the Horn of Africa, and elsewhere during the first decade of the twenty-first century provides a very realistic and grave impetus for the idea that learning from the experiences of other counterinsurgencies from the past is preferable to adapting in contact. Moreover, an important corollary to this is the imperative to learn from and adapt to the current counterinsurgencies, and to capture them in our institutional memory, instead of erasing these experiences because of a perception that counterinsurgency is once again a fleeting aberration. The American military's voluminous lessons in counterinsurgency have been recorded but have not been read or taught very much until recently given renewed impetus as a consequence of the challenges associated with the insurgency in Iraq. This book places the current global war against al Qaeda and others in a more comprehensible context, as a protracted and complex global insurgency waged by networks and groupings of transnational insurgents and terrorists motivated by extremist religious ideology. I borrow my organization for this book from both Clausewitz and Sun Tzu, by fusing together two of their more ubiquitous truisms to arrive at this framework: know the enemy, know yourself, and know what kind of war you are prosecuting.[6]

Chapter 1 examines the current international security landscape using the framework of understanding the enemy, understanding ourselves, and understanding the kind of war that predominates. It offers a distilled analysis of the evolution of insurgency in the context of radical Islamic fundamentalist *jihad* non–state-armed groups. It also offers a short explanation of the challenges that the U.S. military will need to overcome to be successful in this environment. The last part of this chapter examines current counterinsurgency doctrine. Chapter 2 explains the contradictions that have historically plagued the conventional militaries of big powers when they have attempted to wage counterinsurgencies against ostensibly weaker adversaries in the periphery or less developed parts of the world. It also offers some very concise vignettes to demonstrate the dynamics of these paradoxes.

Chapter 3 offers an analysis of Russian military culture. This chapter also explains the impediments that those military cultural preferences have presented when Russia attempted to prosecute counterinsurgencies in Afghanistan and Chechnya. It also provides some short examples of how those paradoxes explained in Chapter 2, along with Russian military cultural preferences, contributed to its failure in those two wars. Chapter 4 examines British military culture. This chapter also provides a distilled explanation of how British military cultural preferences better enabled the British military to adapt and prosecute small wars and counterinsurgencies. Chapter 5 offers an analysis of American military culture. This chapter also explains the impediments that U.S. military cultural preferences have presented when the American Army has attempted to prosecute counterinsurgencies in Vietnam and in the past.

Chapter 6 is the concluding chapter, and it examines previous counterinsurgencies to glean those tactics and approaches that did help achieve some degree of success. It succinctly explains relevant American, British, and French experiences, including the Indian wars, the Philippine Insurrection, Indochina, Malaya, Algeria, Rhodesia, and Vietnam. This chapter also emphasizes the enduring axiom that the early employment of indigenous forces in a counterinsurgent role can be very effective in prosecuting counterinsurgency. The final part of this chapter offers some observations and past and present thoughts on measures of effectiveness within the context of counterinsurgency.

THE ENEMY: OVERLAPPING NETWORKS
OF INSURGENTS-CUM-TERRORISTS

We must make war everywhere and cause dispersal of his forces and dissipation of his strength.—*On Guerrilla Warfare*[7]

Al Qaeda is also characterized by a broad-based ideology, a novel structure, a robust capacity for regeneration and a very diverse membership that cuts across ethnic, class, and national boundaries. It is neither a single group nor a coalition of groups: it comprised a core base or bases in Afghanistan; satellite terrorist cells worldwide; a conglomerate of Islamist political parties; and other largely independent terrorist groups that it draws on for offensive actions and other responsibilities.—*Inside Al Qaeda*[8]

al Qaeda and its associate groups espouse an ideology that can mobilize and animate a broad base of support while minimizing national, class, ethnic, or intra-Islamic sectarian boundaries. The enemies of the United States in this global war are complex, adaptive, asymmetric, innovative, dispersed, networked, resilient, and capable of regeneration. The groups that affiliate with the al Qaeda group function as a loose coalition, each with its own command, control, and communications structures. According to one expert on al Qaeda, "the coalition has one unique characteristic that enhances its resilience and allows forces to be multiplied in pursuit of a particular objective: whenever necessary, these groups interact or merge, cooperating ideologically, financially, and technically." In 1998, al Qaeda reorganized into four distinct but interconnected entities to further advance the goals of radical Islam: The first was a pyramidal structure to enable better strategic and tactical direction; the second was a global network of terrorists; the third consisted of guerrilla warfare bases inside Afghanistan; and the fourth was a loose alliance of transnational insurgent and terrorist groups. Even though al Qaeda is a political entity infused with a radical religious ideology, its operations are founded on a cultural network from which it recruits known persons; it has no formal process by which it recruits and promotes its members. The longevity and resilience of al Qaeda are not predicated on the total quantity of terrorists and insurgents that it may have trained in the past but more simply on its capacity to continue to recruit, mobilize, and inspire both actual and potential fighters, supporters, and sympathizers.[9]

al Qaeda and like-minded Islamist fanatics are waging a global *jihad* that draws on historical roots: Muslim reactions to colonial rule; a series of military defeats at the hands of the West; a profound sense of humiliation and a desire for revenge; a host of failing governments and economies in the Middle East, North Africa, South Asia, and Southeast Asia; an increase in emigration accompanied by the isolation and alienation frequently felt by marginalized immigrant *diasporas*; a vivified sense of unity among all Muslims fueled by charismatic leaders like Osama bin Laden, who use images of suffering Muslims—in Bosnia,

Chechnya, Palestine, and Iraq—to animate followers; and a common sense of purpose and lasting cohesion created by the ultimately successful *jihad* against the Soviet Union in Afghanistan. bin Laden's overarching aim is to supplant the Westphalian secular state system with a medieval caliphate system based on an extreme interpretation of Islam. The foci in this struggle are generally the indigenous populations located in the belt running along the north of Africa, through the Middle East, across central Asia, to the Islamic frontiers of Indonesia and the Philippines—what has been called an "arc of instability." With few exceptions, the states along this arc are failing or have regimes that are unpopular, untenable, or oppressive.[10]

Moreover, bin Laden "provided a suitably inspirational manifesto for a disparate mass of Muslims who saw themselves as victims and as an underclass, and his success restored their self-esteem." He developed a very effective clarion call that essentially cut across a divided Islamic culture. This rallying cry is easily understandable to every Muslim because it is strong in condemnation and it is attractively vague about the future. bin Laden's multipurpose declaration was a necessary instrument to mobilize a very divided constituency of supporters. Active support for al Qaeda hails from a broad range of professional classes, teachers, engineers, and students and from a diverse array of ethnic groups. Even more alarming, however, is the notion that both Sunni and Shiite Muslim groups may support al Qaeda training and initiatives as a result of a June 1996 Iranian initiative to include al Qaeda representation in Hezbollah International. The unusual characteristic of al Qaeda is that its insurgent and terrorist activities come from a wide array of supporters, whose culture, race, and professional background may vary hugely but who nonetheless are so committed to the movement that they will sacrifice themselves for it. In most cases, a radical fundamentalist religious belief provides their common connection or bond. Many Muslim communities may even see the world from the perspective of an underclass, whose most personal sense of identity is also challenged by Western values, the ubiquity and constancy of which highlight an essentially and unambiguously successful culture that visibly dominates the communications, commerce, technology, and global security arenas.[11]

Through his al Qaeda network, bin Laden uses his interpretive and distorted view of Islam as an instrument to mobilize warriors behind the ideological banner of *jihad*. However, *jihad* is one of the basic tasks assigned for Muslims by the Prophet. This word, which essentially means "striving," was usually cited in the context of "striving in the path of God" and was interpreted to mean an armed struggle for the advancement or defense of Muslim power. In theory, *jihad* was divided into two houses: the House of Islam, in which a Muslim polity ruled and Muslim law predominated; and the House of War, the remainder of the world, still populated by, and more saliently, was reigned over by infidels. In the sixteenth century, Ebu's Su'ud, an Ottoman scholar, described *jihad* in language that is not dissimilar from the instrumentally biased version of Islam that radical fundamentalists employ today: "*jihad* is incumbent not on every individual but on the Muslim community as a whole. Fighting should be continual and should last until the end of time." It follows therefore from this somewhat skewed and exclusionary perspective on Islam and *jihad* that peace with the infidel is ultimately not possible, although a Muslim commander or ruler is permitted to make a temporary truce if it is to the long-term benefit of a Muslim community. This type of an instrumental truce is not binding in any legal way, according to this interpretation of Islam. Thus, al Qaeda and some groups affiliated with al Qaeda have sought to use a circumscribed version of Islam and to ignore the fact that the sacred texts emphasized justice and restraint as well. There are also different ways in which to meet the obligation to participate in *jihad*, ranging from fighting a *jihad* with the sword, to participating with the heart or tongue. Another aspect of *jihad* that is omitted from such biased interpretations is that *jihad* can also simply denote a personal struggle to live as a good Muslim.[12]

In fact, the Wahhabi version of the Koran includes a special appendix on *jihad*, the purpose of which is to refute the liberal Muslim notion that *jihad* is not inevitably required of all Muslims at all times. The Wahhabi version thus argues that *jihad* is required of all Muslims at all times and helps buttress the claims of bin Laden and other radical fundamentalists that they are fighting against a Judeo-Christian crusade and that it is the duty of all Muslims to wage *jihad*. Philosophically, spiritually, and physically, then, *jihad* can be subsumed within a mythical and heroic framework of Islamic ideology and is thus a force within Islam that can create a society devoted to the service of God. This is germane in several ways. One, many Muslims espouse the perspective that this is a time of crisis for Islam. For them, it is not only the West that poses a grave threat to the Muslim community but also the apostate rulers, or satraps, who rule oppressive governments within the lands of Islam that pose a threat. Two, *jihad* is a pathway to a renaissance within Islam, but that rebirth necessitates a spiritual as well as an armed struggle. Three, no one is excluded from this struggle because Islam is in peril at its very core. Last, this collective defense of the House of Islam animates a feeling of unity for all Muslims—a panegyric for the perpetual struggle that frames the Islamic experience in mythical terms. As it is applied to *jihad,* this interpretation of Islamic doctrine emphasizes the centrality of perpetual struggle as a condition of the religion.[13]

> We avoid the construct, but it is for America's current jihadist foes a religious war starting centuries ago and lasting until judgment day. It is this mindset that has been grafted upon the tactics of contemporary terrorism. The two now flow together, applying jihadist codes of operation to a terrorist repertoire. It is a powerful and dangerous combination. Today's terrorist adversaries have no intention of matching America's superior military capability. They intend to exploit its vulnerabilities. Like all religious fanatics, they see themselves as morally superior, armed with the sword of God, commanded to wage holy war.[14]

bin Laden has thus wrapped himself in the banner of *jihad* and submerged himself in an endless and "ahistorical story of Islam." That this story has been so fervently and frequently replayed is not astonishing. What is astonishing is how the West ignores its claim and forgets the refrain of an entire community that has experienced a crisis of identity, as well as a complex of inferiority, vis-à-vis Western culture and progress. Even though the United States has characterized al Qaeda as a terrorist network, as though it were a syndicate of criminal gangs, al Qaeda has benefited from the support, sometimes only passive, of millions of Muslims across the globe. It is not difficult to discern how bin Laden and al Qaeda view themselves through their own lenses. Like the Prophet Mohammed, bin Laden sees himself as "the warrior prodigal with his band of *mujahideen*, sweeping out of the desert to renew a degenerate Arabia—an Arabia run by a subverted kingdom, which in turn is run by foreign infidels." bin Laden, moreover, has declared in his decree for the Jews and Crusaders that the duty of every capable Muslim is to kill civilian and military Americans and their allies, wherever possible, until the U.S. armed forces and their coalition allies have vacated the lands of Islam and no longer pose a threat to Muslims.[15]

According to Cheryl Bernard, a RAND expert on Islamic ideology, four ideological positions essentially prevail throughout the Muslim world today: secularists, traditionalists, modernists, and fundamentalists. Two of these positions are most salient in the global struggle against terrorists—the fundamentalists' and the modernists' positions. On the one hand, the fundamentalists reject contemporary Western culture and eschew democratic values. They seek a Draconian and authoritarian state to promulgate an extreme interpretation of Islamic morality and law. They are able and willing to adapt, innovate, and leverage modern technology to achieve their aims. Fundamentalists are not averse to any type of violence against all types of targets. Unlike scriptural fundamentalists, radical fundamentalists "are much less concerned with the literal substance of Islam, with which they take considerable liberties either deliberately or because of the ignorance of orthodox Islamic doctrine." The Taliban, al Qaeda, and a host of other radical Islamic radical movements and groups are subsumed within this fundamentalist category and it is a global phenomenon. On the other hand, modernists want the Islamic world to become part of the modern world. They aspire to reform Islam in order to reconcile it with modernity. They deliberately seek a far-sweeping transformation of the contemporary orthodox interpretation and practice of Islam. Moreover, the modernists' central values—a community based on social responsibility, equality, and freedom, and individual conscience—are congruous with modern democratic principles.[16]

Ideology notwithstanding, the *mujahideen* veterans of the Soviet-Afghan War initially provided the nucleus of al Qaeda's fighting force. Their incentives to continue to fight and to prosecute *jihad* outside of Afghanistan were manifold: an innate desire to continue in meaningful activity, the need to ensure the survival of their organization, and an infatuation with a self-image that was inflated as a result of their defeat of a superpower. Moreover, their like-minded Taliban brethren's subsequent victories essentially guaranteed sanctuary for al Qaeda's holy warriors and its training camps, which graduated thousands more volunteers.

What bin Laden and his associates contributed to this strong but unfocused pool of veterans was a sense of mission, vision, and strategy that conflated the twentieth-century theory of a unified Islamic political power with a renaissance of the Islamic caliphate paradigm. It reframed myriad local conflicts into one singular struggle between a genuine form of Islam and a host of corrupt rulers who would fall without the backing of the West and the United States, in particular. By expunging the conceptual borders between individual states and their wars, al Qaeda then was able to draw its recruits and operatives from a bigger pool of humanity. Secured in the haven of Afghanistan, sufficiently funded, supported by Pakistan, and animated by a powerful ideology, al Qaeda became the rallying banner of Islam's answer to past frustrations, humiliations, trepidations, and defeats.[17]

In their view, they had already driven the Russians out of Afghanistan, in a defeat so overwhelming that it led directly to the collapse of the Soviet Union itself. Having overcome the superpower that they had always regarded as more formidable, they felt ready to take on the other; in this they were encouraged by the opinion, often expressed by bin Laden, among others, that America was a paper tiger. Their hatred is neither constrained by fear nor diluted by respect.[18]

The *mujahideen* from the Afghan war were a proven force as a result of their training and war experiences fighting the Soviets. Although this group was ethnically heterogeneous, its members were linked by al Qaeda's base network as well as by their trust in bin Laden's leadership. "They were a brotherhood, which had come together to face adversity in the same war and had passed to and from Afghanistan through the same al Qaeda system to return as legitimate citizens in their 50 different countries of origin." bin Laden has and does use them as an instrument of his attacks on the West. The largest part of the force, numbering in the tens of thousands, was organized, trained, and equipped as insurgent combat forces in the crucible, the Soviet-Afghan war. A large number in this pool hailed from Saudi Arabia and Yemen. Some also fought in Bosnia, and U.S. forces encountered them in Somalia. Another group, which is approximately 10,000 strong, live in Western states and have received combat training of some shape or form. A third group has approximately several thousand members and is capable of commanding the aforementioned forces. A couple hundred individuals, that include both heads of known terrorist organizations and officials operating with or without the authority of their state governments, comprise the al Qaeda network's top command structure. bin Laden most likely viewed the events of 2001 as a renewal of the struggle for the religious domination of the globe that started back in the seventh century. It created another moment of opportunity for him and his underlings. To them, "America exemplifies the civilization and embodies the leadership of the House of War, and, like Rome and Byzantium, it has become degenerate and demoralized, ready to be overthrown."[19]

Not only did these veterans share a common bond derived from the ordeal of the Soviet war, but many or most members of the al Qaeda group come from the lands of the East, whose warriors for centuries have embraced a way of warfare distinct and different from the Western way of war. The preferred style of combat in the Eastern way of warfare for a span of almost 3000 years was the horse warrior: "that was, indeed, one in which evasion, delay, and indirectness were paramount." The horse warriors elected to fight from a distance and to employ missiles instead of edged weapons; when confronted, they would withdraw with determination and count upon wearing down an enemy by prolongation and attrition rather than by defeating him in one single trial of arms. According to one popular military writer, the enemies we will most likely fight in the future will not be soldiers with the discipline, modernity, and orthodoxy that term evokes in the West but rather warriors, defined as "erratic primitives of shifting allegiance, habituated to violence, with no stake in civil order." These barbaric warriors, unlike Western warrior soldiers, do not play by rules, do not respect conventions, and do not comply with unpleasant orders. Warriors have always been around, but with the rise of professional soldieries their importance was eclipsed. Now, thanks to the confluence of fragmented former empires, stateless global insurgents, and the diminution of a warrior ethos in parts of the postmodern West, the warrior thug has returned to the fore, with more financing, arms, and brutality than since the fourteenth century. A great danger that we face is savage warriors who do not recognize the civilized constraints by which we operate and who will do absolutely anything to achieve their ends. Germinating in the Hobbesian deprivation of overpopulated wastelands or frustrated over their perceived cultural defeat in Muslim lands, these warriors not only commit atrocities but seem to derive immense pleasure in doing so. The decapitation fad was only one of the most recent manifestations of the barbaric proclivities of the stateless "warriors" of the twenty-first century.[20]

At the same time, however, many Muslims may harbor profound feelings of resentment as a consequence of the relatively bloodless seizure of Baghdad and the perceived unchecked projection of American power and influence in the region. al Qaeda's skillful propagandists effectively translated the U.S. coalitions' seizure of Baghdad and the subsequent occupation of Iraq as the latest in a series of humiliating historic defeats of the Muslims by the West that must now be avenged. Although the voice of radical Islamic terrorism speaks of targeting the entire West as its enemy, its offensive is now directed principally against the United States as the very essence of Western civilization's preeminence in the world. What is more alarming, however, is that al Qaeda's resiliency, along with its potential longevity, does not stem from the agglomeration of jihadists who it may have trained or not trained in the past but more from its continued capacity to recruit, to mobilize, and to inspire both current and future fighters and supporters. In a different form and with a different repertoire, the al Qaeda group and its associates are twenty-first century barbarians: they hide at the ends of the earth and the hinterland; they recruit, train, and proliferate from sanctuary; and they collude to plan indirect and insidious attacks against population centers and against symbols of American Imperium abroad. As a footnote, one expert on asymmetric warfare noted a changed form of warfare "may emerge from non-Western cultural traditions, such as Islamic or Asiatic traditions." Moreover, the fact that some non-Western adversaries in the Islamic world are not inherently strong in technology will impel them to develop and employ asymmetric warfare through *ideas* rather than through technology.[21]

WHITHER A REVOLUTION IN INSURGENT WARFARE?

The Pentagon's focus on rapid, decisive operations is largely irrelevant in this type of war.[22]

We wage a global war on terror—a confusing array of threats—while we continue to concentrate on future conventional wars with hypothetical, nation-state foes. We still consign all lesser contingencies to the other war as opposed real war. We still tend to view the enemy through the narrow bores and restricted optics of our existing national security structure.[23]

A strategic paradox exists when an ostensibly militarily superior power confronts a seemingly inferior opponent because the superior power has unlimited means but generally has limited aims; the obverse is true for the ostensibly outmatched opponent. This paradox inheres in the war against al Qaeda because the United States has characterized this war as a war on terrorism. However, this somewhat limited definition of the enemy has formed the basis of a U.S. strategy that uses limited means to achieve its ends and has not properly identified the war's wider scope as an insurgency being waged by non–state-armed groups. An accurate conception about what type of war one is prosecuting is one of Clausewitz's foremost maxims. A more accurate conception of the conflict is as a global insurgency waged against the Westphalian system of states. The enemy commonly uses classic insurgency methods within failing or failed Islamic states. bin Laden has underscored the asymmetric merits of insurgent warfare and has consistently lauded the victory that he argues was realized by using this approach against American forces in Somalia. bin Laden also proclaimed in his 1996 declaration of war "that, due to the imbalance of power between our armed forces and the enemy armed forces, a suitable means of fighting must be adopted, i.e., using fast moving light forces that work under complete secrecy." Thus, the other half of this strategic paradox has al Qaeda and its associates using limited but networked and technology-enabled means to wage total war against the secular regimes in the Middle East, against Israel, and against the West. Its aim is total— to undo the Western state system and to establish a caliphate, imposing an interpretive version of universal Islamic law under its rule. al Qaeda is simply a nucleus group behind various fighting organizations representing the radical Islamic fundamentalist insurgency that is metastasizing within greater Islam.[24]

Fanaticism and barbarism are not novel, but what is novel is the coupling of barbaric and asymmetric methods with a global and radical Islamic fundamentalist ideology that supplies a potentially endless line of recruits and allies for a global struggle. bin Laden and his network have broadened the scope of insurgency to include a "global dimension." al Qaeda's methods are broadly relevant and appealing to other similarly dispersed terrorist groups. al Qaeda has an adaptive model of organization, and its sources of support, the nature of its organization, and the environment in which it operates are all global and transnational. The international scope of their organization, objectives, intent, recruiting base, and organization differentiates global guerrillas from popular guerillas operating within one region or state. As additional examples of the enemy network's propensity for insurgency on a regional and global scale, a 9 April 2003 declaration posted on al Qaeda's phantom Web site (al Neda), under the caption, "Guerrilla Warfare is the Most Powerful Weapon Muslims Have and it is the Best Method to Continue the Conflict with the Crusader Enemy," states "the successful attempts of dealing defeat to invaders using guerrilla warfare were many, and we will not expound on them. However, these attempts have proven that the most effective method for the materially weak against the materially strong is guerrilla warfare." Moreover, a former Egyptian Army special forces officer named Saif al-Adel, one of al Qaeda's most senior operational commanders, has promoted "the use of guerrilla warfare tactics against the American and British forces in Iraq" and provided explicit and copious practical guidance on how to carry them out.[25]

U.S. Army doctrine defines insurgency as "an armed political movement aimed at the overthrow of a constituted government, or separation from it, through use of subversion and armed conflict." It is a protracted political military conflicts aimed at undermining government legitimacy and control increasing insurgent control. Political power is the central issue in an insurgency. The goal of an insurgency is to mobilize material and human resources to establish an alternative counterstate. Effective mobilization enables active and passive support for the insurgency's programs, operations, and goals. Loyalty to the insurgent movement is usually garnered by acts but may also be won by through abstract tenets. On the one hand, pledges to eliminate poverty or end hunger may attract a portion of the people. On the other hand, the desire to eliminate a foreign occupation or to establish a government based on religious or political ideology may attract other parts of the population. Moreover, ideology shapes and animates the insurgents' perception of the environment by providing the lens, to include analytical categories and a lexicon by which conditions are assessed. The effect is that the ideology influences the guerrilla movement's operational and organizational methods. Another study on insurgency by the U.S. Army War College's Strategic Studies Institute underscores the importance of ideology and leaders who can employ that ideology to "unify diverse groups and organizations and impose their will under situations of high stress." Successful guerrilla leaders are so devoted to their movement psychologically that they will persevere although their odds of success are very unfavorable. They become true-faith apostles motivated by vision. Likewise, effective insurgent leaders believe so fervently in their movement that they become absolutely ruthless and capable of doing almost anything to weaken the counterinsurgent forces and to protect their cause.[26]

Unfortunately, globalization and information age technology have enabled a near-revolutionary transformation and conflation of insurgency and terrorism. According to the same Army War College study cited above, "insurgency is likely to continue to mutate or evolve." For example, insurgencies may become increasingly networked, with no centralized command and no common strategy, only a unifying objective. This would make them less effective in terms of seizing power or attaining other political goals but more resilient in the face of host government or global counterinsurgency operations. Information technology and networking have enabled the linkage of a host of various insurgent movements and like-minded organizations, including transnational criminal organizations that operate regionally and globally. The ideological underpinnings of insurgent activities have also metamorphosed. A unifying ideology based on transnational and radical Islam predominates, and there are very few insurgencies still based on the Marxist ideology that heretofore was so central in postcolonial insurgencies. Consequently, radical fundamentalist Islam poses a greater and potentially more complex menace than did Marxism. For example, clerics play a critical role in political and ideological mobilization, but they are not considered acceptable targets. Even still, because radical Islam emphasizes the transcendental and the spiritual, it animates humans of massive destruction—suicide bombers, who were not nearly as common a phenomenon in the previous context of secular Marxist insurgencies.[27]

The resurgence of Islamic ideology is an essential part of this insurgency, making the war as much about Western values as it is about military prowess. Prosecuting a purely military campaign could lead to the extirpation or diminution of those values by the gradual decay of domestic civil liberties. This would also help fulfill one of al Qaeda's war aims to create a divide between the Islamic world and the West. Although the counterinsurgencies in Afghanistan and Iraq certainly have military dimensions, the primary foci should be ideological, political, and economic. The United States will not be successful by using by military force alone; it will be successful if it can strengthen local reformers and allies and if it avoids imposing its own political values. On a macrocosmic level, the war against al Qaeda and radical fundamentalist Islam cannot be won as long as popular anger at the United States in the Islamic world is shaped by perceptions that America is too close to Israel to move forward on the Arab-Israeli peace process. The Western military victory against the Taliban in Afghanistan and the coalition attacks against a host of Islamic fighters in Iraq have further intensified radical Islamic resentment. Although some have viewed Iraq as an imprudent detour from the critical targets in this global counterinsurgency, it has in fact drawn in a host of al Qaeda supporters and *mujahideen* where few existed under Saddam's secular regime. Before Operation Iraqi Freedom, al Qaeda in the Land Between the Two Rivers, Zarqawi's insurgent-cum-terrorist infrastructure and pipeline for suicide bombers, did not exist. Furthermore, many *madrassas* in Pakistan and elsewhere until very recently were still inculcating skewed, interpretive, and unwritten versions of the Koran with the purpose of indoctrinating and mobilizing far more *jihad* fighters daily than the West could ever catch or kill. And al Qaeda, although degraded, still operates as a headless and cross-channeled virtual entity in an elastic alliance with supporters in almost ninety countries.[28]

Some others see this war as a global insurgency that precedes a revolution, where we should view it in the context of Russian revolutionaries in czarist times or in terms of Mao Tse-Tung's theoretical prescriptions for guerrilla warfare. "al Qaeda's 1998 *fatwa* speaks to a scale that mirrors these and many of the other major guerrilla and revolutionary movements that shaped the nineteenth and twentieth centuries." al Qaeda and its affiliates expect to erode America and its allies' economic and social strength sufficiently to cause them to lack the will and the resources to function as international powers. Thus, the world's revolutionary Islamic groups do not ever intend to confront the United States and its allies directly but rather intend to use a guerrilla strategy to attack the West where it is weak and vulnerable—civilians, economic production, etc. Moreover, insurgents and terrorists may use almost exactly the same methods, using force and the threat of force to further their political or ideological agendas. Global insurgents use terror as a tactical instrument, and it is one of several violent tools in their repertoire. According to another report, "al Qaeda represents not terrorism but an insurgency featuring a salafist theology which appeals to significant portions of Muslim believers and which sanctifies terror." al Qaeda and like-minded Islamic fundamentalist revolutionary movements envisage remaking society to be so utterly religious that their faith becomes fundamental, that they can enforce the social stratification therein, and that the clerics are in complete control of an autocratic government apparatus. Through the employment of subversion and armed struggle, with the ultimate goal of establishing a world order ruled by clerics and *shar'ia* law, al Qaeda might be viewed as a non–state actor movement organized with the aim of overthrowing societies, cultures, and values on a global scale. Although religion ostensibly animates al Qaeda, its affiliates, and their recruits, it is essentially a political movement with political objectives. While it may blend some of the tenets of Mao's mass mobilization guerrilla theory with some elements of *foco*'s armed action construct, it also differs in many ways as it is an evolving and mutating insurgency that incorporates transnational networks and a multiethnic international membership.[29]

This war against radical Islam is a guerrilla war: one waged not within a state but across states. Each insurgent guerrilla act is intended to provoke an overreaction that will increase the guerrilla's popular support within Islamic communities. The "base" represents a new wave in warfare because it has adopted a complex organizational structure and because it exploits a powerful mix of high- and low-technology means of warfare. An exponent of unorthodox warfare observed that the origins of a metamorphosing idea-based form of irregular warfare "may be visible in terrorism." Terrorists like those in al Qaeda survive off the land and take haven in their enemies' backyards. Moreover, the global insurgents' highly dispersed battle areas include the entirety of the enemy's society. Many of the characteristics of this global insurgency and terror network indicate a possible shift toward a prototypical form of warfare. One way to identify or discern that war may be witnessing the emergence of a mutation or fusion of insurgency and terrorism is the fact that it seems difficult to arrive at an appropriate moniker for the enemy—names have ranged from noncompliant forces (NCF) and anti-coalition militia (ACM) to opposition militia forces (OMF) or simply "terrorists," "extremists," or "thugs." However, many of the activities of non–state-armed groups without territory-based armies approximate guerrilla warfare. One military expert has commented that the current methods and tactics used by our enemies should not be surprising in view of the last fifty years of Western victories over Islamic armies in conventional wars. Since the Israeli war of independence, when fighting conventional Western-style war, Islamic armies have lost seven wars and won none. However, when fighting unconventional wars against Israel, the United States, and the Soviet Union, Islamic forces have won five and lost none, with the outcome of the war in Iraq as yet undetermined.[30]

The longer that bin Laden and al Qaeda survive, the larger will be their following, as more Muslims across the globe see this *jihad* not as an abstract theological form of hope but as an effective and legitimate way to take action on their anger. The Middle East offers fecund ground in which to foment a revolution, and al Qaeda has harnessed the potential for recruitment in the region more than any other organization. In promulgating its own political agenda, al Qaeda has been able to draw from a reserve of despair and antipathy within the Middle East that has improved its standing within the Islamic community in general. Confronted with repressive regimes, daunting poverty levels, poor educational opportunities, and economic stagnation, Muslims throughout the Middle East have seethed with rage as they perceive their once-magnificent culture as bring marginalized and enfeebled by America and the West. It is in this environment of despondence and anger that bin Laden's call for a renaissance of traditional Muslim values and caliphate rule has found broad appeal. By effectively using psychological warfare or the propaganda war for the "hearts and minds" of the people, bin Laden has made his political aims reverberate throughout the Muslim world. al Qaeda has made media and publicity one of its four operational committees, on an equal footing with its military, finance, and *fatwa* and Islamic study committees. They have prosecuted a successful information warfare strategy that draws on the mythical-heroic framework of Islam to deny combatant commanders' access to the Middle Eastern population for their information warfare. Because al Qaeda's information warfare campaign "emphasizes the idealized return to fundamental religious values and the rejection of both technological and political modernity," the U.S. and coalition's messages of democratization and nation building may not obtain salience with this audience.[31]

Influence of radical Islamic ideology is also apparent among the Chechen separatist fighters, who have, at a minimum, adopted the slogans and garbs of Islamic extremist fighters in other parts of the world. In fact, a segment of the Chechen separatists have blended tribal and nationalist aims with some of the tactics and ideology of al Qaeda–like groups. For example, a merging of the Chechen ethnonational code of *adat* and radical Islamic doctrine of Wahhabism has emerged within the ranks of the Chechen insurgents. bin Laden has proclaimed that the Chechen insurgency is part of his global religious war, and al Qaeda's interest in the region is not disputed. As early as 1997, bin Laden declared that Chechnya was an incubator for religious war and that it was among the regions where infidels were perpetrating injustice against Muslims. It is evident that at least the demonstration effect of Islamic extremism has had an influence on the insurgents' methods in the Chechen war, because the Chechens now perpetrate large-scale attacks and increasingly use suicide bombings, more to spread fear and shock than to achieve military objectives. The Chechen guerrillas have also borrowed al Qaeda's method of acquiring funds that have been channeled through organizations posing as charities. Also, international funds have helped pay and arm Chechen fighters, with significant amounts of monies coming from outside Chechnya, from places like the Gulf, Europe, and even North America.[32]

CONCLUSION

> Even where it is attainable, military victory is ephemeral. That is especially true for counterinsurgency. A guerrilla war is not over merely because the guerrillas disappear. Disappearance is a basic tactic of those who wage guerrilla war effectively. Real victory means an enduring peace. Such a peace cannot be derived from the mere physical cowing of the enemy.—*America and Guerrilla Warfare*[33]

Even though many states in the Islamic world have failed to meet the challenges of political legitimacy, modernity, and economic development, the Islamic world will not long tolerate outside occupation, especially by non-Muslims. There is a tradition in the Islamic world of violent opposition to occupiers. This historical tradition, coupled with the current allure of radical Islamic *jihad*, is combustible, harvesting both recruits who are animated by ideology and contributions from those who are unwilling to fight themselves but are willing to provide money to pay guerrillas. Radical fundamentalist Islam increasingly provides the legitimacy, motivation, and global network of support for insurgents. By using guerrilla tactics and strategies to protract the ongoing insurgencies and to inflict casualties, the enemy has obtained some small sense of legitimacy. As long as many Muslims remain passionate in their perception of the United States as a threat to Islam, an American victory will remain elusive and a sense of frustration and disenfranchisement may continue to fester amid the populations in the Middle East. In addition, the essentially undetectable and unpredictable character of al Qaeda and some of its associate groups, coupled with the potential for increasingly lethal means at their disposal, makes them and any future movements that try to emulate them the greatest threat to international security for the imaginable future.[34]

One conception outlined in this chapter is that the current war against al Qaeda and other non–state-armed groups is a global insurgency requiring a counterinsurgency strategy on a global scale. Thus, in order to achieve some sort of lasting peace in the war against radical fundamentalist Islam, a comprehensive and long-term counterinsurgency strategy that integrates national and international resources and agencies on a global scale is crucial. Many agree that a resolution of the Israeli-Palestinian conflict is a sine qua non for achieving a peaceful resolution to what will be a very prolonged war. Others advocate for regime change, or at least regime modification, in Syria, Iran, and Saudi Arabia as other preconditions for under-mining radical fundamentalist Islam and the ideological rationale behind the *jihad* against the West. Yet, the radical jihadists who comprise the al Qaeda–networked groups are products of the non-Western world; as such, they are a measure of how well the sole superpower and its like-minded Western friends are bringing security to those lawless areas missing out on the benefits of modernity. There are perfectly rational reasons why a group like al Qaeda would seek sanctuary in places like Afghanistan and Sudan—they were two of the least globalized and poorly gov-erned countries on the planet. Part of the solution, therefore, also includes efforts to increase the number of states in the zone of peace while concomitantly decreasing the number of states in the zone of turmoil. This short conclusion distills some ideas about how to approach such a long-term strategy for peace.[35]

One Strategic Studies Institute analysis of insurgency and counterinsurgency challenges whether the question of when and how to engage in counterinsurgency support should be an all-or-nothing issue in U.S. strategy. This study suggests that there should perhaps be a corollary to the Weinberger-Powell Doctrine stipulating that the United States should undertake a counterinsurgency only if the interests are vital and if it is willing to see the effort through to the end, even when that demands a significant commitment of personnel and resources for longer than ten years. This monograph further posits that the United States must determine whether its strategy for counterinsurgency operations is one of management or victory. "Traditional thinking is that victory, defined as the eradication of the insurgency as a political and military force and the amelioration of the factors that allowed it to emerge in the first place, is the appropriate goal." However, a man-agement or containment approach to counterinsurgency may have merit, espe-cially in view of the United States' ongoing commitments to counterinsurgency worldwide and the concomitant resources and time required to achieve total vic-tory in counterinsurgency. A containment strategy would possibly distinguish be-tween different types of insurgencies and commit the American military only to countering those insurgencies related to the support or sanctuary of international terrorism. It may be plausible to "adopt a strategy of intervention and stabilization when necessary without an attempt to transform the societies or a commitment to protracted counterinsurgency." In an effort to decapitate the insurgency's lead-ership while improving security at home, the United States must continue to ruth-lessly pursue al Qaeda and bin Laden. Self-evident though this may be, keeping al Qaeda on the run does allow the United States time to confront the genuine strategic challenge in this war—to establish a long-term peace in the Middle East, the United States ultimately will have to face and counter the broader insurgency occurring within Islam itself. One bold initiative would be to eliminate the global insurgents' external preoccupation with the West and allow their discontent to regress back to internal dissatisfaction. The real strategic challenge is not al Qaeda but the conditions that allowed al Qaeda to germinate in the first place. According to this view, economic support, diplomacy, and cooperation must be extended to those states in the Middle East that are moving toward reform. The essence of the challenge is the disaffected Muslim populations all over the world. Assisting states like Kuwait, Bahrain, Jordan, Yemen, Morocco, Malaysia, and Indonesia means encouraging those populations who "found their own brand of renewal within the construct of Islam without abrogating modernity" to determine their own political future. Diligent support for these populations, using all elements of national power, would create the real possibility of arresting the Islamic insurgency by the example of success in these states. This approach, in fact, could quite possibly defuse the loathing-laden ideology of al Qaeda and diminish its appeal.[36]

Another RAND study has suggested that any information warfare strategy designed for the ideological struggle between the West and radical fundamentalist Islam should see the West supporting the modernists of Islam to propagate their moderate version of Islam by empowering them with a broad platform from which to enunciate and to disseminate their views. Conversely, the West must fully counter the radical fundamentalists by targeting weaknesses in their Islamic ideological credentials. Cheryl Bernard recommends that the United States and its allies oppose the fundamentalists' interpretive and distorted version of Islam in the following ways: contest their interpretation of Islam and reveal their inaccuracies; expose their connections to illegal groups and operations; make public the consequences of their associates' actions; illustrate their inability to develop their countries in positive ways; direct and target the messages to the young, to women, to the devout traditionalists, and to Muslim minorities in the West; depict violent terrorists and extremists correctly as disturbed and pusillanimous, not as heroes; persuade journalists to investigate corruption, immorality, and hypocrisy in fundamentalist and terrorist circles; and promote ruptures among fundamentalists. However, *Islamic Rulings on Warfare* offers the caveat that "a perfectly defined delineation between mainstream and extremist views" in Islam is not readily discernible. al Qaeda and other radical fundamentalist groups convert and recruit their foot soldiers with the same interpretive Wahhabist version of Islam that comprises the principal religion of Saudi Arabia. Wahhabism does include positive emphases on Islamic leadership, social justice, and the importance of the Koran that are welcomed by most Muslims. In contrast, however, Wahhabist doctrine also proselytizes other unconventional and nontraditional views concerning *jihad* (for example, waging continuous *jihad* against all nonbelievers) that may offend many moderate Muslims. This combination of acceptable and unacceptable theory under the aegis of Wahhabist doctrine complicates Western efforts to work with countries, such as Egypt and Saudi Arabia, in order to curb the influence of radical fundamentalist Islam.[37]

The *Islamic Rulings on Warfare* monograph also underscores the requirement to educate U.S. military personnel in Islamic culture, history, and law. Understanding the messages and values of moderate and radical Islam will enable soldiers to much more effectively conduct psychological operations, civil affairs, and information operations. In fact, the U.S. Army has made some progress in this area already, as the U.S. Army Intelligence Center at Fort Huachuca has produced exportable training packages that focus on subjects that increase awareness of Islamic traditions. As important as regional and cultural knowledge is, however, military cultural change is a precondition to making counterinsurgency a central army mission. Military cultural change is imperative in adopting and sustaining a capacity and predilection for stability operations and counterinsurgency in the context of this global counterinsurgency. The U.S. military is adapting from the bottom up, in contact, but it needs to view and value counterinsurgency as a central and core competency, for the long term. All curricula in it professional military education system must dedicate a much larger share to thinking and planning for counterinsurgency. In the area of doctrine, the new *IFM 3-07, Counterinsurgency Operations* is a start, but the percentage and quality of army and joint doctrine for counterinsurgency are still exceedingly insignificant. Doctrinally, there needs to be much more cooperation and collaboration at the joint, interagency, and multinational levels. America does have some allies who have had some successful experiences in small wars and counterinsurgencies. Moreover, a capacity for a unified civil-military interagency approach at the strategic, operational, and tactical level is a sine qua non for success in counterinsurgency. Part of the solution is better and stronger cross-embedded interagency command and liaison elements, down to at least the operational level, in the Combined Joint Task Force (CJTF). Another more innovative solution is to genuinely mobilize the U.S. Department of State and the U.S. Agency for International Development so they can develop off-the-shelf modular units of action that can be plugged into the CJTF before they deploy. The Civil Operations and Rural Development Support (CORDS) used in Vietnam, while not at all flawless, offers some lessons and methods for interagency integration down to the grass-roots level that are germane today. A Civil Operations and Rural Development Support—like U.S. Agency for International Development modular unit of action (UA) is conceivable and not infeasible. It would be a start toward remedying some of the problems that inhered in the Coalition Provisional Authority during the first and critical part of Operation Iraqi Freedom.[38]

Another goal of this book is to show how the prudent tactical use of indigenous forces can also favorably shape the overall counterinsurgency campaign in the intelligence, societal, and political domains, at both the operational and strategic levels of war. When generalizing about previous counter-guerrilla wars it is also important to recognize that in each instance there were unique ideological, social, political, and geographical factors. Even after acknowledging this, however, there are still many potentially valuable lessons to be distilled from those twentieth-century counterinsurgency experiences and to be applied to current and future counterinsurgencies. In fact, one of the cardinal rules of counterinsurgency can be found in the doctrine of the British Army, an institution that has conferred on counterinsurgency a central and valued role: "The first thing that must be apparent when contemplating the sort of action which a government facing insurgency should take, is that there can be no such thing as a purely military solution because insurgency is not primarily a military activity." The British, who have also had fairly extensive experiences with small wars and counterinsurgencies, have delineated six counterinsurgency principles: political primacy and political aim; coordinated government machinery; intelligence and information; separating the insurgent from his support; neutralizing the insurgency; and longer-term post-insurgency planning. To these one may add the timeless lesson that the American military has learned over and over again, from the Indian wars, the Philippine Insurrection, the Banana Wars, and the Vietnam war, to the present: the early and deliberate employment of indigenous forces in a counterinsurgent role can be a very effective method in helping achieve a successful outcome. The global counterinsurgency will be protracted, but the U.S. military, along with its coalition partners, will prevail by adapting and preserving current and previous counterinsurgency lessons and techniques in its institutional culture. The remainder of this book examines how military culture and other factors influence whether armies will be successful or partially successful when prosecuting counterinsurgency. The final chapter presents some successful experiences in counterinsurgency and offers enduring lessons, or truisms, for armies waging counterinsurgency warfare.[39]

Big Powers and Small Wars

The Paradoxes of Asymmetric Conflict

> I will be damned if I will permit the U.S. Army, its institutions, its doctrine, and its traditions to be destroyed just to win this lousy war.[1]

> Organizational structures that encourage the presentation of innovative proposals and their careful reviews make innovation less likely.[2]

THESE TWO QUOTES engender two truisms about the military organizations of great powers: They embrace the big-war paradigm and, because they are large and hierarchical institutions, they generally innovate incrementally. This means that great power militaries do not innovate well. This is particularly true when the required innovations and adaptations lie outside the scope of the conventional-war focus. In other words, great powers do not "win" small wars because they are great powers: their militaries must maintain a central competence in symmetric warfare to preserve their great power status vis-à-vis other great powers; and their militaries must be large organizations. These two characteristics combine to create a formidable competence on the plains of Europe or in the deserts of Iraq. However, these two traits do not produce institutions and cultures that often exhibit a propensity for counter–guerrilla warfare.[3]

In addition to this big-war culture, there are some contradictions that simply derive from the logic that exists when a superior industrial or postindustrial power faces an inferior, semifeudal, semicolonial, or preindustrial adversary. On the one hand, the great power intrinsically brings overwhelmingly superior resources and technology to this type of conflict. On the other hand, the seemingly inferior opponent generally exhibits a superiority of will, demonstrated by a willingness to accept higher costs and by a willingness to persevere against many odds. This disparity in will is one of the most fundamental paradoxes of asymmetric conflict. "Death or victory" is not simply a pithy bumper sticker; it is a dilemma that embodies asymmetric conflicts: the qualitatively or quantitatively inferior opponent fights with limited means for unlimited strategic objectives—independence. Conversely, the qualitatively or quantitatively superior opponent fights with potentially unlimited means for limited ends—the maintenance of some peripheral imperial territory or outpost. Ostensibly weaker military forces often prevail over an overwhelming superiority in firepower and technology because they must—they are fighting for survival.[4]

History offers many examples of big power failure in the context of asymmetric conflict: the Romans in the Teutoburg Forest, the British in the American War of Independence, the French in the Peninsular War, the French in Indochina and Algeria, the Americans in Vietnam, the Russians in Afghanistan and Chechnya, and the Americans in Somalia. This list is not entirely homogeneous and it is important to clarify that the American Revolution, the Peninsular War, and the Vietnam conflict represent examples of great powers failing to win against strategies that combined asymmetric approaches with symmetric approaches. Washington combined a Fabian conventional approach in the North and Nathanael Greene combined conventional with unconventional tactics to wear down Cornwallis in the South. Although the culminating conventional battle at Yorktown brought the Americans victory, it was the guerrilla effort in the south, coupled with some conventional battles, which undermined the British strategy in the Carolinas. Likewise, Wellington coupled the use of his regular forces with the hit-and-run tactics of the Spanish (original) guerrillas to drive the French from Spain. And, even though North Vietnam's final victory over South Vietnam in 1975 was a conventional one, it was the Vietcong's Tet Offensive in 1968 that converted tactical defeats into a political and strategic victory for the Vietnamese. Tet precipitated the loss of American support for the war and the withdrawal of American troops.

However, two qualifications are necessary when generalizing great powers' failures in small wars. First, big powers do not necessarily lose small wars; they simply fail to win them. In fact, they often win many tactical victories on the battlefield. However, in the absence of a threat to survival, the big power's failure to quickly and decisively attain its strategic aim leads to a loss of domestic support. Second, the weaker opponent must be strategically circumspect enough to avoid confronting the great power symmetrically, in a conventional war. History also points to many examples wherein big powers achieved crushing victories over small powers when the inferior side was injudicious enough to fight a battle or a war according to the big power paradigm. The Battle of the Pyramids and the Battle of Omdurman provide the most conspicuous examples of primitive militaries facing advanced militaries symmetrically. The Persian Gulf War was the most recent example of an outmatched military force fighting according to it opponent's preferred paradigm. The same was true for the Italians' victory in Abyssinia, about which Mao Tse-Tung observed that defeat is the inevitable result when semifeudal forces fight positional warfare and pitched battles against modernized forces.[5]

This chapter's purpose is twofold: (1) to identify and explain the paradoxes of asymmetric conflict and (2) to provide historical examples to better illustrate each contradiction. This subject is germane because counterinsurgency-cum-asymmetric conflict is the most probable form of conflict that the United States faces. Four factors point to this probability: the Western powers represented the countries who have the most advanced militaries (technology and firepower) in the world; the economic and political homogenization among these states essentially precludes a war among them; most rational adversaries in the non-Western world would have learned from the Gulf War not to confront the West on its terms; and, as a result, the United States and its European allies will employ their firepower and technology in the less-developed world, against ostensibly inferior adversaries using asymmetric approaches. Asymmetric conflict will therefore be the norm, not the exception. Even though the wars in Afghanistan and Iraq differ from the model of asymmetric conflict presented in this chapter, the asymmetric nature of the war there only underscores the salience of asymmetric conflicts in the present and future.[6]

Although the term *asymmetric conflict* first appeared in a paper as early as 1974, asymmetric conflict now seems to be the strategic "term de jour." However, at the present the term *asymmetric* has come to include so many approaches that it has lost some of its utility and clarity. For example, one author in a magazine article described Japan's World War II conventional, but indirect, attack against the British conventional forces in Singapore as asymmetric. The term should not be that all-encompassing: such a broad approach to defining asymmetric conflict diminishes the usefulness of the term. If every type of asymmetry or indirect approach is subsumed within this definition, then what approaches are excluded? This book circumscribes the scope of asymmetric conflict to analyze conflicts in which superior external military forces (national or multinational) confront inferior states or indigenous groups on the territory of the latter. Insurgencies and small wars lie in this category, and this book uses all three terms interchangeably. Small wars are not big, force-on-force, state-on-state, conventional, orthodox, unambiguous wars in which success is measurable by phase lines crossed or hills seized. Small wars are counterinsurgency, low-intensity conflicts (LICs), and peace operations, where ambiguity rules and success is not necessarily guaranteed by superior firepower. This chapter identifies six paradoxes that characterize asymmetric conflicts. The first two contradictions are closely related and comprise what one historian refers to as a "strategic paradox." Table 1 depicts the paradoxes of asymmetric conflict.[7]

Table 1 The Paradoxes of Asymmetric Conflict

Nature of Paradox	Superior Opponent	Inferior Opponent
Strategic goals	Limited	Unlimited
Strategic means	Unlimited	Limited
Technology/armament	Superior	Inferior
Will/domestic cohesion	Conditional	Unconditional
Tolerance of casualties	Low	High
Military culture	Clausewitzian/direct	Fabian-Maoist/indirect

THE STRATEGIC PARADOX—THE AMERICAN WAR OF INDEPENDENCE

> The guerrilla wins if he does not lose. The conventional army loses if it does not win.—Henry Kissinger[8]

Symmetric wars are total wars wherein the struggle is a zero-sum one for survival by both sides—World Wars I and II are the most obvious examples. An asymmetric struggle, on the other hand, implies that the war for the indigenous insurgents is total but that it is inherently limited for the great power. This is because the insurgents pose no direct threat to the survival of the great power. Moreover, for the great power in an asymmetric situation, full military mobilization is neither politically prudent nor considered necessary. The disparity in military capabilities is so great and the confidence that military power will predominate is so acute that the great power expects victory. However, although the inferior side possesses limited means, its aim is nonetheless the expulsion of the great power. The choice for the underdog is literally "death or victory." The American War of Independence offers a good example of a strategic paradox. In fact, before the Battle of Long Island, George Washington told his rag-tag Continental Army, "we must resolve to conquer or to die."[9]

Since Washington's army was limited in personnel, resources, and training, he soon realized that committing his troops to open battle against the British would invite disaster. Therefore, after the Continental Army's unsuccessful defenses of New York in 1776 and of Philadelphia (Brandywine Creek) in 1777, Washington was compelled to adopt a Fabian strategy. Fabius Maximus' strategy against Hannibal "was not merely an evasion of battle to gain time, but calculated for its effect on the morale of the enemy." According to Liddell Hart, the Roman consul Fabius knew his enemy's military superiority too well to risk a decision in direct battle. Thus, Fabius sought to avoid direct battle and instead sought by "military pin-pricks to wear down the invaders' endurance." Fabius' strategy was designed to protract the war with hit and run tactics, avoiding direct battles against superior Carthaginian concentrations.[10]

Likewise, Washington generally avoided head-on collisions with the British Army. Washington adopted an indirect strategy of attrition whereby he avoided general actions against the British main body but instead concentrated what forces he had against weak enemy outposts and piecemeal detachments. Washington's plan for victory was to keep the Revolution alive by preserving the Continental Army and exhausting the British will to sustain the fight, with raids against peripheral detachments. A strategic paradox necessitated a Fabian strategy: Washington's political objective had to be the absolute removal of the British from the American colonies, but his military means were so weak that he had no other alternative than a strategic defensive. To find a way out of this contradiction, "Washington's hopes had to lie mainly not in military victory but in the possibility that the political opposition in Britain might in time force the British Ministry to abandon the conflict." Since asymmetry characterized the relationship between the American Army and the British Army, Washington's methods were effective in that they generally avoided open battle against the superior British Army until the culminating conventional battle at Yorktown.[11]

To add a footnote, the American Revolution witnessed some of the best unconventional warriors and guerrilla fighting in the history of American warfare. In the northern department, irregulars helped bring about the surrender of British Major General John Burgoyne's army at Saratoga by conducting unconventional hit-and-run attacks on Burgoyne's flanks and lines of communication. In the southern department, Major General Nathanael Greene "developed a capacity to weave together guerrilla operations and those of his regular forces with a skill that makes him not unworthy of comparison with Mao Tse-Tung or Vo Nguyen Giap." In part, Greene's strategy stemmed from the shortage of provisions for his regulars and from the presence of partisan bands in the southern department. He separated his regular forces into detachments simply because three scattered detachments could subsist more easily off the land than one concentrated force.[12]

ASYMMETRY OF TECHNOLOGY—THE WAR IN CHECHNYA

For the Chechens an outright military victory was unlikely, so their goal was to inflict as many casualties as possible on the Russian people and erode their will to fight. The Chechens used an "asymmetric" strategy that avoided battle in the open against Russian armor, artillery, and air power. They sought to even the fight by fighting an infantry war. Time and again, the Chechens forced their Russian counterparts to meet them on the urban battlefield where a Russian infantryman could die just as easily.[13]

This paradox stems from a huge disparity in resource power. Because there are huge differences in the levels of technological and industrial capacities between adversaries in asymmetric conflicts, the big power possesses an overwhelming advantage in military capacity. This disparity inheres in the structure of any conflict that witnesses a peripheral power facing a core power. Some of the most pronounced asymmetries in technology in this century manifested themselves during the Vietnam War and during the Soviet war in Afghanistan. One can certainly conclude from these examples that not only does conventional military and technological superiority not ensure victory, it may even undermine victory in an asymmetric context. One need only ask a veteran of the 1995 Battle of Grozny how superior numbers and technology fare against a guileful opponent using an asymmetric approach.[14]

The Russian forces that assaulted Grozny on 31 December 1994 were technologically and quantitatively superior to the Chechen defenders of Grozny. Perhaps the Russian military's perception of its own invulnerability, stemming from a numerical and technological superiority, even contributed to the haphazard manner by which it ambled into a veritable beehive of Chechen anti-armor ambushes. Just for a look at raw numbers, the Russians employed two hundred thirty tanks, four

hundred fifty-four armored infantry vehicles, and three hundred eighty-eight artillery guns. The Chechens, on the other hand, had fifty tanks, one hundred armored
infantry vehicles, and sixty artillery guns. Yet, despite Russian superiority across
all weapons systems, the Russians were still unable to maneuver the Chechens into
a disadvantageous position. Despite former Russian Defense Minister Grachev's
claim that he could topple the Dudayev regime in a couple of hours with one
parachute regiment, the Chechen forces' skillful resistance in Grozny compelled
the Russian forces to fall back from the city center to regroup. Firing from all sides
and from all floors, from city block to city block, Chechen anti-armor teams
systematically destroyed a large number of Russian tanks with RPG-7s. In fact,
during the New Year's Eve assault, one Russian regiment lost one hundred two of
one hundred twenty vehicles, as well as most of its officers.[15]

Chechen fighters turned every city and town into a network of ambushes and
inflicted serious losses on the numerically and technologically superior Russian
columns. One method by which the cunning Chechens turned Russia's technological superiority to their own advantage was to draw fire from Russian combat aircraft to intentionally precipitate collateral damage. When the Russian aircraft returned fire on the single weapon, in an urban environment, they would invariably
destroy a nearby house or road. Such seemingly wanton destruction inevitably
angered the local population, thus making recruiting much easier for the Chechen
side. Another example of Chechen ingenuity was for Chechen guerrillas to inter-
pose themselves between two Russian regiments during darkness and to fire in both
directions. This often triggered intense fratricidal firefights between the Russian
units.[16]

Whether in the cities or in the mountains, however, the 1994–1996 conflict in
Chechnya witnessed a massive use of Russian technology and firepower—carpet
bombings and massive artillery strikes—most of which exhibited little concern
over civilian casualties and collateral damage. On the other hand, for the remainder
of this war, the Chechen forces continued to avoid direct battles, instead isolating
Russian forces into smaller detachments that could then be ambushed and destroyed piecemeal. For the Russians, unskilled in the techniques and nuances of
counterinsurgency, massed artillery became the substitute for infantry maneuver
and the conventional principle of the offensive "came to be interpreted as the tons
of ordnance dropped on target." It seems, then, that instead of adopting the preferred counterinsurgent approach of separating the guerrillas from the people, the
Russians in Chechnya tried to extirpate the population.[17]

The fact that the Russians' technological and numerical superiority did not
enable them to achieve their objectives only highlights the chimerical nature of
technology. One can argue that guerrilla war negates many of the advantages of
technology because it is more a test of national will and endurance. In addition,
asymmetric warfare is the most effective and rational way for a technologically
inferior group or state to fight a great power. One author offers a cogent conclusion on technology and asymmetric conflict: "technology offers little decisive
advantage in guerrilla warfare, urban combat, peace operations, and combat in

rugged terrain. The weapon of choice in these conditions remains copious quantities of well-trained infantrymen."[18]

ASYMMETRY OF WILL—THE VIETNAM CONFLICT

As far back as two millennia, the professional, salaried, pensioned, and career-minded citizen-soldiers of the Roman legions routinely had to fight against warriors eager to die gloriously for tribe or religion. Already then, their superiors were far from indifferent to the casualties of combat, if only because trained troops were very costly and citizen manpower was very scarce.[19]

This quotation helps highlight a profound disparity that characterizes conflicts between "imperial powers" and non-"imperial powers." Imperial powers are unable or unwilling to accept high casualties indefinitely in peripheral wars. It is the weaker side's national endurance, will, or high threshold for pain, sometimes manifested by a capacity to willingly accept whatever the costs (even if it means "copious quantities of well-trained [dead] infantrymen"), that enables small powers to succeed against big powers. From the Teutoburg Forest, to the Long March, to the Tet Offensive, adversaries who were unambiguously inferior by more tangible measures of military might—weapons, technology, organization—have managed to persevere to ultimately attain victory against superior powers. An expert on Sun-Tzu and Mao Tse-Tung explains why "will" is so salient[20]:

> Guerrilla war is not dependent for success on the efficient operation of complex mechanical devices, highly organized logistical systems, or the accuracy of electronic computers. Its basic element is man, and man is more complex than any of his machines. He is endowed with intelligence, emotion, and *will* [author's italics].

All asymmetric conflicts exhibit this same contradiction of will. No single phrase better captures this disparity than this question posed in *Gardens of Stone*, a movie about the Vietnam conflict: "How do you *beat* an enemy who is *willing* to fight helicopters with bows and arrows?"[21] In Somalia, the enemy used slingshots against helicopters and used women and children as human shields during firefights. In Vietnam, moreover, enemy tactics seemed "to be motivated by a desire to impose casualties on Americans regardless of the cost to themselves." According to one RAND analysis of Vietnam, the enemy was "willing to suffer losses at a far greater rate than our own, but he has not accepted these losses as decisive and refuses to sue for peace."[22]

However, not only does superior conventional military strength not guarantee victory, but under certain conditions it may undermine it. Since the weaker opponent lacks the technological capacity to destroy the external power's military capability but nonetheless has unlimited political aims such as independence, it must look to the political impact on the great power's domestic cohesion. In other words, "the insurgents must retain a minimum degree of invulnerability" to avoid defeat and to win they must be able to impose a continual aggregation of costs on their adversaries. From a strategic perspective, the rebels' aim must be to provoke the great power into escalating the conflict. This in turn will incur political and economic costs on the external power—the normal costs of war, such as soldiers killed and equipment destroyed—but over time these may be seen as too high when the security of the great power is not directly threatened.[23]

The direct costs of lives and equipment lost gain strategic importance only when they achieve the indirect results of psychologically and politically ampli-fying disharmony in the metropolitan power. Domestic criticism in the great power will therefore increase as battle losses and economic costs escalate in a war against an adversary that poses no direct threat to its vital interests: "in a limited war, it is not at all clear to those groups whose interests are adversely affected why such sacrifices are necessary." Equally salient is the fact that the need to risk death will seem less clear to both conscripts and professional soldiers when the political or territorial survival of their country is not at risk.[24]

This problem was particularly acute during the Vietnam conflict, where the Clausewitzian-minded American security establishment incorrectly determined that the destruction of the Vietnamese military means to wage war would make their will to wage it irrelevant. Perhaps U.S. air power would have succeeded in bombing the Vietnamese into the "Stone Age" except for the reality that they were still there. Even though the United States dropped more than seven million tons of bombs on Indochina (this is equivalent to more than three hundred of the atomic bombs that fell on Japan), the enemy's will was resolute and ours was limited. Lacking the military means to destroy our capacity to wage war, Ho Chi Minh and General Giap correctly focused on our domestic political capability to continue to support the war. Mao expressed this as "the destruction of the unity of the enemy," but another author explains it even more lucidly: "if the external power's will to continue the struggle is destroyed, then its military capability—no matter how powerful—is totally irrelevant."[25]

THE PARADOX OF PAIN—TOLERANCE FOR COMBAT LOSSES IN SOMALIA

The enthusiasm of the nation to take an active hand in crafting a new international order through the United Nations and multilateral operations, never strong to begin with, died along with eighteen of America's soldiers on the streets of Mogadishu.[26]

Simply stated, the paradox of pain is this—big powers exhibit much less tolerance for casualties in small wars than do their opponents. This contradiction is cer-tainly a corollary to the asymmetry of will. Because the U.S. experience in Somalia revived the Vietnam specter regarding casualties, this section examines the casualty issue in that context. American participation in Somalia culminated with the 3–4 October 1993 battle of Mogadishu that resulted in 18 U.S. soldiers killed and 84 wounded, compared to 312 Somalis killed and 814 wounded. The entirety of American involvement in Somalia, moreover, witnessed at least 30 U.S. troops killed and over 100 wounded, whereas the figures for Somali casualties range between 1000 and 3000. However, four days after the ill-fated raid, President Clinton announced the end of American involvement in Somalia, "ostensibly because of the public's adverse reaction to the casualties." Why did the world's remaining superpower quit what was essentially a counterguerrilla war against a barbarian warlord who was suffering at least ten times greater casualties? Moreover, after Somalia, the use of force by the United States seemed to be even more afflicted by an overemphasis on force protection. However, the comment below makes clear that even as early as the Korean War, there was embedded in American military culture a concern about minimizing casualties.[27]

> We must expend steel and fire, not men. I want so many artillery holes that a man can step from one to the other.—General Van Fleet, 8th Army, 1951[28]

One can trace the beginning of casualty wariness to the Korean and Vietnam wars, where one lesson learned was "it was politically risky, if not suicidal, to preside over any limited conflict that could not be won quickly, with relatively few casualties." During those two conflicts, both the White House and the Pentagon exerted pressure to minimize combat losses, down to the lowest echelons of command. As both conflicts became stalemates it became more difficult to justify friendly losses: "a heavy reliance on air power, precision firepower, and mobility, and increasingly stringent standards for acceptable friendly-to-enemy casualty ratios, came to distinguish the American way of war." Moreover, the sledgehammer approach of overwhelming force was validated in Panama and the Persian Gulf, giving rise to the new mantra of the American military—"decisive victory and minimum casualties." The decisive victory in the Persian Gulf War, at minimal cost, only reinforced the perception among American elites and the American people that the U.S. military can win wars with few to no casualties: "Pentagon pictures showing the effects of smart weapons led people to think that we really can win with technology." In his 1992 Decisive-Force corollary to the Weinberger Doctrine, then Chairman of the Joint Chiefs of Staff General Colin Powell emphasized "decisive force to overwhelm our adversaries and thereby terminate conflicts—swiftly with a minimum loss of life."[29]

The Battle of Mogadishu raised the concern for American casualties to a new level. However, it is also important to dispel a myth about casualties—there is not necessarily a popular aversion to casualties but there is a perception among elites that there is. This perception causes civil and military leaders to anticipate a potential public outcry over casualties. A cogent Strategic Studies Institute (SSI) study found that casualties are mainly a perceptual issue with the core leaders of U.S. military strategic and political culture rather than with the public. Although casualty aversion is accepted conventional wisdom among elected politicians, pundits, and the country's foreign policy elite, it is not always so among the public. The U.S. public will in fact tolerate casualties if it is convinced there is a consensus among political leaders that the endeavor is in the national interest and if that consensus is considered strong enough to see the operation through to a successful conclusion. However, according to one report, "the elite consensus was obviously missing" in the case of Somalia and, as a result, the Clinton administration's inability to achieve consensus resulted in a policy held "hostage" to public backlash when the soldiers died. Even more alarming, is the implication that senior military officers also bought into the "zero-casualties" myth.[30]

One study finds that perceived costs and benefits are as or more important than casualties in determining and eroding support. It explains that Somalia was exactly the kind of operation that has historically suffered from a low willingness to accept costs—prolonged interventions in complex political situations in failed states characterized by civil conflict, in which U.S. interests and principles are typically less compelling, or clear, and in which success is often elusive at best. Since 11 September 2001, however, and especially since the start of Operation Iraqi Freedom in 2003, with its consequent and attendant insurgency, and in the changed context of a war against unambiguous threats to U.S. security—al Qaeda and the regimes that would provide it sanctuary—the U.S. leadership has thus far demonstrated a willingness to stay the course and to accept the losses in Iraq as the costs of a greater cause.[31]

Somalia influenced the post–Cold War casualty question in an enormous way. It caused the Clinton administration to reassess its approach to peace operations under the United Nations and to issue a policy directive (Presidential Decision Directive 25) reflecting its "new" approach to peacekeeping. PDD 25 was essentially a migration of the Weinberger criteria for overwhelming force into the realm of peace operations. These criteria were best articulated in the 1995 *National Security Strategy of Engagement and Enlargement,* which states that the military is generally not the best tool for humanitarian emergencies but that under certain conditions the use of U.S. forces may be appropriate "when the risk to American troops is minimal." Somalia consequently shaped the American approach to peace operations for the 1990s—a recent and relevant manifestation was Kosovo, where a very antiseptic air campaign exacerbated this notion of using force without bleeding. Moreover, the U.S. forces that deployed to Kosovo to conduct peace operations had "no friendly casualties" as their most important criterion for success.[32]

CLAUSEWITZ VERSUS MAO—THE CONTRADICTION OF CULTURES IN AFGHANISTAN

All great powers exhibit a degree of homogeneity of military thought—since the stunning Prussian victory in the Franco-Prussian War, big powers have embraced Clausewitz as the quintessential oracle of war, and they continue to espouse a theoretical approach to maneuver warfare (conventional and mechanized) that is distinctly German in origin. However, one can also discern a singularly Jominian trait in the military cultures of great powers—there is an inclination to divorce the political sphere from the military sphere once the war begins. This creates two corollary problems for great powers in asymmetric conflicts: (1) poor or non-existent political-military integration and (2) a "go-with-what-you-know" approach, which translates to the preferred paradigm—middle- or high-intensity conventional war. Add to this the tendency of large organizations to change very slowly, and the result is a military that clings to a conventional approach when that approach is not appropriate or effective, such as during asymmetric conflicts.[33]

Nowhere was this more manifest than in the Soviet invasion of Afghanistan. The Soviet Army that invaded Afghanistan was not an army trained to conduct counterguerrilla operations but rather an army trained to conduct conventional high-intensity warfare on the plains of Europe. According to another author, the Soviet doctrine placed "a premium on mass, echelonment, rapid maneuver, heavy fire support, high rates of advance and coordinated, combined arms actions at all levels." Thus, although the Soviet political leadership ordered the Soviet military to invade Afghanistan, the Soviet Army, with a military culture that preferred a big European war paradigm, did not have a mindset or a skill set that was appropriate in that context. Both the mountainous terrain and the enemy were more amenable to guerrilla warfare. There were no conventional "fronts" or "rears" to penetrate with massed advances of heavy armor forces. In fact, the Soviets were up against an unorthodox, tenacious, and elusive enemy. Consequently, the goal of a quick and decisive victory soon became unrealistic.[34]

The Soviet Army exhibited a rigid adherence to a big-war paradigm: "the Soviets invaded Afghanistan using the same military tactics as in the 1968 invasion of Czechoslovakia." In addition, the same officer who commanded the Czechoslovakian invasion, General Pavlovsky, commanded the initial incursion into Afghanistan. The Soviet Army conducted large-scale armor warfare up until 1982. About twice a year, the Soviets launched huge conventional offensives, using motorized rifle divisions trained for battle against NATO in central Europe rather than their lighter and better-suited airborne units. However, in 1982 the Soviets made changes in equipment and tactics to counter the *mujahideen*—the Russians increasingly relied on their three hundred MI-24 combat helicopters in Afghanistan to counter the guerrillas. They also introduced the SU-25 fighter-bomber in 1984, and their standard footprint for an offensive involved intensive air and artillery preparation, the landing of heliborne troops, and direct drives by mechanized forces. If the Soviets had studied and learned anything from the Americans in Vietnam, they might have known that more technology—helicopter mobility and advanced bombers—does not make a military that embraces the big-war doctrine any less conventional or any more successful.[35]

The excessive force and indiscriminate destruction that such an approach entails, however, did not win any hearts and minds. The obverse was true: the Soviet's scorched-earth approach of the mid-1980s offered more utility as a recruiting aid for the enemy. One example was the offensive Panjshir VII in 1984. High-altitude TU-16 bombings and an attack on the Panjshir Valley in April were followed by an offensive near Herat in June when the Soviets destroyed all the villages and suburbs within 20 kilometers west of the city. The Soviets encountered stiff resistance around the city of Mazar-I Sharif, and 1984 was the worst year for Soviet casualties—2060 killed in action. As usually was the pattern, the government forces soon had to withdraw from the objectives they seized during Panjshir VII, only to see the terrain be reoccupied by the *mujahideen*. Another author compared the Soviets' reliance on roads, bombs, artillery, rockets, napalm, and gas to the American Operations Attleboro and Junction City in Vietnam. Both approaches achieved nothing decisive despite the destruction they wreaked. Except for a few minor differences, the Russians applied an approach in Afghanistan that was like the American approach in Vietnam—a sort of counterguerrilla "douhetism." The problem is that big-power militaries are conditioned to use a sledgehammer when in actuality a screwdriver is the more appropriate instrument for asymmetric conflict.[36]

CONCLUSION

> Americans define war as being waged against a uniformed, disciplined opposing state's armed forces, the sort who will fight fairly, the way the Americans do.[37]

One can surmise from the paradoxes explained in here that small wars are very difficult for great powers. This is particularly germane for the United States, as its armed forces are those of the sole remaining superpower. For all of the twentieth century and some of the nineteenth century, the U.S. military almost exclusively embraced the conventional paradigm and eschewed the unconventional one. Furthermore, after the Persian Gulf War—the American version of the Battle of Omdurman—it became unlikely that another second-tier power will be dumb enough to fight us according to our paradigm. The implication is evident: the U.S. military and its allies needed to cultivate a mindset, doctrine, and force that can do things other than wage a conventional war.[38] Even as early as the 1830s, when the U.S. Army fought an asymmetric war against the Seminoles, it exhibited a preference for the symmetric model:

A historical pattern was beginning to work itself out: occasionally the U.S. Army has had to wage a guerrilla war, but guerrilla warfare is so incongruous to the natural methods and habits of a well-to-do society that the U.S. Army has tended to regard it as abnormal and to forget about it whenever possible. Each new experience with irregular warfare has required, then, that appropriate techniques be learned all over again.[39]

According to Sam Sarkesian, an expert on the U.S. military, "in the main, unconventional conflicts do not easily fit into American cultural precepts or perceptions of the external environment." When attempts are made to design strategy and doctrine for unconventional conflicts, "they become suspiciously similar to conventional factors disguised as unconventional." Moreover, Sarkesian asserts,

"U.S. strategy and doctrine for unconventional conflicts not only lack a conceptual base, but are divorced from the broader political-psychological dimensions of unconventional conflicts." It has been argued that the U.S. Army never seriously attempted counterinsurgency in Vietnam, its lack of flexibility being summed up in the memorable remark at the beginning of this chapter: "I will be damned if I will permit the U.S. Army, its institutions, its doctrine, and its traditions to be destroyed just to win this lousy war."[1] The American victory over the Germans and Japanese during World War II "had been so absolute, so brilliantly American, that the notion of losing a war was unthinkable." Thus, the solution for victory in that war—"superior firepower, superior manpower, superior technology"—became the prescribed formula for the rest of the century.[40]

A hubris, or "disease of victory," emerged in the U.S. Army that encouraged its commanding generals in Vietnam "willfully to underestimate their enemies and over-estimate their own battlefield prowess." In fact, one could add yet another contradiction to this list—the paradox of hubris and humility. Great powers always underestimate the will, skill, and tenacity of their adversaries in small wars. The U.S. Army was unable to adapt to the kind of war conducted by the North Vietnamese and the Vietcong. "By its more conventional response, its strategy of attrition and the unceasing quest for the big set-piece battle, the Army became, in effect, a large French Expeditionary Corps—and met the same frustrations." The U.S. Army placed marginal emphasis on unconventional warfare doctrine. With scant interest or recent practice in counterinsurgency on a big scale—and few recognizable payoffs in career promotions or annual budgetary allocations—the evolving U.S. Army strategy was predictable. "The Army was going to use a sledgehammer to crush a fly, while the practice of unconventional war was left largely to the Special Forces."[41]

Eliot Cohen, a respected scholar of military affairs, maintains that the most significant limitations on America's capacity to conduct small wars stemmed from the resistance of the U.S. military to the very idea of participating in such conflicts and from the unsuitability of the American military for fighting such wars. According to Cohen, there is a fivefold requirement to wage small war successfully: expectations, doctrine, manpower, equipment, and organization. However, the U.S. military's understanding of the political context of small wars was distorted by Vietnam. American military officers were shocked and frustrated by the Vietnam experience: they were shocked by the gap that emerged between civil society and the armed forces; they were frustrated by their inability to vanquish an ostensibly inferior Third World opponent with firepower and mobility. The overarching lesson of Vietnam, therefore, was "don't do Vietnams (small wars)."[42]

Another scholar on military subjects and a retired army officer, Andrew Krepinevich, arrived at a similar observation—the "Army Concept" comprises two characteristics: a focus on conventional warfare and the reliance on "high volumes of firepower to minimize casualties." However, the U.S. Army's traditional approach to the use of force does not suit it well for stability operations and support operations (SOSO), where the emphasis is on minimizing firepower and light infantry formations instead of the massive use of firepower and armored divisions. Moreover, the history of U.S. strategy testifies to an American conception of war that best characterizes American strategists as "strategists of annihilation." In the beginning when America had limited resources, there were some strategists of attrition, but America's wealth and its adoption of unlimited aims in war abrogated that development, "until the strategy of annihilation became characteristic of the American way of war."[43]

The victory in the Persian Gulf only served to reinforce this predilection for the big-war paradigm, ironically at the very moment that this paradigm was becoming an anachronism. However, Mohammed Farah Aideed quickly showed the U.S. military that a predilection for the big-war paradigm can be an obstacle to success in asymmetric warfare—a lesson that we consistently refuse to learn. As a result of Somalia, the "No More Vietnams" bumper sticker rapidly evolved into the "No More Somalias" bumper sticker, and almost as soon as the doctrinal cognoscenti at Leavenworth created the acronym OOTW (operations other than war), this concept of OOTW came to be perceived as TWWRA (things we would rather avoid). The Persian Gulf War, on the other hand, was a stupendous feat, "a thing we would rather do: war by the American definition." The second half of the twentieth century, therefore, pointed to another paradox: the U.S. military had trained and organized for the type of war that it would least likely fight. This was necessary during the Cold War to balance and deter the Soviets. However, the Soviet Union has ceased to exist for more 15 years and there is no emerging great power threat over the horizon.[44]

As early as 1988, Jeffrey Record, an expert on U.S. military reform, offered this germane observation about small wars: the promotion of the values of decentralization, lightness, quality of training, and unit cohesion is no less important for the operations short of war of the future than they were for the small wars of the past. Peace operations in difficult terrain amid former enemies also argue for specialized, elite, light, cohesive, and tactically versatile forces. In addition, given the U.S.' ostensible sensitivity to casualties and protracted conflicts, forces must be able to get the mission accomplished at minimal costs.[45]

The good news is that after more than fifteen years of doing things other than war, the culture of the U.S. military is changing. It is becoming more disposed to operations outside its historical paradigm—this is manifest, in particular, by the fact that the army's core leaders (general officers) are reflecting and effecting changed attitudes toward operations other than conventional war. In a U.S. Institute of Peace (USIP) report that interviewed a host of general officers, General Eric Shinseki, who served as the NATO Stabilization Force (SFOR) commander in 1997–1998, observed that he had to face a "cultural bias" in Bosnia because "Army-doctrine based training prepared him for war fighting at all levels, but there wasn't a clear doctrine for stability operations." However, as then U.S. Army Chief of Staff, General Shinseki was driving change in the army's mindset and force structure, to make it more strategically relevant. The USIP report also concluded that peace operations are "the new paradigm of conflict that will confront the army in future deployments as more failed states emerge and peace enforcement and nation-building become staples of the senior military leadership diet." In another study, the former NATO Implementation Force (IFOR) chief of staff expressed the need to "build a military capable of many things—not just the high end." The counterinsurgencies in Afghanistan and Iraq, particularly Iraq, have provided the impetus for significant change in the U.S. military's cultural aversion to stability, reconstruction, and counterinsurgency. All of the cascading national security and national military strategy documents now include explicit reference to the imperative of being competent in irregular warfare. The U.S. Department of Defense has even gone so far as to mandate that the U.S. Army serve as the proponent for doctrine and training for these types of operations, prescribing that the U.S. Army ensure that the emphasis on these missions equals that dedicated to conventional war.[46]

Russian Military Culture and Counterinsurgency

Pavlov Meets Jihad

> The enemy's objective is to have us concentrate our main forces for a decisive engagement. Our objective is exactly the opposite. We want to choose conditions favorable to us, concentrate superior forces and fight decisive campaigns and battles only when we are sure of victory, . . . we want to avoid decisive engagements under unfavorable conditions when we are not sure of victory.—Mao Tse-Tung[1]

ON CHRISTMAS EVE in 1979, Soviet forces conducted a conventional assault on Kabul and other key points in Afghanistan with the aims of implanting a stable Soviet-friendly government and of quelling an insurrection. Almost ten years later, Soviet forces withdrew after suffering close to 14,000 killed, leaving behind a very precarious pro-Soviet government and an ongoing civil war. In December 1994, Russian forces invaded Chechnya, using almost the same conventional template used in Afghanistan. On New Year's Eve 1994, Russian forces launched their main assault on Grozny, initially suffering huge losses and meeting with failure. The goals in Chechnya were almost the same as the goals sought in Afghanistan fifteen years earlier—to implant a pro-Russian government and to stabilize the Chechen republic. Russian forces pulled out of Chechnya almost two years later after suffering close to 6000 killed, having failed to meet their objectives. As a great power, the Soviet Union failed to win a small war in Afghanistan. As a former great power, Russia failed to win in Chechnya.

In both cases, Soviet-Russian forces possessed a technological advantage and a latent numerical advantage in forces. In both cases, Soviet-Russian forces fought conventionally against an adversary who fought unconventionally. In both conflicts, the Russians faced ideologically driven indigenous movements fighting for independence. The significant differences between Afghanistan and Chechnya were that (1) the structure of the international system underwent an enormous change—from bipolar to unipolar and (2) Russia ceased to be a great power. Notwithstanding these two enormous changes, this study postulates that one would observe continuity in Russian military-strategic cultural preferences in Chechnya because not enough time elapsed between the end of the Cold War and the conflict in Chechnya for a cultural change to occur—military cultural change normally takes from five to ten years. Thus, one would expect to observe continuity in Russian preferences for the use of force—these preferences should reflect a focus on the big-war, or conventional, paradigm for war.

The aim of this chapter is threefold: (1) to succinctly explain and define this notion of military culture, (2) to identify Russian military cultural preferences for the use of force, and (3) to explain how these preferences impeded the Russian military's capacity to prosecute the counterinsurgencies in Afghanistan and Chechnya to successful conclusions. Concerning the war in Chechnya, this chapter limits its analysis to the conflict there between 1994 and 1996. Moreover, this subject is particularly germane to the U.S. military and its allies because asymmetric conflict is the most probable form of conflict that NATO faces. In addition, the military organizations of great powers are normally large and hierarchical institutions that innovate incrementally, if at all. This means that one could expect the Russian military to adapt very slowly to a new type of war, even in the face of a changed security environment. This is particularly true when the required innovations and adaptations lie outside the scope of the conventional-war focus. In other words, this chapter will revisit a theme that Chapter 2 examined, the notion that great powers do not win small wars because they are great powers: their militaries must maintain a central competence in symmetric warfare to preserve their great power status vis-à-vis other great powers; and their militaries must be large organizations. These two traits, as manifested in Russian military behavior, likewise did not produce institutions and cultures that were amenable to versatility and adaptation.

CULTURE: POLITICAL, STRATEGIC, AND MILITARY

Before going directly to the concept of "military-strategic culture," it is necessary to clarify some underlying concepts in the fields of anthropology and organizational theory. Clifford Geertz explains cultural anthropology as the study of "the machinery individuals and groups of individuals employ to orient themselves in a world otherwise opaque." Culture, then, is not so much an experimental science in search of laws as it is an interpretive science in search of meaning. In other words, culture is not something to which causality can be readily attributed but it is a context in which patterns of behavior can be intelligibly described. In sum, Geertz identifies culture as the "ordered cluster of significant symbols" that individuals and groups of individuals use to make sense of life.[2]

Moving from the anthropological to the political sphere, Lucien Pye maintains that political culture is "the product of both the collective history of a political system and the life histories of the individuals currently making up the system. Political culture provides meaning and structure to the political realm the same way that culture adds meaning and coherence to the social sphere. Political culture comprises only those central but widely shared beliefs and "patterns of orientation" that give form to the political process. Moreover, Sidney Verba argues that the most important characteristic of political culture is that it is a "patterned set of orientations toward politics in which specific norms and general values are mutually related." In addition, both Pye and Verba maintain that a study of political culture must address both the historical development of the system as a whole and the life experiences of the individuals who currently comprise its core. This is because political culture is learned.[3]

On the other hand, Edgar Schein fuses behavior studies and anthropology to arrive at an explanation of "organizational culture." According to Schein, we must first ascertain whether a given set of people has had enough common history and stability to allow a culture to form. Some organizations will not have an organizational culture because there is no common history or because there have been frequent turnovers. Other organizations will have deep cultures because of shared intense experiences or a long shared history. Schein maintains that culture is "what a group learns over a period of time as that group solves its problems of survival in an external environment and its problems of internal integration. Schein offers a fivefold definition of culture: (1) it is a pattern of basic assumptions; (2) it is invented, discovered, or developed by a given group; (3) it learns to cope with its problems of external adaptation and internal integration; (4) it has worked well enough to be considered valid; and (5) it is taught to new members as the correct way to perceive, think, and feel in relation to those problems. In sum, the consistency and strength of a culture stem from group longevity, stability, intensity of experiences, mechanisms for learning, and the clarity of assumptions espoused by its core leaders.[4]

Moreover, Jeff Legro postulates that military culture is "assessed according to the ideas and beliefs about how to wage war that characterize a particular military bureaucracy." Empirical and measurable indicators include internal correspondence, planning documents, memoirs, and regulations. Likewise, Alan Macmillan offers a succinct definition of strategic culture: it is "a unique combination of geographic setting, historical experiences, and political culture which shapes the formation of beliefs about the use of force." However, the organizational cultures of the military services are particularly strong because these bureaucracies have a closed-career principle—members spend their careers almost exclusively in these organizations. One expert explains, "The services recruit and indoctrinate new members around their core mission and its requirements, thus ensuring cultural continuity across generations." Military organizations also promote career personnel to higher levels with only a limited external veto and no real external competition. Thus, their cultures are institutionalized by the military and internalized by its professionals. Organizational (military) culture influences organizational behavior significantly but not always positively.[5]

Because mission identity is an important part of a military's self-concept, military organizations will seek to promote core missions and to defeat any challenges to core mission functions. Even if other missions are assigned, if the organization perceives them as peripheral to its core mission, then it will reject them as possible detractions from its core focus. Moreover, cultural change occurs in terms of "cultural epochs" that normally range in length from just a decade to as long as a century.[6]

A decade ago, a group of RAND scholars concluded that "the beliefs and attitudes that comprise organizational culture can block change and cause organizations to fail." These authors explained that culture often originates from successes in an organization's history: what worked in the past is repeated and internalized; what did not work is modified or rejected. If the organization survives, historically successful approaches are internalized and gradually transformed into "the way we think." This study asserts that military planners must consider the impact of culture—although it frequently operates outside the realm of observable causation, it can be a powerful and potentially counterproductive influence on behavior. RAND used a comparative approach: "comparisons with other armies can highlight different approaches to the preparation and conduct of warfare, some of which may be culture based." Finally, this study arrived at two important conclusions: first, cultural change requires a significant amount of time—the study determines five years as the minimum time to inculcate a major cultural change; second, major cultural change must come from the top—leaders at the highest levels must unambiguously back the change.[7]

In another study, Williamson Murray argues that military leadership can better influence doctrinal innovations through long-term cultural changes. He contends that the cultural values of a military organization are most crucial when it comes to innovation. However, these values are the most difficult thing to change. Murray defines *military culture* as "the sum of the intellectual, professional, and traditional values of the officer corps." Thus, culture plays an important role in how the military responds to the external environment. Moreover, Murray explains, past traditions are one part of military culture that can frequently block innovation—successful approaches were often worked out on earlier battlefields, at significant cost. As a result, military cultures "tend to change slowly in peacetime."[8]

This chapter thus defines *military strategy* as the art and science of employing the armed forces of a state to secure the aims of national policy by the application of force or threat of force. In war, military strategy encompasses the identification of strategic objectives, the allocation of resources, decisions on the use of force, and the development of war plans. Moreover, organizational culture is the pattern of assumptions, ideas, and beliefs that prescribe how a group should adapt to its external environment and manage its internal structure. Finally, military culture is a set of beliefs, attitudes, and values within the military establishment that shape collective (shared) preferences of how and when military means should be used to accomplish strategic aims. It is derived or developed as a result of historical experience, geography, and political culture. Core leaders perpetuate and inculcate it, but it is most pronounced at the operational level, because when armies have met with success in war, it is the operational techniques and the operational histories, by which enemies were defeated, that are consecrated in memory.[9]

RUSSIAN MILITARY CULTURE

> Russia has always been an empire. Russia has always tried to dominate its surrounding states. Russia has never had separation of church and state, so that the church has really been a state institution. And all of these factors have produced a tremendous tendency toward a solitarianism and toward conquest. And when a nation behaves a certain way for 400 years, you have to assume that it has a certain proclivity in that direction.
> —Henry Kissinger[10]

This section examines Russian history and geopolitics in order to draw some generalizations about Russian military-strategic preferences for using force. The first part briefly provides a short review of Russian history to illuminate its influence on military culture. The second section explains Russian geopolitical continuities with a similar aim. The last part explains Russia's preferred model, or paradigm, for war. One can discern historical continuity in Russia's methods of imperial expansionism, in Russia's self-conception of messianic Eurasianism, and in the host of conflicts Russia has fought against other peoples on its southern periphery. Geopolitically, Russia has been plagued by an apparently irresolvable paradox—the quest for security in a region without natural defensive barriers has historically driven Russia to seek more territory but this territorial expansion, in and of itself, has made Russia more vulnerable on the periphery.

When the Cold War ended and the Warsaw Pact ceased to function, moreover, this paradox was further complicated by Russia's post-Soviet identity crisis as a result of its loss of status as a great power and by the instability on its southern periphery that accompanied the breakup of the Soviet Union. The perception of a perceived Islamic threat in the south was also evident and nearly constant. Finally, and inevitably, one can discern Russian militarycultural preferences and approaches to the use of military force that can be best described as an incessant espousal of the big-war paradigm. Of course, because Russia's long-enduring great-power status stemmed from its geopolitical environment and its history, this focus on a big-war paradigm is not unrelated to both—great powers must embrace a big-war paradigm to compete with other great powers. This military cultural approach is not an exact and quantifiable science, and it will probably not be possible to isolate cause and effect with the precision one observes in the hard sciences. However, it should be possible to discern some preferences, contextually, through inference and interpretation.

HISTORY

Russia's serpentine frontier is both a consequence of the indefensibility of the central Russian plain and an important conditioning factor in the further evolution and execution of its foreign policy. For a weak Russia, such a frontier affords maximum exposure to attack, but for a powerful Russian state, this extended frontier, bordering on nearly a dozen states, offers an enviable and limitless choice for the exertion of diplomatic pressure.[11]

It is beyond the scope of this section, and this chapter, to offer an in-depth history of Russian involvement in central Asia and the Caucasus. The aim of this section is simply to capture the principal Russian historical trends and characteristics that are relevant to this analysis. One unique aspect of Russian history is the manner by which it acquired its empire. Unlike the western European great powers, which acquired empires after becoming nation-states, in Russia, nation building and empire building proceeded simultaneously. Since the seventeenth century, when Russia was already the world's largest state, the immensity of its domain has served the Russians as a psychological compensation for their relative backwardness and poverty. Imperial Russia and her Soviet progeny comprised the largest single continuous intercontinental empire in the world. The Soviet Union occupied halves of two continents and possessed the world's longest and exposed frontier. This frontier was a chimera—it represented Russia's principal asset and its principal liability in international politics at the same time.[12]

Historically, czarist Russia and Soviet Russia were continental expansionist empires, and, despite their ideological differences, one can discern Russo-Soviet imperial continuities. Despite its relative backwardness and despite setbacks, Russia continued to expand, controlling and oppressing its new territories and peoples with the same military force and autocratic rule that were used to command the obedience of the people of Russia itself. As a result, Russia's history reveals one dominant and continuous characteristic—a dual quest for physical and psychological security has produced in Russian foreign policy a unique pattern. This characteristic stems from the paradox that a weak Russia invites attack but a strong Russia stimulates expansion in all directions. Thus, Russia has historically been pulled in two different directions—the first was one was an inward, and hence isolationist, orientation; the second was a tendency toward imperialist expansion.[13]

Describing Soviet Russia in the 1940s, George Kennan once observed that "the powerful hand of Russian history and tradition" sustain Soviet leaders in their ideological belief that the outside world was hostile and that it was their ultimate duty to overthrow the political forces beyond their borders. Historically, this belief stemmed from their Eurasian skepticism about the possibility of peaceful and permanent coexistence of rival powers. This world view translated to an insistence on the submission of all competing power inside and outside the state.[14]

However, the history of Russian expansion is not dissimilar to the history of the U.S. westward expansion: both countries enjoyed a relative invulnerability and a freedom from strategic ambivalence that historically plagued the central European great powers. Both of these future superpowers possessed crumbling frontiers that required watching; but in neither the American expansion across the Alleghenies and the Great Plains nor the Russian expansion across the steppes did they encounter militarily advanced societies posing a danger to the metropolis. In central Asia in the last part of the nineteenth century, Russia faced weak and fragmented principalities to which the principle of balance of power did not apply. In Siberia—until it bumped up against Japanese interests—it was able to expand much as the United States had expanded across a sparsely populated continent. Thus, in Asia, Russia's sense of purpose and messianism were even less impeded by geographic or political obstacles. During the entire eighteenth century and most of the nineteenth century, Russia was alone in the Far East as an expansionist great power seeking Imperialist designs without much competition.[15]

Kindness is only a sign of weakness in the eyes of Asians . . . and I remain inexorably severe.—General Ermolov[16]

The history of Russia's southward expansion through the Caucasus and central Asia in the nineteenth and twentieth centuries shows more continuity than change, compared to the Soviet and Russian tendencies in these two regions in the last part of the twentieth century. Military analysts of the Russian campaigns in the Caucasus in the 1830s and 1840s observed that the Russians would not be able to pacify the mountaineers until they were able to attack their villages with impunity. In fact, General Ermolov once remarked that "not the bayonet but the axe" would prove the key to pacification of the region. However, the Russians' initially poor performance in the Caucasus, as well as the methods that the Russian military subsequently used to subjugate the region, was a harbinger of the Russian military's performance there more than a century later.[17] Captain Mochulskii, who did a tour of duty in the Caucasus in 1837, conducted a study that identified the principal reasons for Russia's failure there. He attributed most causes of failure to Russian shortcomings. Russian officers lacked experience and were not adequately trained for this counter–guerrilla warfare in mountainous terrain. Moreover, because their training focused on European-style war, the Russian commanders continued to rely on heavy artillery and cumbersome supply trains that made them too dependent on the poor road network. Mochulskii also criticized the reliance on over one hundred fifty forts, which he saw as an imprudent dispersion of available manpower. It was impossible for such outposts to control such a large territory—indeed, the outposts themselves were vulnerable to attack. On the other hand, Chechen guerrilla leader Shamil always refused to give battle on Russia's terms, that is, European-style battle. The wily adversary used the forests and mountains of the Caucasus to attack piecemeal Russian detachments, only to vanish into the forests afterward. Russian forces tried, but failed, many times to crush the guerrillas in a single large-scale campaign.[18]

Ultimately, in the 1840s, Russian Generals Freitag and Bariatinski implemented a cut-and-burn policy that resulted in the destruction of Chechen crops and villages, as well as the systematic deforestation of central Chechnya. "Surpassing by far the destructive effects of William Sherman's march to the sea in the American Civil War, Russia's scorched earth policy, coupled with a massive campaign of forced resettlement, stripped Shamil of his greatest assets and permanently transformed the central Caucasus." However, after subjugating Chechnya in 1859, the Russian military made no systematic effort to capture and disseminate the lessons of that war. Russia and the Russian military remained preoccupied with continental Europe and the European model of war and the events in the Caucasus did not become an essential part of the Russian Army's institutional memory.[19]

During the Soviet period, there were two important aspects of Soviet Russia that influenced Soviet strategic thought: the lessons drawn from World War II and those from Soviet Party military relations under Stalin. World War II, with the experience of a devastating war fought on Soviet territory, had a large influence on Soviet strategic nuclear doctrine and, as a result, the Soviet Union attached great importance to making its cities, vital centers, and nuclear rocket forces as invulnerable as possible. However, the impact of Stalin on civil-military relations in Soviet Russia is even more pertinent to this study. Stalin's purges of the officer corps in the 1930s, his bad treatment of Zhukov and other heroes of the Second World War, and his effort to diminish the military's role in the Soviet victory in that war taught the military to distrust the political leadership.[20]

As a result, after Stalin's death the Soviet military sought to reassert its prerogative in the development of strategic doctrine. Thus, after Khrushchev, the Soviet military manifested a willingness to dominate the promulgation of strategic doctrine as well as decisions on force posture. The military's success in defending its interests and asserting its perceived rights, coupled with the military's near monopoly on military-technical information and the development of doctrine, gave the Soviet military enormous influence over strategic decisions. In addition, the Soviet military's tendency to focus on military effectiveness and war fighting instead of the political-diplomatic context led military leaders to resist politically imposed limitations on the use of force. The implications of a strong military influence on strategic and military policy suggest that military preferences for the use of force and for a particular type of war would be less malleable to change directed from the civilian leadership.[21]

Even though the Second World War and Stalin's legacy were significant components of Russia's twentieth century historical experience, any analysis of Soviet strategic culture must recognize the merger of the Soviet experience with the military culture that existed before the Russian Revolution. The attention that Soviet military historians paid to the lessons of Imperial Russia's wars testifies to the relevance of pre-Soviet military culture to its contemporary military culture.

In other words, if the Russian military perceives that its history and military methods are distinct, despite transnational organizational parallels, the Russian approach to basic issues of security policy and military practice is likely to reflect this perception of distinctiveness. Thus, Imperial Russia's historic predilections for messianic expansionism into central Asia and the Caucasus would also remain a characteristic of the Soviet period.[22]

Moreover, Russia's loss of empire is significant, particularly concerning the invasion of Chechnya, because for the Russian political elites this loss of empire was a much more bewildering experience than was the loss of empire for the British, French, or Dutch. Unable to reconcile themselves to the loss, the Russian elites tried in various ways to reassert control over the separated borderlands and to regain great power status for mother Russia. Stated another way, post-Soviet Russia suffered from a lack of national esteem and respect that stemmed from her loss of great power status. A corollary to this had been the need of the Russian Army to show an image of power despite its degraded condition. These two facts together certainly contributed to Russia's imprudent decision and hasty invasion of Chechnya. As Richard Pipes observed, "For the ruling elite and much of the intelligentsia, accustomed to being regarded as citizens of a great power, the country's decline to Third World status has been traumatic."[23] Historically, for Russia's ruling elite, a superior military capacity and imperial splendor translated to power and influence.

According to William Odom, "the trauma and chaos induced in Russian military affairs by the breakup of the Soviet Union are difficult to exaggerate." Russian military elites even hoped that the CIS armed forces would replace the Soviet empire's armed forces. By 1992, however, that hope evaporated and the need to create a Russian national military institution became evident. During the following two years, the defense ministry's goals for force structure and dispositions evolved, ranging to and from full control of former Soviet territories to withdrawing back within the borders of the Russian Federation. Political struggles concerning the nature of Russia's foreign and security policy influenced these goals, but ultimately the defense ministry, with the help of conservative forces in Parliament and elsewhere, prevailed in reasserting Russian military influence in former Soviet territories, particularly in central Asia and in the Transcaucasus.[24]

The publication of the 1993 Russian military and security doctrine reflected this reassertion of the defense ministry's influence—this document asserted Russian security interests in the near abroad and in the military affairs of all CIS states and formed the legal basis for restoring the Russian military to the status of a first class power. Consequently, by 1994 the Russian military had become a large political factor in the face of a weak and fragmented civilian leadership, and it had contributed to Russia's entanglement in renewed imperialism. In fact, an aggressive approach to the near abroad justified a larger share of state resources for the military during a period of decreased spending due to economic turmoil.[25]

GEOPOLITICS

> The irony was that after a certain point, expansionism no longer enhanced Russian security but brought about its decline. Russia continued to identify Great Power status with territorial expansion; it hungered for more land, which it neither needed nor was able to digest.—Henry Kissinger[26]

According to Aymeric Chauprade, the Russian Empire has traditionally sought the domination of its Polish, Baltic, and Ukrainian peripheries as well as its central Asian colonies. For more than two centuries a large continental state, Russia has pushed for access to warm water oceans—the Indian Ocean and the Mediterranean—that would give Russia a more global reach. Moreover, Russia's physical security became ineluctably associated with land space, while its psychological security became inseparable from political centralization. Another expert explains that as a result of its open space, Russia had to stabilize and pacify the indigenous populations on the frontiers of its empire. In addition, Russian strategic culture was characterized by the notion of encirclement and by the notion of unstable populations on its borders that threatened Russia's security. As a consequence, there was an "offensive-defensive" dialectic that also characterized Russian geopolitics. Thus, because Russian expansion was partly offensive and partly defensive, it was always ambiguous and this ambiguity generated debates in the West over Russia's true intentions—debates that lasted through the Soviet period.[27]

As a result, Soviet Russia's approach to its geography and its security was rather paradoxical—its political doctrine was undoubtedly defensive, speaking of war only in the context of an attack on its territory, but its military strategy was undeniably offensive. This tension between political activity and the military offensive has remained largely unresolved since Frunze. Thus, during the Soviet era, Moscow's strategy attempted to make a distinction between military-political doctrine, which is supreme and essentially defensive, and military-technical doctrine (similar to strategy), which upholds the primacy of the offense and the need for surprise and initiative. In addition, the impact of a voluntaristic doctrine like Marxism on the geographical realities of Russia and her historical messianic tendencies not only reinforced the psychological obsession for security but also provided an ideological justification for presuming the implacable hostility of the outside world and sanctified Russian expansion with the "just" mission of liberating the downtrodden peoples of the world from their oppressors.[28]

However, Soviet images of Asia stemmed from both the perspective of Russian nationalism and from its communist ideology. Russian nationalism, coupled with its Eastern Orthodox legacy, its vision of Russia as a third Rome, and its notion of pan-Slavism, provides the connection between Soviet Russia and its Greek and Byzantine heritage. Russians, like Americans, considered their society as exceptional and Russia's expansion into central Asia had some features in common with America's westward expansion, such as the openness of frontiers and the presence of only feudal and primitive societies as barriers to expansion. Instead of manifest destiny, however, Russian expansion was infused by a Eurasianist messianism—a crusade led by Russian leaders to expand and civilize the "barbarians" to the south. In fact, this messianism was a fusion of several concepts, or perceptions: Russia's geopolitical position astride Europe and Asia; Russian nationalism and pan-Slavic literati; and the alleged altruism of Russia's orthodox faith. According to Kissinger, "Russia perceived itself not as a nation but as a cause, beyond geopolitics, impelled by faith, and held together by arms."[29]

In 1904, the British geographer Halford Mackinder, observing the distinct political and geographic characteristics of the Eurasian heartland, called the area "the geographical pivot of history." Mackinder's heartland theory predicted the rise of the Russian empire as the dominant world power in the future. Mackinder argued that Russia had inherited this strategically key advantage and central position from the steppe nomads and that Russia represented a remarkable "correlation between natural environment and political organization . . . unlikely to be altered by any possible social revolution." Moreover, central Asia became a potential theater of military operations in the late nineteenth century when czarist Russia consolidated its conquest of Turkestan. Central Asia came to serve a twofold purpose in Imperial Russia's security system. First, the region served as a support for Russia's east-west lifeline to Siberia. This conduit connected metropolitan Russia with its Pacific coast and was becoming more important and more fragile. Second, central Asia offered a convenient and relatively secure staging platform on the southern periphery of the Eurasian heartland. During the twentieth century, safeguarding the east-west lifeline, which crosses large parts of inner and eastern Asia, was almost synonymous with the protection of the Trans-Siberian Railroad.[30]

The paradox of Russian geopolitics, however, is found in the continuing ambivalence between a pervasive sense of insecurity and Russia's messianic zeal. The history of Imperial Russia and Soviet Russia is one of war and constant expansion. Its incessant quest for security evolved into expansion for its own sake—a kind of expansionistic inertia. However, the more Russia expanded, the more vulnerable it seemed to be because of the increased size of its territory and borders and because of tensions arising from the various nations it controlled (oppressed), many by force of arms. In its most absurd form, this contradiction translated to this: "unless the empire expanded, it would implode." Moreover, Stalin continued this expansionistic approach, defining his requirements for peace as the widest possible security buffer around the periphery of the Soviet Union. Stalin was a true practitioner of Realpolitik—he did not distinguish between democratic and fascist regimes and he did not have any friends, only interests. After World War II, in insisting on a free hand in establishing a security buffer in central Europe, Stalin was following historical Russian practice—expand in search of security.[31]

All of the nations of Europe were seeking aggrandizement by means of threats and counterthreats. But Russia seemed impelled to expand by a rhythm all its own, containable only by the deployment of superior force, and usually by war.[32]

Russia's southward projection of its empire and power into the Caucasus during the nineteenth century reflected the logic of its political geography. This expansion was inevitable since Russia was not impeded by natural barriers or by the once imperial powers of Ottoman Turkey and Persia. In fact, the Russian suppression of the Chechens in the nineteenth century and the Soviet suppression of the Basmachi in Turkestan in the beginning of the twentieth century had much in common with the Soviet and Russian invasions of Afghanistan and Chechnya in the second half of the twentieth century. According to another author, the historical pattern of Russian expansion into the southern tier was fourfold. The Russian wars in Asia and the Caucasus were protracted, largely by design. These wars were modest and limited—less than three percent of total land forces and less than three percent of defense expenditures. The wars were principally political because the Russians hoped not to lose militarily while they prepared the indigenous cadres to ensure victory in the longer term. Finally, the deeper the Russians expanded into the area, the more troublesome their geostrategic dilemma became. Well before the Soviet period, Russian images of Asia drew on the tension between an expansion considered inevitable and a strategic overextension thought to be insoluble.[33]

Finally, the collapse of the Soviet Union triggered a resurgence of Eurasianist activity in the 1990s. Zealous Eurasianists advocated the concept of a "Eurasian empire" set apart from both the Soviet and Russian empires and established by strengthening of geopolitical power and the unification of a Slav-Turkish community. Eurasianists underline the importance of domination, control, and conflict as concepts of power. Unlike Western realists who emphasize the state as the principal international actors, the Eurasianists support the idea of empires as principal actors. They also focus on international politics as an environment of struggle between different empires for resources and power. The Eurasian school also relies heavily on Russian religious philosophy and the messianism mentioned earlier—it sees Russia as a power with a unique geopolitical location and a unique geopolitical crusade to manage and reconcile military conflicts on its periphery. The impact of this school of thought on Russia's 1993 Military and Security Policy was significant.[34]

PREFERRED PARADIGM FOR WAR

It can be argued that Russian commanders in the 18th century were overly impressed by the Frederician model, which they adopted with great success.[35]

Combined arms doctrine still pervades Soviet thinking and the offensive is still the preferred method of warfare.[36]

There is an old military adage that "armies are always preparing for the last war," but a more accurate truism is that militaries are always preparing for the last good war, or the last successful war. The last good war for the Soviet and the post-Soviet Russian military was the Great War for the Fatherland—a total and conventional war of annihilation fought for the survival of Mother Russia. To be sure, as a great power, Russia had to embrace the big-power paradigm for war at least since the eighteenth century. Also, certainly the Eurocentric model of war evolved based on changes in industrial-technological capacities and due to sociopolitical changes that enabled nations and states to more efficiently harness and train soldiers. However, whether Russia was enamored of the Frederician, Jominian, or Clausewitzian model for war, it had to remain competent in the principal paradigm de jour to compete as a great power. In other words, the Russians, the Soviets, and then the Russians again embraced the big-war paradigm for the better part of three centuries. Likewise, the Soviet forces that invaded Afghanistan and the Russian forces that invaded Chechnya embraced the big, conventional war paradigm—tanks, artillery, and phase lines.[37]

That the Soviet Union inherited some historical baggage from Imperial Russia is evident in Condoleeza Rice's characterization of the Soviet military: "reliance on the military power of the state, acquired at great cost and organized like that of military powers of the past, was handed down to the Soviets by historical experience." Moreover, Soviet military thought, as it evolved from the uncertain days of 1917 to the victory over Germany in 1945, was the basis on which Soviet military power was constructed. Frunze's concept of warfare was total—mass warfare supported by the total mobilization of the state. Believing that the small, professional army characteristic of bourgeois states could not win the future war, he predicted that every member of the population would have to be inducted into the war effort. Frunze underlined the primacy of the offensive and the "centrality of maneuver in warfare." Of the Soviet military, one also observed an odd coupling of offensive military strategy with defensive political doctrine. The Soviets' military strategy sought to gain the upper hand by initiating attack.[38]

The Russian civil war taught the Soviet high command to avoid attritional wars against coalitions and to conduct rapid offensives against isolated enemies. After its victory in the civil war, the Soviet Army codified this experience into formal military doctrine that emphasized offensive warfare employing large-scale combined arms formations suitable to the terrain of the central European plateau. Tanks, infantry, and artillery played the principal role. Moreover, the Soviets established a highly centralized system of command and control and doctrinal development. "However, the problem with centralized control over the doctrinal process is that it stifles initiative and promotes rigid operations."[39]

In the 1920s, the Soviet Army adopted the operational art, precipitating the development of the principals of the deep operation and deep battle, moving from a theory of attrition to a theory of maneuver. In 1928, Tukhachevskii took command of the Leningrad Military District where he started the first experiments with mechanization and the use of parachute troops. Tukhachevskii became an avowed and impassioned supporter of mechanization—the mass, mechanized army implementing the new operational art on the battlefield, would be capable of carrying out the total destruction of the enemy through sequential and deep operations. In autumn of 1931, the newly created Operations Department of the Frunze Academy reexamined the fundamentals of the operational art and began investigating the means for decisive and annihilating operations. Moreover, the 1936 *Provisional Field Service Regulations* embraced the concept of deep battle with modern technology—it called for decisive offensives and the total destruction of enemy forces.[40]

The Soviet and Russian forces that invaded Afghanistan and Chechnya, as well as their force structure and doctrine, were a product of the *Velikaya Otchestvennaya Voyna*. The years 1942–1943 witnessed the evolution of an offensive method in which centrally controlled supporting fires preceded and supported the assault in depth. After 1943, the Soviets resurrected deep battle and the operational art with enormous success. In 1944 and 1945, multifront deep battles of annihilation emerged that conformed exactly to a strategy that pursued both military and political objectives. However, the driving force for the elaboration and evolution of this form of an operational art was technology. After Stalin's death, Zhukov modified the force structure by eliminating the corps and the mechanized army. Thus, from the 1950s until the 1990s, Soviet ground forces principally comprised the tank division and the motorized rifle division. In the 1970s, the Soviets' big-war model culminated with the development of the land-air battle concept that relied on technology to conduct "modern combined arms battle" fought "throughout the entire depth of the enemy battle formation."[41]

The Soviet armed forces that invaded Afghanistan and the Russian armed forces that attacked Grozny were structured and trained for large-scale conventional warfare. Moreover, Soviet military doctrine envisaged the employment of Soviet forces on flat, undulating terrain, like the plains of central Europe. This big-war approach is characterized by "heavy tank and mechanized formations, massed and echeloned to conduct breaches of dense defenses, followed by rapid advance into the enemy rear to encircle and destroy him." These offensives are supported by air-ground attack, long-range artillery, and airmobile assaults throughout the depth of the enemy's defense. The Soviet-Russian doctrine sought quick and decisive victory. Afghanistan confirmed what was already suspected about the general fighting capacity of the Soviet Army—it relied more on a concentration (quantity) of forces and artillery preparation than on flexibility and maneuver. However, there is a more disturbing paradox—Soviet military experts knew what to do to win in Afghanistan but did not do it because of a cultural reluctance, in other words, cultural inertia. There was no desire to change the doctrine, training, and organization of an army that was well adapted for a European war against its principal adversary.[42]

In addition, in 1992 the Russian Ministry of Defense issued a draft security doctrine stating that NATO remained the long-term threat but that regional conflicts and low-intensity warfare were more probable. However, the type of military doctrine and forces required for these two types of conflict seemed irreconcilable. The Russian General Staff also studied the Persian Gulf War in the context of other twentieth-century regional conflicts and concluded that conventional but nonlinear battle was the solution. This type of offensive would require mobile forces, conducting simultaneous operational and tactical maneuvers throughout the depths of the enemy's territory. In 1992, the Russian Defense Minister, General Grachev, adopted a new Mobile Forces Directorate to implement this idea, and in November 1994, President Yeltsin announced that the creation of the Mobile Force was complete.[43]

Finally, the following observation is a lucid and concise recapitulation of the Russian military's traditional role in Central Asia and the Caucasus:

> The Russian military has a long tradition of involvement in little wars on the edge of the empire. This tradition has at times had a positive effect on military innovation and reform. The military reforms of the 1860s–70s originated at least partly in the theater reforms carried out in the Caucasus by Dmitri Miliutin and his commanding general. Yet, more often, this military involvement engendered an independent and imperially minded set of officers, like Cherniaev, who tried to carry out their own foreign policies in Central Asia.[44]

COUNTERINSURGENCY: THE RUSSIAN MILITARY STRATEGIC PARADOX

Symmetric wars are total wars wherein the struggle is a zero-sum one for survival by both sides—the world wars being an example. On the other hand, an asymmetric struggle implies that the war for the indigenous insurgents is total but that it is inherently limited for the great power. This is because the insurgents pose no direct threat to the survival of the great power. Moreover, for the great power in an asymmetric situation, full military mobilization is neither politically possible nor considered necessary. The disparity in military capabilities is so great and the confidence that military power will predominate is so acute that victory is expected. However, although the inferior side possesses limited means, its aim is nonetheless the expulsion of the great power. The choice for the underdog is literally "death or victory."[45]

Interestingly, both the *mujahideen* and the Chechens, confronted with a strategic paradox of unlimited aims and limited means, were compelled to adopt a Fabian strategy against the Russian military. A Fabian strategy normally stems from a huge asymmetry of means that inheres in this strategic paradox. Quintus Sertorius, who during Rome's civil war used the following metaphor to convince his Spanish barbarian troops that it would be imprudent to engage the Roman Army in direct battle, elucidated this paradox well. He brought into the presence of his troops two horses, one very strong, the other very feeble. Then he brought up two youths of corresponding physique, one robust and one slight. The stronger youth was commanded to pull out the entire tail of the feeble horse, while the slight youth was commanded to pull out the hairs of the strong horse one by one.[46] Then, when the slight youth had succeeded in his task, while the strong one was still vainly struggling with the tail of the weak horse, Sertorius observed:

> By this illustration I have exhibited to you, my men, the nature of the Roman cohorts. They are invincible to him who attacks them in a body; yet he who assails them by groups will tear and rend them.[47]

Afghanistan

The overarching component of Soviet strategy beginning in December 1979 was its determination to limit the level of its military commitment. In view of the size force it was willing to commit, a plan of conquest and occupation was not feasible, nor was it ever considered. From the beginning, the Soviet strategy was based on the rejuvenation and the employment of the Democratic Republic of Afghanistan's (DRA) Army. It seems that the Soviets initially believed that they confronted a limited insurgency in Afghanistan. However, they eventually realized that the support of the population for the resistance was so strong that it exceeded the puppet DRA forces' capacity to counter it effectively.[48]

Soviet operations in the Afghan War, in fact, did not aim as much at defeating the *mujahideen* as they aimed to intimidate and terrorize the population into abandoning areas of intense resistance and withdrawing support for the guerrillas. The methods and weapons employed—deliberate destruction of villages, high-altitude carpet bombing, napalm, fragmentation bombs, and the use of booby-trapped toys—testify to the intent of the Soviet military's effort to terrorize the Afghan civilian population. These methods, together with a scorched-earth policy and the heavy mining of the key highways and the perimeters of towns, also resulted in the destruction of a large part of agricultural lands. Moreover, according to a 1984 report by French doctors working in the resistance-controlled areas, more than eighty percent of the casualties inflicted by the Soviet military were civilian.[49]

Afghanistan was a limited or asymmetric conflict because the Soviet Union fought a limited war while the *mujahideen* fought a total war. Moscow intentionally limited both the scope of its operations and the amount of forces it committed. On the other hand, for the resistance it was a total war—a war for the survival and the future of their country. To be sure, the Soviet military did not lose the fight in Afghanistan, it simply failed to win—it did not achieve its goals. Moreover, the army that returned from Afghanistan was battered, physically and psychologically. On the other hand, the *mujahideen* were not victorious but remained unvanquished nonetheless. "The guerrillas quickly established that they would not attain a resounding victory, but could sap the invaders' will to fight on. Essentially, the Afghan guerrillas proved Kissinger's maxim—'the guerrilla wins if he does not lose; the conventional army loses if it does not win.'"[54] The Afghani resistance fighters effectively countered the Soviet strategy of annihilation by conducting a protracted war of attrition.[50]

Chechnya

> There is no winning. We know that if we are fighting, we are winning. If we are not, we have lost. The Russians can kill us and destroy this land. Then they will win. But we will make it very painful for them.[51]

The fledgling Chechen Army defeated a Eurasian great power's ostensibly superior army because it was able to use conventional tactics in an unorthodox manner to concentrate against Russian Army weaknesses. In Grozny, Dudayev successfully used a combination of conventional and unconventional methods to fight the Russians. Since asymmetry characterized the relationship between the Chechen Army and the Russian Army, the Chechens' methods in urban combat were sound because the Chechens avoided open battle against the Russian forces and exploited the advantages of urban defense to inflict enormous casualties against them.

Dudayev's army was limited in personnel, resources, and training, and he soon realized that committing his troops to open battle against the Russians would invite disaster. Therefore, after the Chechen Army's costly defenses of Grozny in 1995, Dudayev avoided head-on collisions with the Russian Army. Acknowledging these limitations, Dudayev adopted an indirect strategy of attrition in which he avoided general actions against the Russian main efforts but instead concentrated what forces he had against weak enemy outposts and piecemeal detachments. Dudayev's plan for victory was to keep the war going by preserving his forces and wearing down the Russian will to fight with raids against the periphery of its forces. A corollary to Dudayev's approach was the notion that his recruiting pool would increase as the Russians used more force less discriminately in their pursuit of the guerrillas. Russell Weigley, a prominent U.S. military historian, first explained this strategic paradox in the context of the American Revolution. The Chechens faced the same paradox and from this contradiction stemmed their "strategy of erosion": on the one hand, the Chechens had a political objective that was absolute—the absolute removal of the Russian military from Chechnya; however, on the other hand, the Chechens' military means were so weak that there was no other alternative than a strategic defensive.[52]

Therefore, the Russian Army in Chechnya was confounded by the "principal contradiction" that characterizes asymmetric struggles. The Russians, moreover, had fallen into the dilemma of a war of posts conceived as a counter to a guerrilla campaign. Once dispersed, their outposts had never been numerous enough to control the country, because partisan raids on the smaller posts had compelled them to consolidate into fewer and fewer garrisons. But the garrisons were too few and too small to check the partisans' operations throughout the countryside.

Notwithstanding Chechnya's relatively small size, there simply were not enough troops to control the entire country against a tenacious opponent fighting for survival.[53]

Thus, the Chechen strategy of erosion against the Russians was not unlike both Mao Tse-Tung's and Henry Kissinger's prescriptions for guerrilla victory. Dudayev's strategic purpose had to be to break the resolve of the Russian government and the Russian population through gradual and persistent engagements against peripheral and poorly organized detachments of Russian forces. The Chechens, on the other hand, conducted a strategic defensive, coupled with tactical attacks aimed at inflicting Russian losses, and "did not lose" by preserving their small army. Dudayev's forces were so weak compared to the Russian forces that he could not afford to confront the Russians in many conventional battles because his soldiers could not win. However, the Chechens' political objectives—to expel the Russian Army and gain independence—were total. To find a way out of this contradiction, Dudayev had to rely mainly not on a total military victory but on the possibility that the political opposition in Moscow might in time force the Yeltsin government to abandon the conflict. The weaker, but more skillful Chechen fighters accomplished this by refusing to confront the Russians on their own terms and by instead resorting to unorthodox approaches.

RUSSIAN MILITARY CULTURE, TECHNOLOGY, AND AFGHANISTAN

This paradox stems from a huge disparity in resource power. As previously argued, there are huge differences in the levels of technological and industrial capacities between adversaries in asymmetric conflicts—the big power possesses an overwhelming advantage in potential combat power. This disparity inheres in the structure of any conflict that witnesses a peripheral power facing a core power. One can certainly infer from this example that not only does conventional military and technological superiority not ensure victory but it may even undermine victory in an asymmetric context. One need only ask a veteran of Afghanistan how superior numbers and technology fare against a guileful opponent using an asymmetric approach. The Soviets brought the entire repertoire of an industrialized power's military technology to bear against the *mujahideen* and the Afghan people. However, the Russians failed to recognize that technology is no substitute for strategy and will. In fact, maximizing technology by using force indiscriminately, coupled with the absence of anything approximating a counterinsurgency campaign, helped undermine the Soviets' efforts in Afghanistan by alienating the population. The Soviets introduced and tested new technology during the Afghan War. The most notable of the new weapons were the BMP-2, the BTR-80, the 82mm automatic mortar, the self-propelled mortar, the AGS-17 automatic grenade launcher, the BM-22 Multiple Rocket Launcher System, the MI-8T helicopter, the SU-25 ground support aircraft, and the ASU-74 assault rifle. In addition, the Soviets introduced several models of the MI-24 attack helicopter during the war. However, despite all this technology, Afghanistan was a war for the light infantry and the Soviets did not have light infantry.[54]

Not only did the Soviets lack light infantry, however, but their motorized infantry troops could not easily transition to light infantry because they were married to their armored personnel carriers and to the heavy technology that such a marriage entails. The Soviet reliance on mechanized forces and massive fire-power made the soldiers' load so heavy that any movement on foot beyond 1 kilometer from their BMP, especially given the terrain and heat in Afghanistan, would exhaust them. For example, the standard flak jacket weighed 16 kilograms and the Soviet emphasis on massive firepower instead of accuracy meant the soldier carried a lot more ammunition. Plus, the weight of crew-served weapons was prohibitive for serious dismounted maneuver—the 12.7 mm heavy machine gun weighs 34 kilograms without its tripod, the AGS-17 weighs 30.4 kilograms, and one AGS-17 ammunition drum weighs 14.7 kilograms. Thus benefiting from all this *technology,* a dismounted Soviet soldier in Afghanistan was so encumbered that he could not catch up with the Afghan guerrillas.[55]

Nonetheless, the Soviets in Afghanistan, like the Americans in Vietnam, discovered that helicopters were very useful for fighting the *mujahideen* because of their mobility, armament, range, and versatility. Considering the vast territory to cover and the decentralized nature of operations in Afghanistan, the Soviets would have done much worse without the helicopter. The helicopter did not enable the Soviets to adapt from a conventionally oriented force to a truly counterinsurgency-oriented force, but it did help them bring the fight to the *mujahideen* much more effectively. "Helicopters provided a mobility of combat power that the rebels in no way could match, enhanced surprise, reduced rebel reaction time, enabled Soviet forces to react to rebel threats rapidly, and provided Soviet forces their best means of exercising the initiative." In addition, the low-air defense threat (until 1986) allowed the Soviets the luxury of seasoning their pilots and testing its helicopters in a relatively low-risk environment.[56]

However, the Soviet strategy in Afghanistan essentially focused on the use of high technology and tactical mobility (mainly provided by the helicopter) as a means to inflict casualties on the Afghanis while at the same time holding Soviet casualties to a minimum. In fact, the Soviets used their technology to conduct a combination of the scorched earth method and "migratory genocide." There were numerous reports that showed that Soviet forces, especially attack helicopters, were used to destroy villages and burn crops to force the population—the main source of support for the *mujahideen*—to leave the country. Other reports implied that the Soviets were declaring free-fire zones in areas where there was a strong presence of resistance forces. According to one expert on the Soviets, "the Soviet monopoly on high technology" in Afghanistan "magnified the destructive aspects of their behavior." The average quantity of "high-technology" airborne platforms in Afghanistan was around two hundred forty attack helicopters, four hundred other helicopters, several squadrons of MiG-21s and MiG-23s, and at least one squadron of SU-25 ground attack aircraft. Afghanistan was also the first operational deployment for the SU-25. The following excerpt helps underline the normal template for the Soviets' use of technology and firepower:[57]

> Notably in the valleys around Kabul, the Russians undertook a series of large operations employing hundreds of tanks, mobilizing significant resources, using bombs, rockets, napalm, and even, once, gas, destroying everything in their path, not accepting any quarter, and not expecting any in return.[58]

Moreover, after Gorbachev's assumption of power in March 1985, the Soviet forces in Afghanistan better employed their technological advantage to improve their performance. They made particularly effective use of the Mi-24 and Mi-25 Hind helicopters and of the insertion of special forces units behind enemy lines. Prior to 1985, the Soviet forces largely remained in their garrisons, and outside their garrisons, they generally only operated in armor vehicles along the main highways connecting the major cities. By 1986, the Soviet military's technological and tactical innovations (although still fixed within a conventional-war paradigm) were getting results against the *mujahideen* resistance. However, in April 1986 the Americans decided to provide the *mujahideen* with Stinger shoulder-fired antiaircraft missiles, and this marked a turning point in the war. The guerrillas were then able to undermine a key Soviet technological advantage—the mobility and firepower of helicopters. Estimated aircraft losses were one per day. As a result, the Soviets were no longer able to use helicopter gun ships in a ground support role and the effectiveness of the Spetznaz was degraded as insertion by helicopter became limited.[59]

The introduction and employment of the Stinger beginning in 1986 showed how guerrillas could inflict heavy losses against a regular industrialized army without having a high level of training and organization. The result was also an increased Soviet reliance on artillery and high-level aerial bombardment. The longer the war lasted and the more the Soviets tried to use technology and massive firepower to limit their losses, the more they caused civilian losses. As a result, the resistance to the Soviets became more galvanized, organized, and effective. Despite the Soviets' relatively high technology and the *mujahideen*'s relatively primitive technology, notwithstanding the Stingers, the Soviets' equipment losses in Afghanistan were as follows: 118 jets, 333 helicopters, 147 tanks, 1314 armored personnel carriers, 433 artillery pieces and mortars, 1138 radio sets and CP vehicles, 510 engineering vehicles, and 11,369 trucks.[60]

Considering the Soviets' huge technological advantage, they certainly lost a significant amount of materiel to the primitive and barbaric Afghanis. This clearly shows that an asymmetry of technology does not ensure victory—for every technological advantage, there is a counter, either technologically as was the case with the Stinger or adaptively as was the case with the RPG. Before the Stingers arrived in theater, the guerrillas had already shot down several hundred helicopters with well-placed machine guns and RPGs modified with a fan tail device (to redirect the back blast) that allowed the *mujahideen* to aim this shoulder-fired antitank weapon at airborne targets. Twenty years later, Somali militiamen trained by *mujahideen* veterans similarly employed RPGs to shoot down two American Black Hawk helicopters, precipitating a U.S. withdrawal from Somalia. As a footnote, the Afghanis also used sheep to clear minefields—a very low-technology solution to a high-technology problem.

RUSSIAN MILITARY CULTURE, COUNTERINSURGENCY, AND WILL

Core big powers are unable or unwilling to accept high casualties indefinitely in peripheral wars. It is the weaker side's national endurance, will, or high threshold for pain, sometimes manifested by a capacity to willingly accept whatever the costs that enables small powers to succeed against big powers. As explained in Chapter 2, all asymmetric conflicts exhibit a similar contradiction of will. Since the weaker opponent lacks the technological capacity to destroy the external power's military capability but nonetheless has unlimited political aims such as independence, it must look to the political impact on the metropolis. In other words, "the insurgents must retain a minimum degree of invulnerability" to avoid defeat, and to win they must be able to impose a continual aggregation of costs on their adversaries. From a strategic perspective, the rebels' aim must be to provoke the great power into escalating the conflict. This in turn will incur political and economic costs on the external power—the normal costs of war, such as soldiers killed and equipment destroyed—but over time these may be seen as too high when the security of the great power is not directly threatened. Domestic discontent in the great power will therefore increase as battle losses and economic costs escalate in a war against an adversary that poses no direct threat to its vital interests: "in a limited war, it is not at all clear to those groups whose interests are adversely affected why such sacrifices are necessary." Equally salient is the fact that the need to risk death will seem less clear to both conscripts and professional soldiers when the survival of their country is not at risk. This consideration is germane to counterinsurgency operations, when great powers employ modern militaries in less-developed areas.[61]

Afghanistan

> The ceiling of intervention chosen by Brezhnev, although rather low, was too high for Gorbachev. Soviet public opinion became more vocal; and in light of the "charm offensive" directed at the West, the war appeared increasingly objectionable.[62]

The paradox of will was particularly apparent in Afghanistan because even from the outset of direct Soviet involvement, the Brezhnev government sought to limit the Soviet commitment to a tolerable level. Moreover, the conventionally-minded

Soviet security apparatus incorrectly determined, just as the American one did during Vietnam, that the destruction of the Afghan villages and crops would strip the guerrillas of their means to wage war, thereby making their will to wage it irrelevant. The Soviets, likewise did not succeed in bombing the *mujahideen* into either submission or the "Stone Age": Afghanistan had a very underdeveloped infrastructure and the will of the people to repel the infidel invaders was too strong. Notwithstanding tons of bombs and hundreds of thousands of dead, the enemy's will was resolute and the Soviets' will to see the war to a successful conclusion was limited. Lacking the military means to destroy the Soviet capacity to wage war, the *mujahideen* focused on raising the costs and undermining Moscow's political capability to continue to support the prosecution of the war. In Afghanistan, just as the Vietcong had in Vietnam, the *mujahideen* attacked the enemy's cohesion and unity because if the counterinsurgents' will was weakened or defeated, then their military capability would no longer be relevant.[63]

In Afghanistan, the domestic dimensions of the conflict were superseded by *jihad*, or a religious war against the invading infidels. Islam and nationalism became interwoven, and a galvanized ideological crusade against the Soviets superseded the more secular tribal perspective. Moreover, instead of gaining support for the more moderate government it installed, the Soviet invasion in fact precipitated a backlash even among those Afghans previously loyal to the government. The invasion fused Islamic ideology with the cause of national liberation. After the invasion, thousands of officers and soldiers of the Afghan Army defected to the *mujahideen* and the insurgents seized hundreds of government outposts, most of which had been abdicated by defecting soldiers. For example, Massoud gained control of the entire Panjshir Valley during the spring of 1980 whereas before the invasion his forces had been confined to a much smaller part of the upper valley.[64]

On the other hand, the Soviets sought to limit their role in the war from the outset because they were not prepared to incur the necessary human costs. The Soviet aim was never to win outright victory on the battlefield but instead to undermine and divide the *mujahideen* with an indirect and long-term strategy. This strategy was threefold: conducting a war of attrition and reprisals; sealing the borders against supply routes, coupled with direct pressure on Pakistan by bombing and terrorist operations; and penetrating the resistance movement. In addition, aware of the American debacle in Vietnam, the Soviets wanted to avoid the "Vietnam syndrome" by keeping the war local and at a low level and avoiding escalation or direct spillover into adjacent countries. Moreover, the Soviet Union could not afford to commit its best units for a long time in Afghanistan because the "maintenance of its empire depended on a heavy and permanent military presence in its satellite states." This unwillingness to commit significant forces there made the Soviets very cautious and conservative militarily, at all levels. During their ten-year war in Afghanistan, not once did the Soviets endeavor to build a counterinsurgency force or establish counterinsurgency doctrine.[65]

To keep the Afghan war at a low level, therefore, the Soviets had to limit the human, economic, diplomatic, and political costs. As a result, they put the troop ceiling at 115,000, did not pursue the enemy into his sanctuary in Pakistan, tried to minimize casualties as much as possible, tried to avoid extended diplomatic isolation, and tried to consolidate the Kabul government militarily and politically in order to limit the direct involvement of Soviet troops. However, the political will even for this limited level of commitment was not sustainable in the long term. Although the actual costs of the Soviet war in Afghanistan did not change in 1985, Gorbachev's new policies could not bear this level of commitment because the costs were less bearable for the following reasons: Soviet public opinion became more vocal under Glasnost; the war appeared objectionable vis-à-vis the "charm offensive" toward the West; and the Soviet government became more reluctant to subsidize ineffective governments in the Third World, such as Cuba and Vietnam.[66]

In the end, "the Kremlin's leadership simply was unwilling to make a larger troop commitment when the numbers that might be necessary for victory were unclear in the first place, and the political and economic costs of such escalation would be too high." As a result, the Soviets chose to conduct the war with a heavy reliance on bombing and air power—an approach that surely kept the *mujahideen* from achieving quick victory but which by itself could not destroy the resistance. As long as the *mujahideen* were willing to suffer the punishment required to sustain and to protract their struggle for national survival, and as long as neighboring states provided sanctuary and external support, the inevitable outcome was a stalemate.[67]

Chechnya

> The Chechens knew it would be very difficult to actually destroy Russian armed forces in battle; they sought to destroy their opponent's *will* to fight.[68]

A principal reason why many observers and the Russian government underestimated the Chechen will to resist was because the Dudayev regime appeared so ramshackle and his troops seemed so unimpressive and so disliked by the majority of the Chechen population. What the Russian government missed "were the deep underlying strengths of Chechen society and the Chechen tradition, as tempered and hardened by the historical experience of the past two hundred years." Although these same characteristics have impeded the creation of modern and democratic institutions, they have afforded the Chechens a very formidable capacity for national armed resistance. The Chechens are, in fact, one of the great warrior peoples of modern history. However, this underestimation of the Chechens was very characteristic of some colonial approaches to ethnography and in "an equally common pattern, this was related to a view of the enemy society as not just primitive but also static." This capacity of the Russians to underestimate less-developed adversaries is a bit surprising because the first conflict in Chechnya came only six years after the Soviet withdrawal from Afghanistan, an event that should have taught the Russians not to underestimate semiprimitive opponents in the context of counterinsurgent warfare.[69]

From the outset of the conflict in Chechnya, there was a conspicuous Russian lack of will to prosecute the conflict. Oddly enough, it was initially most acute among the Russian forces that entered Grozny: they were underpaid, poorly equipped, poorly clothed, and uninformed about the purpose and goals of the operation. In addition, the average Russian soldier and some Russian officers were not enthused about shooting at whom they viewed as fellow Russian citizens. Contrariwise, there was not a lot of support for Dudayev's corrupt and inefficient government before the conflict began. However, the Russian invasion, coupled with the inappropriate and excessive methods employed by the Russians, quickly catalyzed a consolidation of Chechen resistance. As a result, there was a great asymmetry of will: the Chechen tactics and techniques inflicted huge casualties on the Russians who had no strong desire or clear reasons for fighting there, whereas the Russians' excessive and indiscriminate use of force, causing much death and destruction among noncombatants, increased and reinforced the will of the Chechens to continue the struggle.

> Their god is liberty and their law is war.—Lermontov

There are also some unique Chechen cultural characteristics that contribute to the will of the Chechen people to resist foreign domination. Two principal traditions are *adat* and *teip*. *Adat* is an ancient system of retribution, an unwritten code based on revenge that incorporates "an eye for an eye" sense of justice. *Teip* is a tradition that requires clan members to fight fiercely to preserve their clan's independence, culture, and separate identity. In addition, there is another very old Chechen tradition of looking to older men for wisdom and to younger men for the warrior spirit. These two characteristics unite Chechen society and explain their will to resist foreign domination. This kind of will can outlast superior combat forces and superior technology. To the Chechens' warrior culture, one can add intense historical hatred of Russia and Russians among elements of the Chechen population. Beginning with General Yermelov's scorched-earth policy in 1816, continuing with several decades of Russian cut-and-burn counterinsurgency and deportations, and ending with Stalin's 1944 deportation of the entire Chechen population to central Asia, no other people evokes the enmity of the Chechens more than the Russians. Inexplicably, and exacerbating an already strong Russophobia among the Chechen population, in 1949 Soviet authorities erected a statue of General Yermelov in Grozny. The inscription on the statue declared, "There is no people under the sun more vile and deceitful than this one."[70]

In addition, the Russians did nothing to win the battle of wills in Chechnya—there was no effort to "win the hearts and minds" of the people. Even though most experts in counterinsurgency would underline the importance of winning over the population, the Russian Army entered Chechnya without any civil affairs or psychological operations units and this complicated their difficulties. The Russians failed to take into account both the will and the skill of the opponent they would face in one of the most difficult venues for combat—urban combat. On the other hand, the lack of leadership and political conviction on the Russian side created a vulnerability that could be exploited by the Chechens. Since political support for Yeltsin's decision to invade was weak from the outset, both the Yeltsin administration and the Chechens realized that the will of the Russian people was an important target. Yeltsin tried to bolster public support for the war through a disinformation campaign—the government provided distorted accounts of friendly casualties, civilian casualties, and types of weapons used.[71]

However, the Chechens very effectively used two psychological operations instruments to undermine Russian support for the war: the media and dramatic raids into Russian territory. Chechen guerrillas conducted two raids against urban areas—Budyonnovsk and Pervomaiskoye—raids that were highly publicized by the media and that triggered intense public outcries about the conduct of the conflict among the Russian people and world opinion.[72]

CONTRADICTION IN MILITARY CULTURES: CLAUSEWITZ, MAO, AND CHECHNYA

> One execution will save the life of a hundred Russians and prevent a thousand Muslims from committing treason.—General Yermolov[73]

The historical continuity manifested by the Russian invasion of Chechnya, just five and a half years after Soviet troops withdrew from Afghanistan, is remarkable. To be certain, Russia was much weaker and the Russian armed forces that went into Grozny in December 1994 were even less trained and more poorly equipped. Nonetheless, however much Russia had fallen from superpower status and however much Russian military power was degraded, the Russian forces that invaded Chechnya still exhibited the military cultural preferences of a great power. Whatever training level the Russian military had sustained was still focused on fighting big wars because of the cultural inertia attending the large military bureaucracies of big powers. Being consistent with the Russian great-power tradition, Yeltsin adopted a hard line against the Chechens and surrounded himself with advisers who were hawks. He removed hesitant military commanders, fired the doves in the Ministry of Defense, and denounced his critics in the press. Moreover, the Russian military employed massive force, including heavy aerial and artillery bombardments of Grozny and other cities, excessive force, in fact, that created a level of indiscriminate carnage that reminded many observers of the Afghan war. After weeks of such methods, which resulted in thousands of military and civilian casualties, the Russians took control of Grozny and began a string of very costly but successful attacks on other cities using the same approach. General Yermelov would have been smiling in his grave.[74]

Russian forces surrounded Grozny on three sides and entered the city from the north, moving headlong into hell. The Chechen force was not a regular army but rather a composite force of armed militia (guerrillas) and a few regular forces. Much of the equipment they used had been left behind by Russia's armed forces when they departed in 1993. However, the Chechens spoke Russian, had served in the Russian armed forces, and had Russian uniforms. This made it easier to understand Russian plans and tactics and to use deception against the Russians. Clearly, the Chechens also had an enormous advantage as a native defender in the battle of Grozny. In addition to the guerrillas' knowledge of the city's sewer, metro, and tram systems, they also knew the back alleys, buildings, and streets. On the other hand, the Russians did not know Grozny, they lacked the right maps, and as a result they often got lost, stumbling into Chechen ambushes or firing on friendly forces. Unit boundaries were virtually impossible to coordinate because of the lack of good maps. Although the guerrillas fought the Battle of Grozny more conventionally than they did operations subsequent to this battle, they nonetheless used an unorthodox Fabian approach, harnessing the advantages of urban sprawl to undermine the Russians' technology. Their preferred tactic was to isolate Russian forces in some alley, than to ambush and destroy the Russian force in a piecemeal fashion.[75]

After the battle of Grozny, the Chechens chose to conduct a battle of successive cities, intending to repeat the pain they inflicted on the Russians in Grozny elsewhere. They moved their operations to Argun, Shali, and other urban centers because they realized that they could accomplish two goals with urban warfare: they could negate the Russian advantages in firepower in open terrain from helicopters, combat aircraft, and tanks and they could blend in with the local population to their advantage. This not only made it very difficult to discriminate between civilians and combatants, but it also helped the Chechens recruit more warriors and win the support of the population, thanks to the Russians' use of force. When Russian forces entered a city, they typically killed and wounded civilians and destroyed property—not the ideal way to "win hearts and minds."[76]

On 9 February 1995, the Chechen command decided to withdraw the largest portion of its forces from Grozny because the balance of forces was shifting against them and because the Russians were getting smarter about fighting there. Even though the Chechens had inflicted significant Russians, they also had suffered serious losses in Grozny. In the true Maoist style of "hit and run to fight another day," the Chechens decided to cut their losses and move their base of operations to the mountains—another milieu in which mechanized conventional forces are at a distinct disadvantage. Once in the mountains, the Chechen Defense Committee made a deliberate shift to partisan methods that included attacks against isolated Russian outposts, ambushes along roadways, diversionary attack against railway lines, and attacks against lines of logistics. Moreover, the guerrillas consistently avoided direct battles with Russian forces and focused instead on surprise attacks, always withdrawing with their dead immediately afterward.[77]

In addition, there are several anecdotal examples of how the Chechens employed Maoist-asymmetric methods to exploit the weaknesses of their conventional Russian enemy. One such method was to use the seams between the Russian units, coupled with the poor coordination between Russian formations, to provoke the Russian elements to fire ate each other. A small group of Chechen warriors would infiltrate between the Russian units at night and fire their weapons in both directions, with machine guns and grenade launchers. Sometimes the Chechens would even use trotyl-enhanced antitank grenades. As soon as the Russians troops responded with fire, the Chechens would withdraw. As a result, the Russian units would continue to fire at each other for a long time before they realized they were committing fratricide. Often enough, they kept firing at each other until sunrise the next morning, when helicopters providing assistance could observe and clarify the situation. The guerrillas also intercepted nonsecure Russian radio transmissions; as a result, the Chechens were sometimes able to deceive Russian aircraft into attacking their own troops.[78]

The Russians also had difficulty pursuing dismounted infantry in an urban environment. Chechen infantry consistently eluded Russian troops for the duration of the war. Every time a Russian mechanized task force surrounded a Chechen village, most Chechens were able to exfiltrate through the surrounding Russian units. The Chechen advantage stemmed from the fact that they used an asymmetric approach that fused Fabius with Mao. Their tactics were simple; they had light and portable grenade launchers, machine guns, and antitank weapons, and as a result they were mobile. In addition, the Chechens avoided situations in which Russian numbers and conventional forces would be at an advantage—they avoided strengths and attacked weaknesses. On the other hand, the Russian Army was Clausewitzian, trained to fight according to the conventional rules against other regular army units on the plains of Europe. The Russians were not trained to fight against an enemy composed of small groups, in either urban terrain or in mountainous terrain.[79]

TIME AND SPACE—THE DISPERSION AND CONCENTRATION CONUNDRUM

> The enemy, employing his small forces against a vast country, can only occupy some big cities and main lines of communication and part of the plains. Thus there are extensive areas in the territory under his occupation which he has had to leave ungarrisoned and which provide a vast arena for our guerrilla warfare.—Mao Tse-Tung[80]

Time and space present another paradox for the big metropolitan power that is endeavoring to counter an insurrection in an underdeveloped peripheral country. In the vast expanses of China, Mao masterfully manipulated time and space to cause Japanese forces to disperse. By inducing the dispersal of the Kwantung Army, Chinese guerrillas could attack isolated outposts and attrit Japanese forces piecemeal. Essentially, the weaker opponent can use time and space factors to shape the concentration-dispersion chimera to its advantage. The asymmetric strategist uses space to draw his enemy out to the countryside, making it difficult for the big power to concentrate its numerical superiority. The conventional force, then, must use more and more troops to secure its lines of communications, resulting in a host of isolated outposts. The weaker adversary is thereby able to locally concentrate his inferior numbers against overextended detachments. B. H. Liddell Hart refers to this as an inversion of the orthodox principle of concentration and offers this description:

> Dispersion is an essential condition of survival and success on the guerrilla side, which must never present a target and thus can only operate in minute particles, though these may momentarily coagulate like globules of quick-silver to overwhelm some weakly guarded objective.[81]

In other words, a prudent peripheral opponent harnesses time and space to disperse the great power's military forces, thereby protracting the conflict: "Mao and Giap have repeatedly emphasized that the principal contradiction which the imperialist army must confront on the ground derives from the fact that forces dispersed to control territory become spread so thinly that they are vulnerable to attack." Also, if the big power concentrates its forces to overcome this vulnerability, then other areas are left insecure. A massive increase in metropolitan forces can help resolve this operational contradiction, but it also immediately increases the domestic costs of the war. Conversely, if the great power wants to placate domestic opposition by withdrawing some forces, the contradiction at the operational level becomes more acute.[82]

Mao explained that the "guerrilla can prolong his struggle and make it a protracted war by "employing manpower in proper concentrations and dispersions" and by concentrating against dispersed enemy detachments that are relatively weaker. For every territorial space, there is an inevitable mathematical logic that dictates how many troops are required to exert control. For example, T. E. Lawrence claimed that it would have required twenty Turkish soldiers for every square mile (600,000 total—a prohibitive number) to control the Arab revolt. Similarly, although the Russian forces were far superior in numbers, they were unable to concentrate against their enemies because of the terrain and because of the ability of the *mujahideen* and the Chechen guerillas to use the terrain to protract the war. Both guerrillas compelled the Russians to disperse in order to protect their vulnerable lines of communications.[83]

Afghanistan

> We must make war everywhere and cause dispersal of his forces and dissipation of his strength.—Mao Tse-Tung[84]

The absence of a well-developed transportation infrastructure and the difficult terrain in Afghanistan dictated the terms of combat to a large degree. Although there were single major highways that connected the major cities and despite the route to the Soviet frontier, Afghanistan lacked a serious road network. Consequently, the mobility of modern mechanized and motorized forces in the rugged terrain in the central and northern regions of Afghanistan proved exceedingly difficult and vulnerable to attack by small guerrilla bands. Nevertheless, the Soviets did carry the war to the resistance by conducting air and helicopter operations into rebel-controlled areas. "Aerial bombing, sometimes massive, typically accompanied such campaigns and contributed to a population exodus on such a scale that one Afghanistan expert used the term 'migratory genocide' to describe it." The Soviets, like the Americans in Vietnam, bombed potential resistance pockets, destroying crops, villages, and anything else that might support guerrilla operations. However, even though the Soviets showed that they could go wherever they wanted, they could not hunt down and rout the guerrillas, who melted away into the mountains and ravines. When the Soviets withdrew, the insurgents returned.[85]

It was not the capabilities of the guerrilla fighters alone that prevented the Soviets from winning in Afghanistan. The Soviet's conventional doctrine did not work in that type of physical environment. Instead of the open terrain and moderate climate of Europe, the Soviets found desert and very restrictive mountainous terrain, with very extreme variations in temperature and weather. Also, the road, rail, and logistical infrastructure were very underdeveloped. This environment was an advantage for the *mujahideen* because it restricted the movement and fires of the heavy Soviet forces and it caused huge command and control problems. Moreover, the Soviets' own air and ground logistical organizations were not initially capable of supporting dispersed forces in such difficult terrain.[86]

The vast space of Afghanistan and the limited quantity of Soviet troops practically guaranteed a temporal and spatial enigma for the Soviets. For most of the war in Afghanistan, Soviet troop strength was between 80,000 and 115,000, but at least thirty to thirty-five percent of that was dedicated to securing lines of communication and bases. For example, the defense of convoy units against ambush, "the most venerated tactic in the guerrilla repertoire," posed an enormous security problem. Even still, the lack of good highways and the frequency of *mujahideen* ambushes had already congested the transportation network in Afghanistan. However, the Soviets' principal priority was the control of their lines of communication back to Soviet territory. Their second priority was the disruption of the *mujahideen*'s logistics. As a result, the paradox of concentration and dispersion, which stems from unfavorable time and space factors, was clearly manifest in Afghanistan: the majority of Soviet forces were concentrated on their bases and their lines of communication and the rest of their forces were inevitably overdispersed in the valleys and the mountains, hunting guerrillas.[87]

Chechnya

> And if I concentrate while he divides, I can use my strength to attack a fraction of his. There, I will be numerically superior. Then if I am able to use many to strike few at a selected point, those I deal with will be in dire straits.—Sun Tzu[88]

The Chechens made good use of urban and nonurban terrain to delay the Russian forces, to inflict significant casualties, and to protract what Russian political and military leaders hoped would be a quick and decisive war. Russian Minister of Defense Grachev was so confident in a quick victory that he boasted it would require only one Russian parachute regiment to remove the Chechen leadership in short measure. There were two aspects to the Chechens' conduct of the war: urban guerrilla and mountain guerrilla. Certainly, the urban terrain was very different than the terrain that either Mao or Sun Tzu envisaged when they explained the notions of dispersion, concentration, time, and space. However, the Chechens' knowledge of Grozny, combined with their guileful guerrilla methods, allowed them to exploit the concentration-dispersion conundrum. For example, in Grozny, whenever the Russians occupied defensive positions, they usually placed several people in every building—in the urban version of an outpost. Consequently, such Russian forces were dispersed and vulnerable and the Chechens generally exploited this by concentrating a single strike force, or "fist," to attack these urban outposts piecemeal.[89]

There was also the notion of urban defense as "defenseless defense." The Chechens chose not to defend from strong points but to remain absolutely mobile and difficult to find. Their hit-and-run tactics in the cities made it very difficult for Russian troops to locate, fix, and bring overwhelming firepower against them. As a result, the Russians' strengths were mitigated, and the Russians often attacked with piecemeal forces. According to another author, the battle for the cities showed that the urban forests of the nineteenth century have been replaced with the "urban forests" so skillfully exploited by the Chechens. The Chechens simply applied their mastery at the art of forest warfare, so evident in the eighteenth and nineteenth centuries, to the urban forests in Grozny and other cities. In the nineteenth century, the Russians had shown that they could cut down enormous swaths of forest and make the land unsuitable for asymmetric strategies, but a city destroyed by artillery and bombs is just as good as an intact one for conducting guerrilla operations against conventional forces. Anatol Lieven convincingly explains this phenomenon:[90]

> For a guerrilla-type defensive force, this new urban forest therefore provides many of the same possibilities as the old natural one in terms of opportunities for sniping, mines, booby-traps, and ambushes, and of negating the enemy's superiority in cavalry, armor, air power and artillery.[91]

Although the Chechens used urban and mountain guerrilla methods to avoid direct battle against Russia's quantitatively superior forces, there was not enough suitable (urban and forested mountains) space to protract the conflict and still preserve the Chechen guerrillas as a fighting force. Yermelov's successors had deforested such a large part of Chechnya in the nineteenth century that the amount of forested terrain suitable for a protracted guerrilla struggle was limited in the 1990s. Moreover, in both 1995 and 1996, when the Chechens were in dire straits as a result of losses due to superior (quantitatively) Russian forces and the Russians' use of massive firepower, the Chechens chose to conduct terrorist raids against Budionovsk and Pervomaiskoye, inside Russian territory. The Chechens opted for an ingenious and perfidious asymmetric technique—they used Russia's space and porous borders to conduct raids inside Russia—raids aimed at shock effect, to undermine Russian political and popular support for the war. In June 1995, a Chechen detachment under the command of Shamil Basajev infiltrated the Stavropol District of Russia in Russian military trucks and attacked the city of Budinovsk, shooting soldiers and civilians, taking hostages, and occupying the city hospital. The raid came right after the Russians had taken the mountain villages of Noshi Jurt and Shatoja—the Russian commander had already declared the last phase of the mountain war against the Chechens to be a success.[92]

In January 1996, Salman Raduyev led another raid into Dagestan with two hundred fifty guerrillas—they attacked the city of Kizlyar and seized about 3000 hostages. After some negotiation, the Chechens loaded up several buses with the hostages but were stopped at Pervomaiskoye, where the Chechens dismounted and entrenched themselves. This raid was a big media disaster for the Russians because it showed how ineffective they were against a detachment of lightly armed Chechen warriors. After the Russians reinforced the position, Russia's "elite" Alpha unit attacked the village and was repulsed several times even though it had the support of Russian helicopters, tanks, and artillery. After three days passed without successfully seizing the Chechen-held village, the Russians pulled back their infantry and pulverized the city with firepower. However, the Chechens had already exfiltrated through the Russian positions before the village was destroyed. The media covered the assault and reported the excessive military and civilian casualties, causing a general public condemnation of the Yeltsin government's conduct of the war.[93]

Budionovsk had shown the Yeltsin government the very high political price it might have to pay for continuing the war as well as the Chechens' capacity to inflict serious public humiliation through asymmetric attacks. The debacle at Pervomaiskoye showed the Russian public and the world how poorly trained and unwilling the Russian troops were to risk their lives in taking a small village, even against an outnumbered and surrounded enemy. In March 1996, the Chechens launched a counterattack against Grozny—they seized the center, killed about one hundred fifty Russians, and withdrew after three days. Finally, on 6 August, the day of Yeltsin's second inauguration, the Chechens launched their "zero option"— they simultaneously attacked Grozny, Argun, and Gudermes in what was the largest Chechen offensive of the war. In Grozny, the guerrillas quickly occupied the center, captured the "government headquarters," and surrounded or overran

Russian military outposts even though the Chechens were outnumbered by the Russian defenders by three to one.[94]

This was a pivotal use of urban terrain and psychological shock to attack the Russians' will to continue the war—by the second day, the Russians had suffered 500 killed and 1500 wounded and were pushed back to their preassault positions of December 1994. This huge defeat caused the Russians to negotiate for peace and end the first campaign against the Chechens. It is worth mentioning how analogous the Chechens' "zero option" assault against the principal cities in 1996 was to the Vietcong's Tet Offensive against the cities of South Vietnam in 1968. Both offensives were decisive in causing two great powers to quit small wars and both were quintessentially asymmetric in that they were indirect attacks against the two great powers' centers of gravity—their will to continue these limited wars.[95]

CONCLUSION

In both Afghanistan and Chechnya, Russian forces demonstrated a conspicuous lack of agility because they remained tied to mechanized-heavy forces and to a conventional doctrine, both of which were unsuitable for counterinsurgencies in rugged mountain terrain and urban terrain. The *mujahideen* and the Chechens, on the other hand, were much more agile and adept. The guerrillas in both conflicts were able to use Maoist hit-and-run tactics to mitigate the Russians' superiority in combat systems. According to Edward Luttwak, "the Romans evidently thought it was much more important to minimize their own casualties than to maximize those of the enemy," one need only substitute "Russian troops in Afghanistan" for "legionary troops" and "BMP" for "full breastplate," and the comparison becomes alarmingly apparent. The following quotation, about the Romans' role in peripheral wars, underscores why the Russians' lack of agility was germane.[96]

> It is enough to recall images of legionary troops to see how far offensive performance was deliberately sacrificed to reduce casualties. The large rectangular shield, sturdy metal helmet, full breastplate, shoulder guard, and foot grieves were so heavy that they greatly restricted agility. Legionnaires were extremely well protected but could hardly chase enemies who ran away, nor even pursue them for long if they merely retreated at a quick pace.[97]

The asymmetry of will and the tolerance for losses that inheres in the logic of small wars were determining factors in the Soviet and Russian failures in Afghanistan and Chechnya. The Soviet Union and Russia were less willing to accept casualties than were their guerrilla adversaries. In asymmetric struggles, the weaker side has two options—victory or death. The great power's options, on the other hand, are victory or go home. Even in the Soviet era, under a totalitarian regime and with complete government control of the media, Moscow was not able to sustain the will required to commit a sufficient amount of troops for a sufficient duration to succeed. The lack of will was even more manifest in Chechnya, where the Russians essentially lacked any indigenous troops to do some of their fighting for them and where the losses inflicted were more acute, over a shorter period of time. In two years in Chechnya, the Russians suffered almost half the total number of soldiers killed during ten years in Afghanistan (6000 versus 14,000). In addition, in Chechnya the Russian military was suffering from huge morale problems due to the poor quality of life, poor pay, and poor training. It is important to underline this as an important difference between the war in Afghanistan and the war in Chechnya: the state of readiness of the Russian forces who entered Chechnya in 1994 was significantly degraded compared to the state of readiness of Soviet forces that entered Afghanistan in 1979.[98] One author explained this very lucidly:

> A rickety, corrupt, and collapsing military machine was to be pitted against a keenly motivated and well-armed warrior people adept at guerrilla tactics. The results should have been predictable.[99]

This is the essence of the paradox of will—few great powers ultimately demonstrate the will to stay in a protracted war, not in defense of vital national interests, and against an enemy who does not fight by the great power's rules. However, the U.S.-led global counterinsurgency in Afghanistan differs significantly from the Soviet war there because we are fighting against an enemy who has attacked our homeland and who continues to threaten the security of our population.

Imperial Russia, Soviet Russia, and present-day Russia have manifested continuous geopolitical and strategic predilections to assert control over their perceived spheres of influence along Russia's southern rim. For Imperial Russia, it was a messianic crusade to expand, "civilize," and "russify" a multinational empire. Soviet Russia also continued to dominate and subjugate the peoples of the Caucasus and central Asia but did so under the pretext of ideological consolidation and of securing a vast land empire inherited from the imperial period. Since 1991, it has been Russia, the former great power, who has been using military force and economic coercion to reassert its influence over the "near abroad" as a method of reclaiming its great power status. The "patrimonial mentality embedded in the Russian psyche" that posits that everything inherited from previous epochs is "inalienable property" argues against accepting the separation of the former republics as a fait accompli. However, for the last several centuries of Russian Empire, one thing remained constant—Russia maintained an empire solely through brute force. In fact, both Russia's and the Soviets' great power status did not stem from cultural or economic prowess—it stemmed from raw military power and from the fact that Russia is a huge country that dominates the Eurasian land mass.

An expert on Russia emphasizes this point: "Russia's claim to be a world power has traditionally rested on military prowess, and the temptation is to resort to this expedient once again."[100]

The Soviet and Russian Federation forces exhibited more continuity than change, and this was manifest in the prosecution of counter–guerrilla warfare with conventional doctrine and conventional forces. In Afghanistan, the Russians did modify their approach with the use of helicopters and the insertion of special units, but their approach remained conventional nonetheless. Also, during their second war in Chechnya, the Russian military has employed an improved, but nonetheless conventional, approach. Interestingly, during the second Chechen war, the Russians did ultimately reexamine some of the lessons for which they paid with the blood they spilled in Afghanistan, but ones they also had ignored and paid for with similar losses during the first Chechen war. For example, during the subsequent second Chechen conflict, the Russians relied more on their technological advantages in artillery and bombing standoff ranges to avoid close urban combat, because they had suffered huge losses in urban combat during the first Chechen war between 1994 and 1996.[101]

One can surmise from the examples provided in this chapter that small wars and counterinsurgencies are very difficult for great powers. This is particularly germane for Russia as a long-time continental great power. For most of the previous two centuries, Russia and the Russian military have embraced the conventional paradigm and eschewed the unconventional one. The implication is evident: if the Russian military wants to be successful in small wars, it needs to cultivate a culture and doctrine that does not focus exclusively on the big-war paradigm and it needs to become an institution that can learn, innovate, and adapt. As the Russian military accelerates its transformation and restructuring, it would do well to place a preponderant amount of thought, resources, and training into stability and counterinsurgency operations.

The Russian military should have learned from the British and American lessons in counterinsurgency, good or bad. These militaries have had much experience in prosecuting counterinsurgencies and asymmetric wars. Counterinsurgency in difficult terrain against tenacious mountain fighters also requires specialized, elite, light, cohesive, and tactically versatile forces. Thus, asymmetric conflicts require the opposite type of military culture, force structure, and doctrine that the Soviet and Russian great-power militaries brought to those wars. It also requires good intelligence and a very precise and restrained application of lethal force. This conclusion, in particular, is also germane to the U.S. military's counterinsurgencies in Iraq and in Afghanistan.[102]

In fact, the paradox of hubris and humility mentioned as a postscript in Chapter 2 was also salient for the Russians in Afghanistan and Chechnya. Great powers often underestimate the will, skill, and tenacity of their adversaries in small wars. The following closing quote, however, cogently underlines Russia's geopolitical and strategic cultural continuity in the southern periphery where it continues to operate and machinate to this day:

The goal of preserving a "Great Russia" was always at the heart of the Russian Federation's efforts [in Chechnya]. The basic contours of this policy had remained unchanged since tsarist times with only the tools of modern warfare being added to the methodology. All the old ramifications of empire went with it and, in essence, hegemony by force of arms remained its key ingredient.[103]

British Military Culture and Counterinsurgency

Less Is Better

> The British excelled in small-unit, anti-guerrilla warfare as they did in other aspects of counterinsurgency. History had given them an army that was relatively small and decentralized, and therefore ideally suited to such warfare. Since Britain is an island nation, the navy and not the army has been its first line of defense. Distrusted and underfunded, the junior service was thus relatively unaffected by the revolution in size and organization experienced by continental armies during the nineteenth century.[1]

THIS QUOTE APTLY highlights the underlying reason for examining British Army culture and ascertaining how some characteristics of that military culture have historically influenced the British Army's approach and capacity for counterinsurgency warfare. The historical context of the British experiences in small wars and counterinsurgencies during the nineteenth and twentieth centuries is topical and salient because the twenty-first century sees the U.S. military and its coalition partners, to include sizeable British forces, prosecuting multiple counterinsurgency campaigns in Afghanistan, Iraq, the Philippines, the Horn of Africa, and elsewhere. It should also be evident why an analysis of British military cultural predilections in the context of counterinsurgency is also germane and potentially useful. The U.S. Army is transforming in contact and a large part of that transformation is about military cultural change. If American military culture has traditionally exhibited a preference for a big, conventional-war paradigm and if this preference has impeded its capacity to adapt to small wars and counterinsurgencies, then there may be something to gain or learn from examining the cultural characteristics of another army that may favor adapting to counterinsurgency.

Oddly, the British Army's strategic puzzle in the American War of Independence was a harbinger of the perplexity engendered by later asymmetric conflicts.

This chapter also revisits the notion presented in Chapter 2 that great powers can lose small wars when their opponents refuse to fight them conventionally. The rebellion in America was unprecedented because a conflict between an ideologically motivated insurgent population and a metropolitan state 3000 miles away had never been seen. For a long time, the British Army acted as though it was conducting the kind of limited war it had successfully fought since 1689. However, British Army culture was shaped more by its host of small (asymmetric) wars of the nineteenth century than it was by its one conventional and symmetric conflict of the post-Napoleonic period—the Crimean War. Washington's strategic purpose was to break, or erode, the resolve of the British government through gradual and persistent engagements against peripheral detachments of the British Army. The Americans, on the other hand, conducted a strategic defensive and "did not lose" by preserving their inchoate army. Washington's army was so weak compared to the British Army that it could not even pursue a battlefield attack in the tactical realm, because his soldiers could not win. Yet, the Americans' political objectives—to expel the British Army and secure independence—were total. To find a way out of this contradiction, "Washington's hopes had to lie mainly not in military victory but in the possibility that the political opposition in Britain might in time force the British Ministry to abandon the conflict." Likewise, local nationalist forces in the post–World War II period won against opponents with overwhelmingly superior military capabilities by not losing—indigenous forces protracted the conflicts and increased the costs (economic and political) for the great power. Weaker military forces accomplish this by refusing to confront the modernized armies on their own terms and by instead resorting to unorthodox approaches. As Britain approached the peak of its great power status, it suffered a humiliating defeat at the hands of a fledgling American military that combined asymmetric guerrilla war techniques with symmetric employment of the Continental Army. But subsequent to this, Wellington was able to leverage a similar combination of conventional and guerrilla operations to harass and defeat the French on the Iberian Peninsula.[2]

THE BRITISH ARMY—THE INFLUENCE OF GEOGRAPHY AND HISTORY

It is likely that no other country in modern history has aggregated as broad an experience in counterinsurgency in its client-states of the less-developed world as Britain did during its long devolution of empire. The British Army never had an overarching manual for colonial tactics. After much experience in imperial policing, the British devised a basic approach to both rural and urban insurrection that, when applied properly, served to reduce the level of violence to manageable proportions. The British understood that military tactics alone were of little use in counterinsurgency unless they were integrated with the political tactics. As Bell explains, military tactics that had been refined over a generation of men with differing experiences could be learned and applied but could not be effective unless those tactics were used in the context of a political formula to isolate the rebels from the population. The British Army realized and was sensitive to both the ultimate power of the cabinet and the political aspects of revolt. The military recognized that the bounds of political strategy and action were delimited in London, based on advice from and not as a result of the direction of the general staff. Notwithstanding, the British Army always sought the authorization to pursue the insurgents with a robust campaign that was centralized under one command (ideally that of a military officer) and unrestricted by local authorities.[3]

British Army culture has also been characterized by a cycle not unfamiliar to the U.S. Army experience: "instead of continuous development of a national army, as on the continent, there is a succession of sudden expansions to meet particular emergencies, followed by a relapse into peacetime stagnation and national neglect." This approach to military policy, pitfalls notwithstanding, was a luxury afforded only to insular great powers, and only until the middle of the twentieth century. The central dilemma for British military policy has been the choice between defense of global empire and involvement on the continent. However, a commitment to NATO has been a big part of the British Army's role since the Paris agreements of 1954. Even though the British Army developed a more continental ethos in the 1970s and 1980s, colonial legacies still remained relevant. In 1991, British troops and ships were still deployed in twenty-five different locations around the globe. In fact, the end of the Cold War witnessed a reassertion of Britain's role beyond Europe. Britain agreed to contribute two divisions to NATO's new Rapid Reaction Corps, a unit whose parts were more likely to see, and actually did see, service outside of NATO's traditional area. In fact, Britain's 1992 Defense White Paper reasserted a global role for the British Army.[4]

The neglect of Great Britain's army is also attributable in part to its insularity—as an island nation, British survival had never really been threatened by anything more significant than tribal conflicts with the Welsh and Scots. While continental states relied on armies to secure their existence, Britain relied on its navy for security. Because Britain had a long-standing naval tradition, its people could not understand why they should have to pay professional soldiers to do what amateurs had always performed since the time of the Norman Conquest. "Any such institution as a standing army was regarded as entirely unnecessary, and in fact the whole history of the British Army reflects this attitude." Because it was fully neglected during peacetime but expected to accomplish miracles during war, the only discernible periods of reform were during or immediately after an emergency when the army had been unable to meet all the demands made on it, through no fault of its own.[5]

Britain's fundamentally maritime strategy took shape between the fifteenth and eighteenth centuries, when the main concern became the maintenance of a fleet that could defeat any other power. The Royal Navy thus became the priority of effort, receiving the most money and attention. Once Britain acquired a trading empire with colonies and bases for the fleet, she required garrisons to protect them. Britain would deploy infantry battalions from home, and later from British India, to man the garrisons and serve as armed policemen. Thus, unlike other armies of Europe, imperial policing became the main task of the British Army. Moreover, because Britain's territorial security depended on her insularity, her policy was also to provide balance against whatever continental power was seeking to dominate Europe. Britain did this by supporting coalitions of rival states with money and troops. As long as Britain was safe from invasion, the British could afford to engage in prolonged warfare with every confidence in victory. "The regiments of an army could be created and disbanded as necessary around a nucleus of permanent troops, and the Army needed to be no larger than was necessary to demonstrate Britain's commitment to her allies." Thus, the British Regular Army evolved as a disparate group of individual regiments, accustomed to isolated locations and long service. By the middle of the nineteenth century, the regular army saw eighty percent of its troops stationed abroad, with imperial policing, as well as occasional internal policing, dominating its development.[6]

The late professionalization of the British Army officer was another salient factor in the development of British military culture. Recognizing the need for professionalism, the British Army established the Staff College in 1858. However, in actuality it was merely an annex to Sandhurst until 1870 and the absence of a general staff until the early twentieth century mitigated its effectiveness anyway. The Cardwell reforms were the next major attempt at reform. The dilemma presented by the exigencies of imperial warfare and continental warfare was theretofore addressed on an ad hoc basis until Edward Cardwell became the secretary of state for war in 1868. When Cardwell took office, the British Army comprised long-service troops that were appropriate for the imperial demands but provided almost no reserve for future expansion. "Cardwell brought the number of troops overseas into balance with those at home, reduced the terms of service from twenty years to six years with the regular army and six years with the reserves, and reorganized the infantry regiments of the line. Linking the battalions, with one at home for every one overseas, was in many respects a brilliant solution to meet both the needs of empire and the potential exigencies in Europe."[7]

Insofar as these reforms influenced the British Army's military culture, the War Office Act of 1870 and the Localization Act of 1872 were the most salient. The War Office Act clarified and centralized the relationship between the secretary of state for war and the commander-in-chief of the army by subordinating the latter to the former. What this act ultimately did, though, was to centralize civilian control over the army and thus make the army more responsive to the policy decisions of its civilian masters. The Localization Act, on the other hand, was designed to improve the effectiveness of home defense battalions while also generating from the home units trained replacements for imperial policing battalions. This act established sixty-six territorial districts, each of which would man two line battalions, two militia battalions, and several volunteer units. Although this act did improve the efficiency of the home units, it did not fulfill the purpose of providing adequate replacements for colonial battalions. This would only have worked if there had been parity between the number of line units at home and those overseas. However, a host of small colonial wars in the 1870s helped create an asymmetric situation wherein fifty-nine battalions were at home and eighty-two battalions were overseas. Home battalions were also often cannibalized to keep imperial units manned, thereby reducing home battalions to skeletons.[8]

The organization of the British Army that resulted from the Cardwell Reforms of 1870–1872 was geared toward colonial policing rather than large-scale conventional war in Europe. Although Cardwell's reforms were conceptually sound, there were problems with them in practice. For example, the amorphous array of battalions that represented the home army was suitable only for providing drafts for and rotating with overseas units. Moreover, launching any protracted expedition overseas tended to throw the system out of whack. Also, Cardwell's system mandated homogeneity among linked battalions—this definitely constrained the British Army in carrying out both of its two roles because it could be organized to do either imperial policing or continental warfare but not both. In the aftermath of the Boer War debacle, Secretary of State for War Hugh Arnold-Foster tried to implement a permanent fix to the imperial-continental dichotomy by establishing a long-service army for imperial policing and a short-service army that could serve as home defense as well as an expeditionary force on the continent in the event of war. This was a viable solution but it was anathema to the Army Council and to Edward VII—it was offered on a trial basis but abandoned in 1905 when Campbell-Bannerman's liberal government took office.[9]

For reasons beyond the Cardwell reforms, the British Army was able to win a series of late nineteenth-century colonial wars and to meet the security needs of the empire. For one, Britain's colonial wars did not stir much opposition at home because they were cheap in terms of lives and monetary outlays. This David French attributes to the fact that colonial expeditions were normally small—between 1815 and 1899, the largest deployment comprised a force of 35,000 sent to Egypt in 1882. Moreover, the diversity both of Britain's nineteenth-century colonial adversaries and of the terrain where the British Army fought precludes generalizations about the conduct of colonial campaigns. It is important to point out, however, that the whole nature of the British Army's nineteenth-century colonial wars differed markedly from the more ideologically driven insurgencies that the British Army would face in the twentieth century. The British Army's approach to colonial warfare was much more orthodox and conventional in the nineteenth century, partly because many of its colonial enemies tended to fight the British Army on its terms.[10]

The Battle of Omdurman in 1898 represented both the culmination and the apotheosis of Britain's nineteenth-century style of colonial warfare. This battle for the Sudan in September witnessed 11,000 Dervishes killed compared to 48 British killed. By fighting the British European style, "the Dervishes invited the British to indulge their own preconceptions of what constituted proper combat."

Kitchener's army, equipped with rifled artillery, twenty machine-guns, and breech-loading rifles, decimated the Dervish Army, which had opted to attack the entrenched British by frontal assault, in human waves. For his success, Kitchener received the Dervish commander's bleached skull and a peerage from Queen Victoria while the British Army rested on its laurels. The British regulars espoused the old Wellingtonian aphorism that "her Majesty's enemies would always come in the same way and be dispatched the same old way." However, as Bolger points out, the battle was anachronistic even as it occurred and, unfortunately, it encouraged the British Army to continue fighting the way it preferred instead of the way it should. "The eventual corrective measures had to be lubricated by a generous application of British blood." There were, however, some common elements to these imperial campaigns. Whether the British Army was fighting the Arabi Pasha, Zulus, Ashanti, Pathans, or Afghans, the British normally assumed the strategic offensive as early as possible because they worried that if they delayed too long, it would encourage others to join the opposition. The British Army also preferred battle in the open because it was the best way to translate its superior discipline into the largest possible casualties for the enemy. The British Army could maintain soldiers in the field indefinitely and apply continuous pressure until attrition wore down their enemies.[11]

Conversely, the Boer War was the harbinger of a more difficult and cunning approach to insurgent warfare, one in which indigenous opponents would prove unwilling to fight the British Army in European style. The tenacious Boers elected not to be Dervishes or Ashanti or Zulus, and they fought their own style of war on the hills and plains of South Africa from 1899 to 1902. As Kitchener later observed, "The Boers are not like the Sudanese who stood up to a fair fight. They are always running away on their little ponies." Although British horse soldiers continued to operate in World War I, the ways of the Union Brigade at Waterloo or the Heavy Brigade at Balaclava had outlasted their usefulness. To defeat the Boers, it would take a complete purge of senior British commanders, additional troops, an overhaul of the British Army, and concentration camps for Boer families.[12]

The fallout from the Boer War provided the next impetus for reform, and as a result the general staff was established in 1904 as a necessary addition to the Staff College. In fact, in his memoirs the first chief of the general staff, Neville Lyttleton, remarked, "I have seen or taken part in the development of our Army from an occupation to a profession."[13] In 1904, the British government took a significant step toward reform with the Esher Report. The Esher Committee analyzed the ineffectiveness of a military bureaucracy that had been built piecemeal since 1660. This report laid down the foundations of the War Office organization and general staff system that have endured essentially to the present. Correlli Barnett referred to the recommendations of the Esher Report as "the reconstruction of the brain of the Army on clear functional lines." The substantive recommendations and consequent reorganization that resulted from the Esher Report were the creation of an army council, a general staff, and the division of department responsibilities inside the War Office on clearly defined and logical principles. The army council would provide a single collective body to review and decide questions of policy in place of the amorphous responsibilities of the war secretary. Moreover, the secretary of state for war was placed unambiguously in charge—all military policy recommendations to the Crown would go through him, thus consummating civilian and parliamentary control of the army. The creation of the army council and the general staff also necessitated the elimination of the post of commander-in-chief of the army. As a result, the last incumbent commander-in-chief was removed in 1904 and responsibility for preparing the army for war was vested in the new post of chief of the general staff (CGS). The creation of a general staff also gave the Staff College at Camberley a new sense of purpose— the residual traces of the old dry curriculum were swept away in favor of practical training in different staff duties in the field. The end result of the Esher Report recommendations was that the British Army was instilled with a sense of professional purpose not witnessed in peacetime since the days of the Commonwealth.[14]

When Richard Haldane became the secretary of state for war in 1905, his challenge was to continue military reform and reduce expenditures. He restructured and standardized military organizations and manuals throughout the Empire and he created an expeditionary force of seven divisions. Haldane also reorganized the volunteers into a new territorial force of fourteen divisions, transformed the old militia into a special reserve to reinforce the expeditionary force, and streamlined the command and control of the infantry regiments. By any measure, Haldane's feat was not insignificant. Only a few years after the Boer debacle, Britain, historically a dominant naval power, had acquired a formidable army at a decreased cost. Subsequently, Britain employed this new army in its leading role of fighting a war against the major European land power of the day. Yardley and Sewell help explain the unprecedented character of World War I for Britain. "It was a total war in which, for the first time, much of a nation's private industry was mobilized toward the single aim of victory, and airships attacked concentrated civilian targets." "Fundamentally, it was a war of attrition where being a winner was less important than not being a loser."[15] One of the most salient lessons of World War I for the British was that the cost of victory had been too high: nearly a million soldiers were killed in action. The end of the war saw the British Empire larger than any time in history and the possibility of an early return to fight in Europe seemed remote.

The British Army existed in an extremely antimilitary environment from 1920 until early 1939. On the one hand, Liddell Hart's polemical concept of a "traditional British way in warfare" emerged as an attractive alternative to revisiting the bleeding the British had suffered in World War I. Hart's limited liability concept was a strategic approach that relied on naval supremacy and a small army for attacks on the periphery. Such an approach, Hart maintained, had historically allowed Britain to avoid the heavy casualties that accompany continental war. Moreover, it was this "traditional" approach that had enabled Britain to influence the outcome of continental conflicts during the same time that it was creating a global empire. On the other hand, all of the political parties rejected the experience of World War I and the literati's novels and war reminiscences reinforced antiwar and antimilitary attitudes. By the mid-1930s, Murray explains, "Much of the educated population in Britain fervently believed that nothing was worth the price of war."[16]

The result was a hostile environment for the British Army at the very time when the international security environment was becoming increasingly menacing. From the mid-1930s, army leaders identified Germany as the most probable enemy and they recognized that such a conflict would require a commitment of troops to the continent. However, the willingness of the government and the nation to expend resources on defense remained minimal. To make matters even worse, the British Army's sister services received the priority for equipment, personnel, and training. Moreover, when Chamberlain came to power in 1937, he completely embraced Hart's concept of "limited liability." After a series of defense reviews, the Chamberlain government essentially stated that Britain would not commit an army to the continent under any circumstances. As a result, work to prepare the army for a continental role halted and the government assigned the following priorities to the army: (1) to protect the home islands; (2) to secure trade routes; (3) to garrison the empire; and (4) to cooperate for the defense of British allies but only after it had addressed the first three priorities. Moreover, the government described the army as a general-purpose force, a vague term that made it difficult to requisition equipment or supplies for any theater of operation.[17]

This political environment had a significant impact on the British Army's willingness and ability to confront the issues about war on the continent. For one, the political guidance did not direct the army to focus on war in Europe since the government indicated that the army would not be used there under any circumstances. On the other hand, when the army finally received political direction to prepare for war on the continent, the government demanded that it accept a huge number of conscripts and create a mass army. To complicate matters, military reformers like Fuller and Hart, who should and could have helped innovate doctrine and forces, had so vilified the army leadership during the interwar years that that leadership was hardly amenable to Fuller's and Hart's ideas on the eve of war. Social and political indifference impeded the development of armored warfare in Britain, as well as military conservatism and the imperial defense mission. Military conservatism, according to one definition, is "the tendency to preserve existing military institutions and practices"; this conservatism clearly played a role in the development of doctrine leading up to World War II. The cavalry's attachment to horses and its determination to have a cavalry officer command the Mobile Division are other facets of military conservatism. It was also Montgomery-Massingberd's desire to preserve the cavalry as a branch that played a significant role in his decision to use the cavalry as the core of the Mobile Division. However, it was neither the antimilitary milieu nor military conservatism that was the principal obstacle to the development of multiple armored divisions in the interwar years. The principal obstacle was a historical focus on the imperial defense mission and an army organized primarily for imperial defense with its bulk comprising one hundred thirty-six infantry battalions.[18]

Winton is unambiguous in this finding: "Of these various factors, the imperial defense mission was the single most significant impediment to the development of armored formations. So long as the Army's primary mission was to garrison the Empire, armored divisions were of little utility." The organization of the British Army that resulted from the Cardwell Reforms of 1870–1872 was one geared toward colonial policing rather than large-scale conventional war in Europe.[19] As highlighted earlier, the Cardwell system mandated a one-for-one match of units deployed garrisoning the empire and units in Britain for home defense (war in Europe). Winton, moreover, argues that the principal effect of the imperial policing mission, coupled with the Cardwell system, was to almost completely rule out the creation of a large organization for armored warfare. The Tank Brigade was in actuality an add-on to the Cardwellian British Army, and it could be maintained only by maintaining a commensurate number of armored car companies overseas. However, the colonial defense mission assigned to the overseas armored companies was entirely unrelated to the Tank Brigade's mission for war in Europe. "Vehicles that worked well on English roads and in English climates often did not perform well on Indian roads in Indian climates." Nor were men trained for mechanized warfare in Europe necessarily well suited for imperial policing.[20]

During the period leading up to World War II, several military-strategic and political-cultural factors combined to influence Britain's strategic response to the German threat. First, the British Army's cultural preferences, especially the regimental system, impeded innovation in armor operations and slowed transition to larger formations. Second, British political culture was averse to direct or frontal approaches, largely as a result of exorbitant British casualties during World War I. Third, Liddell Hart, although marginalized in the intrainstitutional innovation debate, wrote books and articles prescribing an indirect-Fabian British strategic approach that certainly influenced British military thought. Finally, Churchill himself had been an advocate of Fabian strategy since his time in the admiralty during World War I. He, consequently, was amenable to Liddell Hart's prescriptions for British strategy vis-à-vis continental Europe. More fundamentally, however, all of these factors resulted in one strategic reality in 1940—any confrontation in Europe between German forces and British forces would be an asymmetric one.[21]

After World War II, neither the political nor the military leaders of the United Kingdom shrank any longer from a continental commitment. "They had learned their lesson; though it was not until 1954, ten years after the Normandy landings, that a final, binding commitment was undertaken to maintain substantial British armed forces on the continent in time of peace." At the end of World War II, the British Army comprised three million men scattered all over the world. It was inevitable that the British Army would be reduced in size—the total strength of the postwar army was 305,000 but by 1951 it was increased by 100,000 due, in part, to the Korean War. The postwar army was also a conscript army as a result of the 1947 National Service Act—it remained so until 1963, when it became an all-regular army. For the British Army, the period 1945–1970 was a "transitional phase whereby the Army lost its overseas role and gained one in Europe; when it fought small wars but became ever more focused upon" the defense of mainland Europe and "when it lost its large number of conscripts, reverting to a small regular force to be expanded by reservists and Territorial Army volunteers in time of war." "Although both the Heath and Thatcher governments attempted to retain a vestigial world role for the Army, the Army's ability to intervene in conflicts outside Europe was strictly limited."[22]

Several key lessons emerged from the British Army's experience of major war prior to the Korean War: (1) the army lacked a formal doctrine for war and tended toward intellectual indifference and (2) the decentralized regimental system was well suited to imperial policing, and in particular it helped to promote a strong esprit de corps, but it was less well suited to modern warfare. In particular, the regimental system impeded combined arms cooperation and standardized procedures for training and operations. (3) The army focused on the tactical level of war and it paid little attention to the strategic or operational levels. However, this did not necessarily translate into tactical competence—instead the army's tactics were often simple and unimaginative compared to the best continental armies; (4) the army demonstrated a distinct preference for set-piece, attritional battles, emphasizing artillery and infantry; and (5) the army almost invariably fought its major wars as part of a coalition. Although Britain proved skilled at the strategic and political dimensions of coalition warfare, it was not always successful at the military-operational level."[23]

The Korean War seemed to reaffirm the British way of warfare. "The British fought according to traditional methods, adapting them as required, rather than developing a coherent body of ideas in advance of war which covered both training and operations."[24] The British Army's experience in the Korean War highlighted several issues. First, despite the large size of the British Army and of the threats consequent to the Cold War, the army had difficulty finding the forces for Korea and it was not prepared for war. The war in Korea revealed the army's difficulty in responding promptly and in strength to major overseas crises.[25]

Between 1950 and 1955, significant new developments began to influence the military policies of Britain. The creation of NATO and the emergence of the "Lisbon Goals" to put ninety divisions in Europe eliminated the possibility of a smaller occupation force there. During the same period, the Korean War reinforced U.S. arguments for large armies. However, it was the requirements of Britain's empire that decisively pointed to the need for a conscript army in peacetime. The Malayan campaign kept thousands of British troops occupied in countering the Communist insurgency, and as soon as the campaign approached a successful end, the Mau-Mau rebellion in Kenya and the E.O.K.A. crisis in Cyprus occurred.

Initially, empire maintenance simply required numbers, more troops to act as reinforcements for the police in Palestine or to conduct punitive anti-bandit operations in Eritrea. However, on the Malay Peninsula, for the first time, the British Army confronted a guileful opponent trained in the Maoist model of guerrilla strategy. Soon the troops were learning the counterinsurgency trade on the ground. For example, the Far East Land Forces training center in Malaya developed a coherent philosophy of counterinsurgent warfare and trained every arriving officer and soldier before they began jungle operations. In Kenya, British officers and soldiers operated for long periods in the forests, using unconventional techniques against an unconventional enemy.[26]

However, although the advent of nuclear weapons and the emergence of Maoist guerrilla warfare were both transforming the character of military operations, no real changes in the training of the British Army at home came about. As Gwynne Jones explains, "The training and doctrine of the British Army in 1955 were still essentially that of a nation in arms, dedicated to the principle of unlimited war fought by massive forces and only reluctantly discarding the organization and tactics of El Alamein and the Normandy beaches." Moreover, Gwynne Jones asserts, the 1956 Suez campaign, notwithstanding the political fallout, unambiguously demonstrated that the British Army was unable to get the right forces in place on time. The implicit basis of the 1957 White Paper was that British overseas commitments would gradually be eliminated. The new professional army was to be concentrated into a strategic reserve in England: a small, mobile, hard-hitting force. "This belief, based on a mistaken reading of the strategic effects of constitutional advance in the colonies, remained an article of official faith for about five years."[27]

By the early 1960s, British Army tactics and training were absorbing the valuable lessons of its wide experience in counterinsurgency. Past experience demonstrated that success in counterinsurgency depended on first-rate political and military intelligence, effective modalities for integrating the political and military spheres, and the training of local forces. In its "Cold-War role," the British Army, Gwynne Jones asserts, "achieved an enviable expertise, partly because of its imaginative use of the lessons of the past, and partly because operations of this type were quite its favorite occupation."[28] British soldiers adopted a very pragmatic approach to colonial warfare. "The British, of course, could draw on a very substantial body of experience—greater than any other colonial power—and their rather ad hoc attitude toward fighting colonial campaigns reflected its length and diversity."[29] The 1980s witnessed a significant change in the British Army's approach to high-intensity warfare. The impetus for this change was twofold: first, by the early 1980s the political priority of forward defense and the reliance on the early use of nuclear weapons were no longer tenable; and second, Sir Nigel Bagnall, through strength of personality and intellect, was able to push reforms through within the British Army.[30]

During the Persian Gulf War (Operation Granby for the British Army), the 1st British Armored Division fought a war of maneuver with a coherent plan of operations, in close cooperation with the Americans, and drew heavily upon the doctrinal ideas developed in the 1980s and the idea of doctrine itself. Again in this war, the British approach revealed an emphasis on flexibility. "Whether this is a conscious decision or one forced upon the Army by financial limitations and poor planning is, to some extent unimportant because the result is the same: the British Army has responded to crises by adapting what it has rather than by advanced preparation."[31] As a result of the end of the Cold War, the focus of British defense policy shifted "to what was termed wider security interests," so the army came to be seen as increasingly important in roles ranging from humanitarian assistance in Bosnia to high intensity war in the Gulf.[32]

PREFERRED PARADIGM FOR WAR

The success of British counterinsurgency has stemmed from a combination of fortuitous circumstances and historical development that produced a military establishment well suited to combating internal unrest. Out of this favorable context, the British developed methods and more importantly, principles upon which these methods were based.[33]

During the Napoleonic Wars, Britain was faced with a strategic dilemma since it had a superior navy but an army inferior to the French Army. "If, because of the Royal Navy's supremacy, the British Isles were invulnerable to invasion, Britain's geographic seclusion and the defeat of her continental allies left her facing impotency on the strategic level, too." Britain could pluck at the periphery of Napoleonic Europe but she could not roll back Napoleon's forces alone. This asymmetric situation on land, therefore, compelled Britain to adopt a Fabian strategy against the French Army in Spain. Wellington's methods in the Peninsular War were uncannily similar to the methods that Nathanael Greene had employed in the Carolinas against the British during the American Revolution. Wellington recognized Napoleon's superiority too well to risk a decisive battle, so he indirectly used "pin-prick" attacks in order to induce the French to concentrate against him while the Spanish guerrillas consolidated control over the Spanish countryside, attacking French outposts and lines of communication.[34]

In the Peninsular War, Britain's most significant impact was in aggravating the Spanish insurgency against French occupation and encouraging the source of it. "Rarely has she caused a greater distraction to her opponents at the price of so small a military effort." The presence of the British Expeditionary Force (BEF) facilitated success, but Wellington's battles were materially the least effective part of his operations. The overwhelming majority of French losses were as a result of Spanish guerrilla operations. Wellington was successful in harrying the French and making the countryside a desert where the French forces could not sustain themselves. He fought very few battles during the five years of campaigning on the peninsula. The initial purpose of the BEF, in other words, was for 26,000

British soldiers to distract 100,000 French soldiers from the main theater of war in Austria. "Wellington's greatest influence came through his threats rather than his blows. For, whenever, he threatened a point, the French were forced to draw off troops thither, and thus give the guerrillas greater scope in other districts." For example, in 1810 the French had 350,000 troops deployed in Spain but could only use 90,000 of them to attempt invading Portugal, because the rest had to be used for counterinsurgency and to guard their lines of communications. Wellington's force, by 1810, comprised 50,000 troops.[35]

Although the French forces were far superior in numbers, they were unable to concentrate against Wellington's combined Anglo-Portuguese force because Spanish guerrillas compelled the French to disperse in order to protect their vulnerable lines of communications. Logistics was also a problem for Napoleon's forces—they were accustomed to living off the land, but Spain was too poor to support any large foraging army. The Royal Navy, on the other hand, supplied Wellington's forces. The Iberian Peninsular represented a theater ideally suited to Britain's naval supremacy and small army—it was surrounded by water on three sides and the Navy both convoyed ships to supply the BEF and prevented the French from moving men and supplies around the coast. The Peninsula War granted the British Army of the best opportunities it ever had to exploit its sea power. The navy precluded the French from moving supplies and forces around the coast, compelling them to use roads that were vulnerable to attacks from Spanish guerrillas. The guerrillas helped Wellington's army survive by supplying him with valuable intelligence and by preventing the French from concentrating in sufficient numbers to crush his field army.[36]

The circumstances that Wellington's success created on the Peninsula and his subsequent victory at Waterloo "profoundly affected the development of the British Army, both positively and negatively, for much of the nineteenth century." Because Britain's hegemony was to remain unchallenged for almost four decades of peace in Europe, the army was marginalized, compared to the Royal Navy, as an instrument of foreign policy. Its preparedness to fight a large-scale land war deteriorated and it commanded little public attention. The improbability of foreign invasion even diminished the army's importance as an instrument of home defense. Faced with an economizing parliament and an indifferent public, the British Army was left to run itself with minimal interference. This, Peter Burroughs explains, had deleterious consequences: "Here the collective memory of victory over the French exerted a detrimental influence, since it strengthened and legitimized the forces of habit and torpor so ingrained in the operations and ethos of an authoritarian, hierarchical institution." Burroughs argues that complacency and traditionalism were not subjected to the test of battle until the Crimean War because in the many small wars of the period: "British numbers, discipline, and firepower were usually sufficient to secure comforting victories."[37]

During the eighteenth century, moreover, fighting in the colonies was not peripheral to Britain's war efforts in Europe but central to them. Colonial operations were not separable from European war because Britain's opponents outside Europe were not indigenous peoples but rival imperial powers: in 1739 Britain fought Spain for control of the West Indies; the Seven Years War saw Britain fighting France for control of North America and India; and Britain's break with the American colonists lured France into a renewed struggle with Britain for maritime control of the Atlantic. In the nineteenth century, the pattern changed as no serious European challenge to Britain's colonial hegemony emerged until the 1880s. The British Army then fought its nineteenth-century battles against the native populations of Britain's Asian and African possessions. The British Army's central role during the nineteenth century was to "ensure security, stability, and consolidation of empire."[38]

The British Army's nineteenth-century experience of colonial wars had a significant influence on the British military culture as it evolved into the twentieth century. The British way in war as embodied in the campaigns of the three Victorian heroes, Roberts, Wolseley, and Kitchener, reflected essentially all the British people knew of war. It was in fact a highly specialized form, which contrasted sharply with war as fought between great industrial powers. The British approach emphasized small scale instead of large scale, the soldier rather than the system, and small casualties and easy victories instead of prolonged fighting and heavy losses. But small wars against savages really could not test an army, as evidenced by the British Army's problems in the Boer Wars and its experiences in the world wars. These colonial victories created a dangerous perception in Britain, that wars were "distant and exotic adventure stories, cheaply won by the parade-ground discipline of the British line."[39]

According to Eliot Cohen, "one reason for the success of British small wars has been Britain's development of a military manpower system uniquely suited to such conflicts." In the early nineteenth century, British statesmen created a regimental system that was quasi-tribal in which officers and enlisted men served together over extended periods of time, rotating between overseas and home assignments. Moreover, the regimental system provided an "emotional substitute" for the sense of public approval relied on by the U.S. military. Another reason for the success of the British Army in small wars, Cohen explains, has been Britain's "near-exclusive reliance on volunteer professional soldiers rather than draftees or reservists." Cohen maintains that regular soldiers are more adept at the challenging types of operations that inhere in small wars. The use of volunteer professionals to fight low-intensity but protracted conflicts mitigates domestic political constraints because they are not unwilling participants.[40]

Another British expert also proffered that in the twentieth century it was Britain's empire, and not Europe, that had been the more continuous element in soldiers' experiences. The years between the world wars reinforced the idea that war on the continent was an aberration rather than a norm. In the interwar years, the British Army was conducting imperial policing from Palestine to the northwest frontier of India. The practice of counterinsurgency in the 1950s and colonial withdrawal in the 1960s shaped the careers of senior British Army officers who were still serving in the 1980s. Even as the twentieth century drew to an end, "Britain's recent military experience has more in common with its colonial past than with the Army's declared commitment to Europe." The persistent low-intensity conflict in Northern Ireland was viewed as the last stage of imperial withdrawal. In addition, the Falkland Islands War in 1982 was limited in scope as far as geography and means were concerned.[41]

The British Army in 1918 and in 1945 was able to resume its role in imperial policing. It was also significant that after 1918, the British political and military establishment was determined to never again sacrifice the British Army in a continental role. The imperial style in which the army had been cast before 1914 had been modified and not transformed by Haldane's creation of a European expeditionary force and the concept of depending on territorial as well as regular army reserves to support it. In 1939, the rapidly assembled BEF deployed to France was less well equipped, armed, and trained in every way. Moreover, the memories of World War I casualties, coupled with an emphasis on imperial policing between the wars, ensured that the British commanders of World War II were required to husband their manpower. According to one scholar, the imperial perspective of and a need to avoid high casualties led Churchill to prefer any peripheral and indirect (Fabian) approach to a direct European one.[42]

By the end of the World War II, large numbers of British soldiers and colonial policemen had equal familiarity with the actual conduct of guerrilla warfare. Many of the techniques involved in a politico-military insurgency, particularly of guerrilla warfare, were merely adaptations of traditional rebel tactics against which the British had often fought in their imperial past. In addition to its experience in this area, "the British advantage laid in a tradition of flexibility, based upon the fact that throughout the colonial policing campaigns of the past they had been forced to make do with only limited resources." "Global responsibilities had spread a relatively small volunteer army thinly on the ground and precluded the maintenance of a strategic reserve, while financial parsimony had made the soldiers aware of a need to husband their supplies of ammunition and equipment." Therefore, once the British were confronted with a revolt, they were more likely to take a low-profile response, using their armed forces sparingly and searching for solutions that did not necessitate large expenditures of men or materiel. Moreover, "the wide range of threats to imperial rule and the different geographical conditions encountered, produced a constant need to adapt responses to fit local circumstances and avoided the development of a stereotyped theory of policing."[43]

Thus by 1945, as the British faced a host of threats to their rule or influence, they already possessed three important characteristics for low-intensity conflict: experience, appropriate military skill, and flexibility. The British Army during this period never compiled an elaborate theory to which it rigidly adhered, but "a series of responses which, when adapted to fit specific conditions, proved successful in maintaining at least a measure of political stability." The pattern of British counterinsurgency was therefore well established, founded upon flexibility and experience and comprising the key components of political primacy, appropriate military response, and isolation of the guerrillas.[44]

The key to the British Army's success in counterinsurgency conflicts was its integrated civil-military approach. Civilian officials remained in control of emergencies and were responsible for the broader political strategy and for propaganda. The British Army operated under civilian control and accepted the requirement of employing minimum force. Moreover, even though a preference for large-scale operations can be discerned in the early phases of its campaigns, the British Army tended to be flexible, adapting to meet local circumstances. The British Army was flexible enough to switch to small-unit operations with decentralized control after it became evident that large-scale sweeps did not succeed. A similar pattern emerged in the subsequent British Army experience in Northern Ireland. According to Colin McInnes, "The civil authorities remained in control; minimum force was generally used; new tactics were constantly developed and tactical control devolved; close relations were established with the police; and finally the Army recognized that it could not resolve the conflict on its own, but that a broader-based political strategy was required."[45]

Thus, the British approached insurgency with the critical assumption that insurgency was not principally a military problem. "If necessary soldiers would be brought in to bolster the police, but the soldiers would always be acting in aid to the civil power and would be bound, like the police themselves, to use only that degree of force" that was essential to restore order and should never exceed it. "Close cooperation between colonial administrators who implemented reform, police who maintained order, and soldiers who fought the insurgents was essential." According to Thomas Mockaitis, these operations required a degree of decentralization of command and control, "which was further encouraged by the tendency of the insurgents to operate in small, highly mobile bands." Moreover, British success in counterinsurgency is also attributable to a society that had created an army "ideally suited to counterinsurgency and to cultural attitudes about how that Army might be used." The character of the British Army, Mockaitis contends, also set it up for success in counterinsurgency operations.[46]

Success in countering guerrillas requires the ability to deploy small units on an area basis and to decentralize command and control. However, conventionally minded officers and armies are usually averse to such dispersion because they have been taught to mass and concentrate their forces. The British, though, had a somewhat unconventional army. The British Army's history of imperial policing made internal security the norm and conventional war the exception. Operating with a regimental system also facilitated decentralization: "The British were used to deploying smaller units throughout the empire for extended periods, which enabled these units to mesh with the civil administration and police within an area." Ian Beckett maintains that Charles Callwell's 1899 *Small Wars: Their Principles and Practice* played a significant role in capturing the lessons learned from the imperial experience of the nineteenth century. Callwell was able to discern several principles of counterinsurgency; although some became less relevant in the context of twentieth-century insurgencies, others had lasting relevance for the British Army's role in low-intensity conflicts.[47]

Callwell's extensive use of historical examples as a way of suggesting lessons was also significant because this was also a characteristic of the traditional British approach to the study of counterinsurgency. Charles Gwynn's 1934 *Imperial Policing* followed in the footsteps of Callwell and derived lessons from the revolts in Amritsar in 1919 to Cyprus in 1931 to demonstrate the principles of minimum force, firm action, civilian control, and the integration of civilian and military efforts. After 1945, the British Army faced a new form of insurgency "firmly based on political revolutionary ideology and often eschewing direct military action against security forces for political indoctrination among the population." The fundamental versatility of the traditional British approach assured that what were by then accepted tenets of military subordination, use of local resources, intelligence gathering, and a recognition of the need to divorce active insurgents from their local supporters were very adaptable to unique conditions and generally effective in maintaining at least a modicum of political stability, even against the pressure of fervid nationalism or communist revolutionary challenges.[48]

The British Army fought its post–World War II campaigns in predominantly rural conditions, varying from jungle conditions (Malaya, Kenya, Borneo, Guyana, Dhofar) to desert conditions (Palestine, Muscat and Oman, Radfan, Kuwait). The most salient common characteristic of these campaigns was how successful the British Army was in conducting small-scale and medium-scale operations. The British Army helped bring about favorable political outcomes for Britain. In almost every case of devolution, the newly independent states allowed the British Army to retain facilities in their countries. According to Michael Dewar, the British were successful in small wars because they were willing to fight like their indigenous adversaries. For example, in Malaya and Borneo, the British Army fought the guerrillas not with air power and artillery but by inserting small patrols that operated like the insurgents. The army used stealth and cunning and on the few instances when bombers or artillery were employed they were remarkably unsuccessful.[49]

In assessing British Army attitudes in the post–World War II period, Correlli Barnett observed that the British Army's social structure, its values, and its way of life survived the years 1939–1960 with surprisingly little change. The British officer corps was still dominated by the "gentleman." It remained essentially a working-class army officered by the upper classes. The continued power of regimental loyalties signified that the British Army had survived the social revolutions of the mid-twentieth century with its traditions in tact. The counterguerrilla struggle in Malaya lasted from 1948 to 1960, and "it ended with the only victory won by a Western power against practitioners of revolutionary warfare." The British fought this war like their guerrilla opponents, with limited resources, and adapting themselves to living and fighting deep in the jungle for long periods and with minimum supplies. They outfought and outsmarted the Communist insurgents at their own game of camping, ambush, and jungle tracking. Notably, the insurgents' ability to live off the local population was undermined by resettling villagers in model villages under government protection. In fact, in all the operations during the British retreat from empire, the army's techniques of riot control avoided unnecessary shooting and the systematic brutality that characterized the experiences of other armies in similar situations.[50]

The British Army's campaign in Malaya was in many ways the archetypal counterinsurgency campaign, although it took several years to adopt a good counterinsurgency strategy and a total of twelve years to ultimately defeat the guerrillas. Although regular troops, aircraft, and sophisticated equipment played no small part in defeating the insurgents, the British could not have achieved success without the support of the indigenous population—the Federal Army, the Home Guard, the Police Force, the Malayan Chinese Special Branch, and a preponderance of the civilian population. Military measures, emergency regulations, and winning hearts and minds together defeated the Communist insurgents. The British defeated the guerrillas in Malaya because the British Army was willing to beat them at their own game. All in all, in Malaya the British Army lost 509 soldiers and the insurgents lost 6710 of its 12,000 members killed.[51]

Notwithstanding the Korean War and the Falklands, almost all the campaigns the British Army fought during the Cold War were counterinsurgency in character. "Of all the former colonial powers, the British experience in counterinsurgency is probably the richest." The British Army's experiences in small wars had been gained over a long period when the Empire was established, maintained, and devolved. According to one scholar of British Army history, however, even the strategic focus on Europe after 1967 and the shift to a maneuver-oriented doctrine in the 1980s did not detract from the British Army's cultural affinity for operations other than war. The Northern Ireland commitment essentially pulled manpower toward the imperial policing mission, with tankers and artillery men functioning as infantry since there was nobody to take their places.[52]

In August 1969, the British Army was called in to give military aid to the civil power in Northern Ireland. The troops' initial task was to protect the Catholics in Londonderry. However, after the Provisional IRA split from the IRA, it aimed to kill as many British troops as possible in order to influence British public opinion to force the British government to pull out its troops. The Provisional IRA adopted tactics that were a mixture of terror and guerrilla warfare. They were so successful that the traditional IRA decided to join the shooting and ambushed an army patrol in May 1971. However, despite recent counterinsurgency experiences in Kenya, Malaya, Cyprus, and Aden, the British Army was unsure of an approach. It initially alienated most of the Catholic community with its policy of internment without trial and bad intelligence—imprisoning the wrong people. This went from bad to worse, however, when on a day early in 1972, which came to be known as "Bloody Sunday," the Parachute Regiment killed thirteen men and wounded thirteen others. In March 1972, the British dissolved the Ulster Parliament and implemented direct rule from Westminster. The British Army was subsequently compelled to reconsider its intelligence methods and training. Frank Kitson reexamined and revised tactics and improved training facilities. After 1975, the British Army successfully contained the troubles by improving its tactics and making its intelligence operations more sophisticated. Moreover, the army was employed to support civil police efforts, which remained primary. This was a corporal's war, with great responsibility place on young NCOs. As a result of Northern Ireland, the British Army has unique experience in urban patrolling, covert surveillance, and bomb disposal. Until 1995, the commitment to Northern Ireland occupied about 18,500 British soldiers, of which 11,500 were regulars and 6000 comprised the Ulster Defense Regiment.[53]

Colin McInnes, an expert in British military policy, asserted that British military culture "would suggest certain continuities in underlying approach between colonial insurgency and Northern Ireland because of deep-seated beliefs and attitudes held by the Army as a result of its historical experiences, despite the different pressures unique to the Army's role in the province." Gavin Bulloch and Thomas Mockaitis also support this assertion. According to Bulloch, "The experience of numerous small wars has provided the British Army with a unique insight into this demanding form [counterinsurgency] of conflict." Mockaitis adds, "Although the hey day of British counterinsurgency ended with the Malayan Emergency in the 1960s, the examples of Oman and Northern Ireland suggest that the principles upon which it is based are as valuable today as they were 30 years ago." Succinctly stated, the British principles for counterinsurgency are (1) minimum force; (2) civil and military cooperation to win support of the population; and (3) decentralization of command and control, which is nurtured by the regimental system and creates initiative in junior leaders.[54]

The low-intensity function of the British Army remained central to this institution even after the Healey decision to withdraw the British military from east of Suez. According to Strachan, even though this decision was thought to have settled the dilemma between Europe and empire in favor of the continent, the colonial legacies remained. Institutions of the British Army have been shaped far more by colonial continuities than by the intense but infrequent periods of continental warfare. Moreover, the periods between major European wars have not been characterized by peace but by continuous fighting in imperial wars in the 1840s, 1890s, 1920s, 1950s, and 1970s. Others have also emphasized the influence of Northern Ireland in perpetuating the British Army's experiences and attitudes about low-intensity conflict: "Despite subsequent distractions like the Falklands Islands and the Gulf, we should not underestimate the profound influence of Ulster on soldiers' lives." This apparently endless commitment called much of the tune. According to Strawson, this commitment conditioned training, movement, deployment, logistics, and morale. It shapes the soldier's life.[55]

In sum, "only the British have enjoyed notable success in counterinsurgency." Against the Communist insurgents in Malaya, the Mau Mau in Kenya, and the EOKA nationalist insurgents in Cyprus, the British Army successfully defeated indigenous movements. The British Army was involved in two post-imperial campaigns: from 1970 to 1975, British soldiers advised the Sultan of Oman's

armed forces against Dhofari nationalists, and it conducted internal security operations in Northern Ireland from 1969 to 1995. The lessons derived from the
British Army's earlier campaigns helped influence its response to these more recent insurgencies. According to Mockaitis, Frank Kitson successfully applied insights he gained during the Mau Mau emergency in Kenya to Belfast in the early
1970s, where he commanded British troops. Although much of the official British
doctrine was not formulated until the last quarter of the twentieth century, it built
on experience gained doing imperial policing in the Middle East, India, and
Ireland during the first three quarters of the century.[56]

Even so, the culture and organization that made the British Army amenable
to changes required to successfully counter insurgencies or control internal unrest
also made it very difficult for the British Army to prepare, innovate, and successfully conduct symmetric-conventional wars in Europe. The conventional wars
that the British fought against continental powers—the Napoleonic, Crimean, and
world wars—testified to a mediocre record in this operational milieu. Although
the British Army was ultimately victorious in all of these wars, it embarked on
each one unprepared in size, doctrine, or mindset. Even during the Napoleonic
Wars, the British Army found itself on the inferior side of an asymmetric relationship and was therefore compelled to use an unorthodox (indirect) approach to
gain a foothold on the peninsula, combining a Fabian conventional strategy with
guerrillas to disperse and overextend the French. Moreover, the Crimean War and
World War I underscore the problems the British Army faced when operating
outside of its principal imperial defense role. The British Army, in size, organization, and doctrine, certainly was not prepared for conventional war against
Germany in 1940. The history of the British Army's thus reveals a culture whose
attitudes, experiences, and preferences see major wars as the exception, or aberration, and low-intensity conflicts as the norm.

However, even after the creation of a general staff and the Haldane reforms, at
the beginning a World War I the British Army was not capable of fighting a major
war on the continent. "Doctrinally, the British Army before 1914 was poorly
prepared, as its major experience of war since the Crimea had been colonial wars, of
which the latest was in South Africa." After the Boer Wars, the infantry improved
its shooting skills and field craft, but new doctrine did not emerge. "Indeed, there
was no institution through which the Army could engage in serious thinking about
war before 1914, and army manuals were often written by poorly prepared staff—
thus one officer before 1914 found himself writing three manuals at once: one on
infantry training, the songbook of the British Army, and the handbook of the 4.5-
inch gun!" Leadership and staff work above the regimental level were also inadequate. Although the British Army improved its performance from 1914 to 1918
and subsequently played a major role in winning the war, "there was a yawning
chasm between Britain's chosen strategy and her actual military organization or
long-term planning." According to Peter Simkins, even though the BEF was
committed to fight in a continental war, the implications of that commitment had

not been thoroughly considered and no plan existed for raising a mass army or expanding ammunition production.[57]

AN EMPHASIS ON MINIMUM FORCE IN COUNTERINSURGENCY

Since at least 1945, the basic principle of minimum force has underpinned the British Army's approach to operations short of war. In 1961, the situation in Georgetown, Guyana, did not escalate because the British troops did not over-react. In 1967, in Aden, General Tower did not re-occupy Crater right away because it would have required significant force, probably including 76 mm armored car guns. In Londonderry and Belfast, Northern Ireland, the British Army did not immediately storm the "No-Go" areas because it would have required maximum force. Moreover, the Yellow Card (rules of engagement) limitations imposed on British soldiers in Northern Ireland laid down very strict conditions for when a soldier was authorized to use deadly force.[58]

Initially, the principle of minimum force did not apply to insurgency but to all situations up to and including riots. However, in the aftermath of the Indian massacre at Amritsar in 1919, this principle was also applied to most forms of internal unrest except those types of counterguerrilla operations that approximated conventional combat. According to Mockaitis, the Hunter Committee, which investigated the Amritsar massacre in 1919, discovered what the United States discovered a half-century later in Vietnam: "The employment of excessive measures is as likely as not to produce the opposite result to that desired." Restraint, or circumspect selectivity on when to use force, is essential to succeed in counterinsurgency operations because they require security forces to hit the insurgents without harming the population at large. "Amritsar profoundly affected the attitude of British officers toward internal conflict and encouraged a steady evolution of the principle of minimum force to include every form of disturbance from riot to revolution."[59]

In fact, a quick recapitulation of the Amritsar incident helps illuminate why it was so central in embedding the minimum-force principle in British Army culture. In April 1919, Brigadier General Dyer ordered his men to open fire on a crowded assembly in the Jallianwala Bagh in Amritsar. Within ten minutes, the soldiers expended 1650 rounds, killing 379 and wounding over 1200. Dyer did not have a martial-law imprimatur when he acted but he did have the authorization of the deputy commissioner of Amritsar to use force "if necessary." The official inquiry into this massacre had limited the military's responsibility in cases of civil disorder and found that Dyer had violated the principle of minimum force. As a result, the interwar army came to embrace the notion that military force was to be used only as an instrument of discrimination and restraint. Sir Charles Gwynn's *Imperial Policing*, published between the wars, also argued that minimum force was a sine qua non of counterinsurgency operations. Moreover, the British Army's experience in

Ireland in 1919–1921 and Palestine in 1946, wherein it focused more singularly on military measures and where it used greater force, proved unsuccessful. "It had seen the situation in military terms: in looking for an enemy it had gone some way toward creating one."[60]

Consequently, minimum force became a central principle in the British approach to intrastate conflicts, to include peace operations. Until the events at Amritsar in 1919, the principle of minimum force was applicable only if the uprising was still under the control of the civil authorities. Until Amritsar, if the civil authorities had handed the situation over to the military, the principle of minimum force was no longer necessary. However, after Amritsar, the principle of minimum force was codified in the *Manual of Military Law* and remained embedded in the British approach to intrastate emergencies. This principle was also clearly manifest in Malaya where the British response to the Communist insurgency reflected their colonial traditions: "tight integration of civilian and military authority, minimum force with police instead of army used when possible," and a predilection for the use of "small, highly skilled troops in well-planned operations rather than [the] massive use of large numbers and heavy firepower."[61]

A CULTURAL AND ORGANIZATIONAL INCLINATION TOWARD COUNTERINSURGENCY

The nineteenth-century experience of imperial policing fixed the regiment as the British Army's valued organization, and fighting a varied host of indigenous warriors in adverse environments made the British Army adaptable, locally. Moreover, in the one instance when the British Army faced a European power in a symmetrical and conventional war after Waterloo—the Crimean War, it showed itself to be poorly prepared. The regimental system is key to understanding the British Army's culture. The British Army still makes the regiment the focus of emotional attachment and individual loyalty. For senior British officers, the regimental system reflects a constellation of attitudes rather than a specific structure. In addition to geographic and historical factors, the structure and values of the army also contributed to British strategic culture. The most salient of the British Army's organizational features is the regimental system. The army's separate regiments engender two cultural values: respect for tradition and particularism. These values, moreover, derive from the value that the British place on continuity and from the relative stability of British society. The infantry and cavalry regiments trace their lineage way back to their origins and seek to maintain an esprit particular to that heritage. As one student of the British Army explained, "the inculcation of regimental histories, the wearing of distinctive uniforms, the formation of regimental associations, and the appointment of regimental colonels commandant made the individual feel much more part of his regiment than the Army at large." Although difficult to prove, British soldiers justify the centrality of the regiment with the proposition that loyalty to the regimental family makes British soldiers continue to perform effectively under duress when otherwise they would not. On the other hand, the family spirit embodied by the regiment is not conducive to military innovation. "The regimental system tends to perpetuate established procedures, narrow men's outlooks, and, most significantly, complicate organizational change."[62]

Individual soldiers identify with the regiment as their clan or tribe. The regiment is associated with one special role instead of being an integrated combined arms unit. Regiments generally have an affiliation with a particular region in the United Kingdom and one or more territorial army (TA) units may share their regimental identity. There is a body of sacred history, a host of sacred possessions, a special dress code, and a rigid hierarchy wherein individuals clearly know their place. The origins of this hierarchy are considered feudal, with the social organization and regimental practices and traditions generally reflecting those of old England. The royal link is sustained and regiments have developed very arcane customs. In fact, Yardley and Sewell explain that it was during the period between 1870 and 1914 that the regiment as apotheosis, as the twentieth century knew it, was realized. "Sadly, it was also the same period in which Britain's transition from a rural county-based society to an urban, technological society was completed, and in which the nature of warfare changed as small colonial conflicts gave way to clashes on a titanic scale."[63]

The regimental system is a significant component of British military culture, and it was certainly a variable in influencing the army's ability, or inability, to meet its bifurcated strategic demands. The regimental system can help account for the absence of militarism in England. The definition of militarism is twofold: the army's intervention in civilian politics or a veneration of the military beyond the exigencies of warfare. Partly as a result of continual overseas service, Britain has had a professional regular army that has remained separated from civilian society. Moreover, because loyalties in the British Army are alleged first to the regiment rather than the army at large, the army has tended not to act a unified front in a political context. In other words, loyalties that lie first and foremost to individual regiments have essentially precluded the army from acting as one voice and, as a result, have made it in some ways less threatening, and more responsive, to civilian leadership. Loyalty to regiment is inculcated from the very beginning of an officer's career when the individual regiment is a powerful influence in molding an officer, helping him make the transition from civilian to military life and from school house to profession. The regiment's mess, distinctive regimental traditions, and the paternalism inherent to the regimental system all helped place the officer's loyalty first with the regiment as an institution, rather than the British Army.[64]

World War I as a harbinger of massive industrialized warfare between divisions, corps, and armies should have for all intents and purposes been the death knell of the regimental system. World War I made it clear that the Cardwell system was not successful in balancing British Army resources and training between Britain's dual strategic requirements of imperial policing and countering continental powers aspiring to hegemony. However, World War I buttressed the centrality of the regiment in two emotional ways. First, when the British Army expanded from its 161 regular infantry battalions extant in 1914 to its wartime peak of 1750 battalions, the new battalions were attached to existing regiments. Therefore, virtually every family in the country was related to someone who had served with an infantry battalion associated with a regiment, with its history, tradition, and distinctive cap badges. The result of adding a hugely increased number of battalions without increasing the number of existing regiments was to propagate the regimental spirit from the old British Army to the widest scope. Second, the war more closely linked nationalities to the regiments. The adjutant general's policy of assigning personnel by nationality into nationally affiliated regiments reinforced the national identities of the regiments and further ensconced the regimental system as a subculture of the British Army. For example, in 1914 Scots comprised forty-two percent of the Scot Guards, whereas by 1918 Scots comprised sixty-two percent of that regiment.[65]

The fact that the British Army became a servant of the empire during the interwar period partly justified the reassertion of the regiment—colonial policing again validated the regimental system in the infantry and the cavalry. However, World War II revealed the flaws in the Cardwell regimental system: the needs of the whole army dictated that men were posted to understrength units notwithstanding regimental links; and a narrow military education as defined by the experiences and expectations of regimental life may have contributed to operational-level ineptitude during the North Africa campaigns of 1941–1942. During the Korean War, the disadvantages of the regimental system were also evident: the British clearly preferred to operate at brigade and battalion level, and indeed for the first critical months of the war operated as independent brigades. Even when the Commonwealth Division was established, operations tended to be thought of more in terms of a series of brigade or battalion-sized actions rather than the entire division operating under a coherent and unified concept of operation. Also, Williamson Murray asserts that the insularities of the regimental system and its concomitant influence on British Army culture created a parochial anti-intellectualism that impeded an understanding of operations beyond the battalion level and that derided intellectual professionalism.[66]

In 1957 when the new defense policy included measures to cut the conventional forces and to abolish conscription, the army's senior leadership equated the regiments with the essence of the army as a whole and fought to defend them. By making the needs of the army equal to the needs of the regiments, these senior officers politicized the regiment. Sir Gerald Templar, chief of the imperial general staff between 1956 and 1958, was a key figure in this fight. Templar himself was shaped by the regimental system and imperial policing—his own regiment, the Royal Irish Fusiliers—had been scheduled to be disbanded in 1921 but was saved by a compromise that enabled it to continue as a single-battalion regiment. Sitting out most of World War II due to a serious injury, Templar's reputation was made in Malaya where small units (battalion-size regiments) were most adaptable and best suited for prolonged counterinsurgency operations in the jungle. "As in the nineteenth century and between the wars, the empire gave the single-battalion regiment a tactical and administrative relevance it could not sustain in European warfare." And even though the British Army shifted focus toward European war in the 1970s and 1980s, defense of the regiment persisted, as officers who had reached the top of the army in the 1970s and 1980s had earned their spurs under Templar.[67]

"That Britain possesses not an army but a collection of regiments is a truism which has long outlived the obvious reasons for the system itself." Even by 1990–1991, when the Ministry of Defense released its post–Cold War review, *Options for Change*, leaving to the army the decision on which regiments remain and which amalgamate, the army failed to address the broader questions of its shape and size. The army board continued to espouse the single-battalion regiment even though lessons from NATO and the Persian Gulf War pointed to the desirability of thinking in terms of larger formations and of the army as a whole. Not surprisingly, the then chief of the general staff and his successor were both products of the regimental system (Gurkhas and Green Howards) as was the chief of the United Kingdom Land Forces (Gloucestershire Regiment). One can infer that their regimental loyalties did not predispose them to support a fundamental restructuring that threatened the regiment. The institution's justification for this unusual reversal of priorities was, that "the regiment, by virtue of the fierce loyalties which it generated, was the receptacle of the Army's history and traditions, and was therefore the bedrock of the Army's morale and fighting qualities." Since the end of the Cold War, the combinations of reductions in number of units and troops has driven the British Army to orient contingency planning along the lines of reinforced brigade structures.[68]

Although the twentieth century witnessed the advent of mass armies, with their attendant combined arms formations of divisions and corps, the continued importance of imperial garrisoning to Britain continued to confer a functional validity or utility on the infantry regiment that was disappearing elsewhere. The battalion was an appropriate load for a troop ship, a sensible organization for a colonial outpost, and a reasonable component unit of the relatively smaller sized regimental formations used for imperial policing. What's more the separation of imperial regiments from the home society through overseas service made the regiment more that just a military unit. "It saw itself as an enlarged family, a self-contained community, with its own welfare arrangements, its own recreation and sports." By the end of the twentieth century the regiment became the focus of the British Army's political activity. Officers and soldiers were readily enticed into defending their regiments because most of their professional careers were centered on the regiment. They also understood the value of regimental symbols, badges, and uniforms as instruments to rally support from the wider community.[69]

CONCLUSION

This conclusion summarizes the salient characteristics of British military culture. First, history and an insular geography have helped shape a pragmatic and indirect

British approach to strategy. Second, imperial policing, intrastate security, and counterinsurgency have been considered normal roles for the British Army. Stability Operations (small wars and counterinsurgencies) have dominated the British Army experience and the British military has embraced them as central to the institution. Next, although the British Army has been successful in almost all of its conventional wars, for the historical, cultural, and organizational reasons elaborated in this chapter, for most of its history the British Army has viewed its expeditionary role to fight on the Continent as aberrant and peripheral. Imperial policing, and subsequently internal security/counterinsurgency, have been the mainstay of British Army operations. Likewise, the regimental system has proved responsive and adaptable to the exigencies of intrastate operations. However, as Winton explained, imperial policing and the regimental system were impediments to preparing for conventional conflicts on the Continent. The regimental system is embedded in British Army culture.

Additionally, years of experience in low-intensity conflicts and counterinsurgency have over time imbued the institution with certain principles about the use of force in such operations. As a result, the British have wholeheartedly accepted that they should use minimum force and only when required. The British Army also seems to exhibit more patience when it comes to protracted internal security problems—this is probably attributable to a tradition of operating in small, autonomous units in isolated and far away places. The British approach to casualties, moreover, is best described as a "stiff-upper-lip" attitude: a history of taking a limited number of casualties in remote places for unclear reasons has made the British more tolerable of casualties. This is not to say that the British Army did not try to avoid casualties, but that it did not seem to be averse to them in the context of small wars and counterinsurgencies. Also, due in part to a history of limited resources for the army, the British Army has not come to over rely on technology as a be-all and end-all solution.

American Military Culture and Counterinsurgency

Another Street Without Joy

> The deplorable experience in Vietnam overshadows American thinking about guerrilla insurgency.[1]

IN 1961, BERNARD FALL, a scholar and practitioner of war, published a book entitled *The Street Without Joy*. The book provided a lucid account of why the French Expeditionary Corps failed to defeat the Viet Minh during the Indochina War and the book's title is derived from the French soldiers' sardonic moniker for Highway 1 on the coast of Indochina—"Ambush Alley," or the "Street Without Joy." In 1967, while patrolling with U.S. Marines on the "Street Without Joy" in Vietnam, Bernard Fall was killed by an improvised explosive mine during a Vietcong ambush. In 2003, after the fall of Baghdad and following the conventional phase of Operation Iraqi Freedom, U.S. and coalition forces operating in the Sunni Triangle began fighting a counterguerrilla-type war in which much of the enemy insurgent activity occurred along Highway 1, another street conspicuously without joy. Learning from the experience of other U.S. counterinsurgencies is preferable to the obverse.

The U.S. military has had a host of successful experiences in counterguerrilla war, including some distinct successes with certain aspects of the Vietnam war. However, the paradox stemming from America's unsuccessful crusade in the jungles of Vietnam is this—because the experience was perceived as anathema to the mainstream American military, hard lessons learned there about fighting guerrillas were neither embedded nor preserved in the U.S. Army's institutional memory. The American military culture's efforts to expunge the specter of Vietnam, embodied in the mantra "No More Vietnams," also prevented the U.S. Army as an institution from really learning from those lessons. In fact, even the term "counterinsurgency" seemed to become a reviled and unwelcome word, one that the doctrinal cognoscenti of the 1980s conveniently transmogrified into "foreign internal defense." Even though many lessons existed in the U.S. military's historical experience with small wars, the lessons from Vietnam were the most voluminous. Yet these lessons were most likely the least read since the U.S. Army's intellectual rebirth after Vietnam focused almost exclusively on its military-cultural preferred paradigm of big, conventional war in Europe.[2]

Americans faced no serious external military threat for most of their history until the late 1990s. Therefore, many Americans could afford to dedicate most of their energy and thought to the pursuit of peace, whereas other states devoted much thought and energy to preparing for war. "But the United States won its independence in the course of a global war, found its security threatened for several decades thereafter by other global wars, and then, following the long interval of safety, discovered itself caught up in the global wars of the twentieth century." According to Weigley, a focus on naval power was implicit to a country of large ocean frontiers—this very focus appeared early and persisted. However, the United States is a continental power as well, and U.S. concerns over security have also turned to the establishment of an American Army.[3]

Although the history of the U.S. Army is replete with many years of experiences with nontraditional types of conflict, its culture, until now, had preferred a concept of war akin to its World War II approach to war. For example, the U.S. Army has consistently refused to seriously consider any type of war except a European-style conventional war. "When the U.S. Army has nevertheless had to participate in unconventional, insurrectionary, or guerrilla wars, the experiences have soon been dismissed as aberrant." Long before the Vietnam war, the American Army culture had virtually erased the Philippine Insurrection (1899–1902) from its memory. Ostensibly, it allowed this to happen based on the assumption that the kind of warfare engendered therein—counterinsurgency waged in difficult terrain and in a terrible heat—was not likely to revisit the U.S. Army. Likewise, even though the U.S. Army had a long history of warfare against the Indians, it never bothered to develop a doctrine suited to the particularities of counter-Indian warfare because that kind of irregular war diverged too greatly from the European style of war.[4]

Similarly, in 1989 Carl Builder observed that the experiences of the two world wars combined to form within the Army a strong perception of the U.S. Army in the role of "defender and liberator of Europe."[5] In the interwar years, though, the U.S. Army resumed its role as the government's handyman, patrolling the Mexican borders, quelling veterans' riots, running the Civilian Conservation Corps camps during the Depression, and so forth. However, Builder asserts, the Army's experience in its final and best year of World War II influenced the institution so significantly that it has persisted to the present day. The Army's experiences in Korea and Vietnam have been consigned to the "wrong kinds of wars," disquieting aberrations because they either lacked public support or limited the military's use of force with onerous political constraints. World War II, Builder observes, was an experience the Army liked, the last successful absolute crusade—a self-image very distinct from its subsequent experience during the Cold War. One sage aphorism, in fact, alludes to this: "military men are forever preparing to refight the last *satisfactory* war."[5]

However, although the Cold-War U.S. Army focused its force structure, training, and doctrine on fighting the big battle for central Europe, the Army had still conducted a diverse array of missions: constabulary forces in Japan and Germany, a United Nations "police action" in Korea, a contingency operation in the Dominican Republic, the Sinai peacekeeping commitment, Vietnam, Grenada, and so forth. According to Builder, "none of this long list of duties—for the recent past or the likely future—includes the war toward which the Army has devoted so much of its energies and equipment designs."[6] Although, Builder was not pre-scient enough to foresee the Persian Gulf War back in 1989, Saddam Hussein provided the United States with a war that was perfectly congruous with the Army's favorite paradigm. According to another military historian, the Persian Gulf War gave the U.S. Army what it had longed for since 1945: "It was a war of clear aims, well-defined means, and circumscribed duration, fought in happy concert with many allies."[6] However, this same author argued, "Strategically, operationally, and tactically, this one was a museum piece—exciting, militarily impressive, and in the long run as sterile and unimportant as Omdurman."[6]

In another work, this same military expert maintained that World War II and the Persian Gulf War were actually the aberrations in the American Army experience. "The American military's artificially narrow definition of war has never matched the real world or its own heritage of small, ambiguous wars." The preferred American paradigm for war has typically been one that is a declared war against a conventionally organized enemy. The U.S. Army has preferred to prepare for wars where its adversaries come to fight division against division, with tanks and jets, the kind of foe that fights fairly, kind of a mirror image. However, the U.S. Army has experienced about six hundred hours worth of what it defines as war (in contrast to "operations other than war" and limited war) since 1945. In addition, the U.S. Army's experience in and after Vietnam, coupled with its success in the Persian Gulf War, reaffirmed a propensity for the big-war model. As Eliot Cohen once posited, "the American armed forces' understanding of the domestic political context of small wars has been shaped, and in fact distorted, by the experience of Vietnam." U.S. officers, Cohen asserts, were shocked by their military's apparent inability to annihilate an enemy who had less mobility and less combat power.[7]

A preponderance of officers in the U.S. Army derived from Vietnam the determination to never again prosecute a war without the degree (full) of public support more characteristic of a world war than a small war. As Michael Vlahos observes: "Ironically, Vietnam brought us back more intently to the myth of World War II, to the restatement of the just war, or as Studs Terkel cunningly sensed, *The Good War*, that it represents." Vietnam was America's least successful war and it was the single most important cause of uncertainty and turbulence for the U.S. Army in the 1970s and 1980s: "The manner in which the war was fought also generated profound misgivings within the service as well as among the American people at large about the possible erosion of the Army's tactical, operational, and strategic skills."[8] After Vietnam, the U.S. Army redoubled its focus on planning and doctrine for war in Europe. Although focusing on Europe helped to ultimately renew the U.S. Army, it also helped recreate an army that was not very agile in the conduct of wars other than the conventional type.[8]

During the 1970s and 1980s, in examining past wars to derive lessons for future conflicts, the U.S. Army generally tended to eschew both Vietnam and Korea as unpleasant anomalies. Revisiting World War II and embracing the recent technological developments of the conventional 1973 Yom Kippur War, the American military hoped that the next war would prove to be like World War II. In fact, the principal architect of the first post–Vietnam army doctrine, General William Depuy, was a product of the U.S. Army's success in World War II and its failure in Vietnam. In describing him, one study observes: "Depuy was skeptical of the relevance of the Korean and Vietnam experiences, except as they reinforced his ideas." Depuy engendered armored warfare and combined arms operations, and he was enamored of the German methods of warfare. It was this experience and these ideas that appeared in the post–Vietnam doctrine, and around which Depuy sought to renew the army. In addition, the new technology and lethality augured by the Yom Kippur War helped reinforce the fear of Depuy and his assistants that "Vietnam had been an aberration in the historical trend of warfare, and that the Army had lost a generation's worth of technological modernization there while gaining a generation's worth of nearly irrelevant combat experience."[9]

Added to Depuy's renewed focus on Europe was a book by then Colonel Harry Summers in which he argued that civilians had made a mess of the strategy for fighting Vietnam. Summers highlighted in his book the fact that the United States cited 22 different reasons for fighting the war. As a result, political and military leaders could not arrive at a consensus on strategy or properly identify the nature of the war, which, according to Summers, would have been the application of overwhelming U.S. conventional force to defeat the North Vietnamese Army. Summers' "lessons" became the predominant school of thought and devolved into, and perpetuated, the "Never Again School." Moreover, in the 1980s the Never Again School dominated American military culture: it was articulated in the Weinberger Doctrine in the middle of the decade; and it was subsequently embodied by General Colin Powell as the chairman of the Joint Chiefs of Staff (JCS) at the end of the decade. The "lessons" of Vietnam, coupled with the lessons from the 1983 bombing of U.S. Marines in Beirut, were (1) the United States should not commit troops without public support; (2) if America does commit the military, it should have clearly defined political and military objectives; (3) the United States should use force only in an overwhelming manner and with the intent of winning; (4) America should commit force only in defense of vital national interests; and (5) the United States should use military force only as a last resort.[10]

The history of American military's suboptimal performance in low-intensity conflicts during the 1980s is also a testimony and a litany of military and political failures: the aborted hostage rescue in Iran, the invasion of Grenada, and the bombing of the Marines in Beirut. As one author cogently stated it, "rather than squarely face up to the fact that Army counterinsurgency doctrine had failed in Vietnam, the Army—and the governments of the 1980s and 1990s—decided that the United States should no longer involve itself in counterinsurgency operations." Instead of resisting change to counterinsurgency doctrine, the more influential groups in the U.S. Army opposed participation in low-intensity conflicts entirely and sought to peripheralize the supporters and doctrine for low-intensity conflicts. Richard Duncan Downie uses the moniker "War is a War" to identify Summers' Never Again School. According to Downie, this powerful and predominant group looked to army big-war norms and domestic popular support to avoid involvement in low-intensity conflicts. Consequently, the Weinberger Doctrine codified the criteria that, when followed, essentially proscribed the use of the U.S. military in anything other than its preferred paradigm, conventional mid- to high-intensity conflict in which the U.S. military could exert technological prowess and overwhelming combat power to annihilate the enemy.[11]

The U.S. military's success in the Persian Gulf War, moreover, was viewed as a vindication of the War is a War and Never Again Schools. "The Gulf War, although waged against a Third World country, was a classic conventional war fought along the lines of strategies and tactics developed in World War II, Korea, and the Arab-Israeli wars of the previous four decades, and America's military is very good at conventional combat." Many also thought that the Gulf War had finally expunged the ghosts of Vietnam. As the ground war took shape, in fact, President George Bush claimed, "by God, we've kicked the Vietnam syndrome once and for all." Another observation was simply, "the Gulf War simply confirmed the Army's Jominian concept of fighting purely military battles with high technology weaponry and overwhelming firepower." Cori Dauber at University of North Carolina at Chapel Hill explained the significance of the Weinberger Doctrine and the success of the U.S. military in the Gulf War: "Desert Storm is represented by a variety of authors in a variety of venues as being successful precisely because the U.S. military learned—and applied—the appropriate lessons of Vietnam." Despite the fact that the army essentially conducted peace operations for a decade after the end of the Cold War, the first Persian Gulf War had so reinforced the culturally preferred, technologically enabled, decisive conventional war model, that by 11 September 2001, the U.S. military still predominantly viewed its mission essential tasks as being focused on conventional war. Even as late as March of 2002, the National Training Center (NTC), the U.S. Army's premier desert collective training opportunity, still focused exclusively on conventional battles with linear boundaries and phase lines. Since Operation Iraqi Freedom, however, the Army has radically changed its training paradigm at NTC—it is now adaptive and very asymmetric.[12]

THE AMERICAN ARMY—THE INFLUENCE OF GEOGRAPHY AND HISTORY

American ways of war were offshoots of European ways of war, and American strategic thought was therefore a branch of European strategic thought.[13]

It is important to emphasize from which European military-strategic thinkers the American military tradition stemmed—more so from Napoleon and Jomini than from Clausewitz. From the outset, Weigley explains, "one of the American changes of emphasis was toward less restraint in the conduct of war, in both means and ends, than became characteristic of European war after the close of the Wars of Religion and before the Wars of the French Revolution." Although wars in Europe after 1648 were fought by professional armies for limited ends, the wars between the colonists and the Indians, at least after King Philip's War, were wars of cultural survival fought with absolute aims wherein European restrictions on attacks against the property and lives of noncombatants were frequently disregarded.[14]

George Washington was foremost among those Americans who sought to import European models of war. Washington modeled the Continental Army as closely as possible after the rival British Army, and he fought the American Revolution as a conventional war with the American prototype of an eighteenth-century professional army. However, since Washington's army was limited in personnel, resources, and time to train up, he soon realized that committing his troops to open battle against the British would invite disaster. Therefore, after the Continental Army's unsuccessful defenses of New York in 1776 and Philadelphia (Brandywine Creek) in 1777, Washington avoided head-on collisions with the British Army. Acknowledging his limitations, Washington adopted an indirect strategy of attrition whereby he avoided general actions against the British main body but instead concentrated what forces he had against weak enemy outposts and piecemeal detachments. Washington's plan for victory was to keep the revolution alive by preserving the Continental Army and wearing down the British will to resist with raids against the periphery of its armies. According to Weigley, this "strategy of erosion" stemmed from a strategic paradox: Washington's political objective had to be the absolute removal of the British from the insurgent colonies but his military means were so weak that he had no other alternative other than a strategic defensive.[15]

The subsequent course of U.S. history—characterized by a rapid increase in power and resources—curbed any further development of both guerrilla and counterguerrilla methods. Nathanael Greene "remains alone as an American master developing a strategy of unconventional warfare." After the war, the influence of Washington's orthodoxy prevailed. Greene and the other unconventional warriors who performed so well in the revolution did not play a role in influencing the development of American military strategic culture. "Whenever after the Revolution the American Army had to conduct a counter-guerrilla campaign—in the Second Seminole War of 1835–1841, the Filipino Insurrection of 1899–1903, and in Vietnam in 1965–1973—it found itself almost without an institutional memory of such experiences, had to relearn appropriate tactics at exorbitant costs, and yet tended after each episode to regard it as an aberration that need not be repeated."[16]

In fact, when the Seminole War started, the professional U.S. officer corps was preparing the army to fight with new skills in campaigns of the conventional

European style. It did not really try to prepare the American Army for an un-conventional, irregular war. The U.S. regular army was modeled sufficiently on European and British patterns by 1835 that it was "not much better prepared for a guerrilla war against the Seminoles in Florida than Napoleon's army had been prepared to fight guerrillas on the Iberian Peninsula." This was true despite the experience the Army had gained fighting Indians in the French and Indian War and the irregular campaigns that American soldiers had themselves prosecuted against the British in the American War of Independence. As it turned out, the U.S. Army, in its campaigns against the Seminoles, had to learn counterguerrilla warfare all over again, as the Seminoles adopted a guerrilla approach in Florida. "The Seminoles refused to stake their future on showdown battles but preferred instead to wear out their adversaries by means of raids and terror, and by turning their forbidding homeland itself into a weapon against their foes."[17]

In the first part of the nineteenth century, moreover, the West Point envi-ronment of Sylvanus Thayer and Dennis Hart Mahan was essentially divorced from the main intellectual trends of Jacksonian America. West Point's isolation allowed it to establish high standards of performance, but the price of isolation was high. Because American military leaders stood apart from American civil life, they failed to reconcile themselves to the development of military programs that were congruous to that life. Very satisfied with the U.S. Army's performance in Mexico and of the regulars' professional growth, these officers were growing more confident in the prowess of the regular army. However, they avoided any serious thought about preparing a military policy designed to achieve the greatest effectiveness from an armed citizenry, despite the fact that any major war would have to be waged mostly with militia and volunteers. To be certain, it was unlikely that Jacksonian America would authorize either a larger regular army or even an expansible army of regular officer cadre. If the professional officers were to lead Americans to war, they would have to lead armed citizens, deficiencies notwithstanding; otherwise, they would lack the numbers to fight a serious war. Dennis Hart Mahan was one of the original oracles of American military thought. Mahan received part of his military education in France and his hero was Na-poleon. His book, *Outpost*, revealed Mahan's personal preference for the offen-sive mode of war and the commitment of professional officers to regular troops because no other troops could ensure the fulfillment of an offensive role.[18]

In other words, the pre–Civil War U.S. Army culture was divorced from realistic thought about how to fight an American war. The army's senior (cor-porate) leaders expected civil society to adapt to their way of war fighting, and they made little effort to adapt their ideas on warfare to civil society in America. These officers were ill prepared for the full scope of the Civil War, a total war that witnessed mass armies of armed citizen soldiers waging a war of annihilation for survival. The absolute character of the Civil War would have been anticipated by Clausewitz, but not by the American military's preferred oracle of military strategy before the Civil War—Jomini. In fact, the Civil War would become the harbinger of a solely American fusion of Jomini's separation of the military from politics and Clausewitz's precept that all wars incline toward the absolute. This fusion would be engendered by a hero of the Civil War, a protégé of Sherman's, and "the single most influential officer in sealing the commitment of the officer corps to the conservative, professionalist view of war"—Emory Upton. After the Civil War, paradoxically, the isolation of the U.S. military was the principal precondition for the development of professionalism. "Withdrawn from civilian society and turning inward upon itself, the U.S. Army came under the influence of reformers like Sherman, Upton, and Luce." They looked abroad for most of their ideas. Upton, in particular, focused on the Prussian military system. In fact, the years between 1860 and World War I saw the emergence of a distinctive professional military ethic in the U.S. Army.[19]

Emory Upton was the most influential younger officer among the U.S. Army reformers. After the Franco-Prussian War, the U.S. military's reverence for French military institutions abated and U.S. Army officers became interested in the military institutions of Germany and other countries. Sherman, in fact, played a pivotal role in sending Upton on his inspection of foreign militaries in 1870–1871, with instructions for a particular emphasis on German military institutions. Upton's *The Armies of Europe and Asia*, the first study to emerge from his tour, revealed in a comprehensive fashion to American officers the degree to which the U.S. Army was behind its European counterparts in the process of professionalizing. Upton recommended that the U.S. Army establish advanced military schools, a general staff, a system of personnel evaluation reports, and promotion by examination. While Upton studied the experiences of many militaries, he was particularly enamored of German military institutions. Upton contrasted the backward state of American military education with the fact that, in 1866, every Prussian general was a graduate of the Kriegsakademie. Sherman, who thought that the German system of military organization was "simply perfect," agreed with Upton wholeheartedly.[20]

Also, Clausewitz's magnum opus, *On War* was translated into English in 1873, and many articles about Prussian military topics began to appear in the U.S. professional military journals. Huntington maintains that American officers tended to accept the German methods unquestionably and that by the end of the century, American military thinkers fully accepted the German general staff model. Even though American officers frequently misinterpreted and misapplied German military theory, the desire by the U.S. Army to emulate German institutions was an important factor in the development of American military professionalism. Weigley identified and summarized the confluence of three factors that explain this period of professionalization in the U.S. Army's history: (1) as the post–Civil War U.S. Army was left to languish on the frontier, it was impelled to turn inward and professionalize; (2) when Clausewitz's work was translated into English in 1873, his ideas spread among U.S. officers; and (3) the oracle of total war, Sherman, established the Army's postgraduate professional schools between 1869 and 1883.[21]

In 1878, Major General Winfield Scott Hancock established the Military Service Institution of the United States, with the purpose of promoting "writing and discussion about military science and military history." In 1879, the *United Service Journal* also began publication. Sherman encouraged these institutions to supplement the school system. In 1881, Sherman established the School of Application for Infantry and Cavalry at Fort Leavenworth. The purpose of the postgraduate school system was to establish a "pyramid of institutions through which the officer could learn the special skills of his own branch of service and then the *attitudes* and principles of high command." The journals and the schools cross-fertilized each other, with the journals affording an outlet for ideas and studies nurtured at the schools. Army officers John Bigelow and Arthur Wagner wrote for these journals and their work had a significant influence in shaping professional attitudes. Bigelow also published a textbook, *Principles of Strategy*, in which he included principles "drawn from Sherman's warfare against civilian populations." Moreover, Wagner, who taught at the Leavenworth school from 1888 to 1904, eventually helped transform Leavenworth into the General Service and Staff College. Wagner was also one of the founders of the Army War College. Wagner admired the excellence of the Prussian military system and he regarded the Prussian school system as a "model for American military schools to emulate."[22]

However, it was Emory Upton who had the most influence in shaping U.S. Army professional attitudes during the late nineteenth century. For many years, anyone interested in U.S. military history consulted his *Military Policy of the United States* as the standard work in the field. "He argued that all the defects of the American military system rested upon a fundamental, underlying flaw, excessive civilian control of the military." As officers were alienated from the country, they embraced Upton's ideas in the late nineteenth century. Articles written in the new professional journals that suggested approval of Upton's work became more frequent. According to Weigley, Upton did lasting damage "in setting the main current of American military thought not to the task of shaping military institutions that would serve both military and national purposes, but to the futile task of demanding that the national institutions be adjusted to purely military expediency."[23]

Published after his death, Upton's *The Military Policy of the United States* argued for a strong regular military force. Sherman endorsed Upton's recommendations for reform, and the U.S. Army embraced *The Military Policy of the United States* in its disputes with the militia advocates. Upton considered the Prussian model to be excellent because of its general staff system, mass army, and freedom from civilian control. For the rest of his life, he endeavored to get the U.S. Congress to implement reforms based on the German Army. All of Upton's recommendations had a single aim—the creation of a modern professional U.S. Army. However, according to Stephen Ambrose, Upton was incapable of realizing that one could not simply graft a European-style professional army onto the American liberal system. This was so, Ambrose explains, because Upton failed to grasp the interrelationship between the political and military spheres in a democracy.[24]

Upton seemed to misinterpret Clausewitz and to misunderstand the nature of a liberal democracy. In *Military Policy*, he argued that officers alone should be entrusted with directing armies in the field. Moreover, through his vitriol against the secretary of war, Upton was advocating a complete independence of the army from civilian control. Enamored of the German war machine, Upton wanted the U.S. Army to achieve a similar status. Upton was willing to let the president retain the title of commander in chief, but his remarks about the defects in the U.S. Constitution (that encourage the President to assume the character of military commander) bespoke his real intentions. According to Ambrose, Upton renounced the military policy of the United States as one of imprudence and weakness, largely because uninformed civilians dominated the military. In Upton's opinion, the United States needed a professional, expansive, and autonomous army.[25]

Deborah Avant also emphasized the influence that Sherman, Upton, and other military reformers exerted on the cultivation of the U.S. Army's cultural preferences. The U.S. Army developed a very deductive method for understanding warfare and it stemmed largely from the Prussian "science of war." "The Army objected to the use of the armed forces as a police force (because it was beneath the soldiers vocation) and argued that the Army must always be governed by classic military principles." As a result, Avant asserted, the U.S. Army developed an approach to war that was biased toward decisive and offensive doctrine that was derived from Europe and suitable for the European theater. Moreover, the efforts of Sherman and Upton helped the army institutionalize an officer educational system that focused on the principles of war and cultivated uniformity of thought. The principles of war, as taught in the educational system of the U.S. Army, led more and more to a rigid conception of war. As in the Prussian Army, the American Army favored the science of war over the art of war, resulting in a stiff adherence to principles and a bias against individual initiative.[26]

U.S. Army leaders were able to professionalize, unencumbered by congressional oversight, because they deliberately formulated proposals for reform that would not require budgetary increases. "Military leaders learned that budgetary requests would prompt congressional scrutiny and acted to shape the development of the military institution without request increases in their budget." Recognizing that the chances for a budgetary increase during the post–Civil War period were unlikely anyway, U.S. Army leaders opted for autonomy to focus on professionalism. As long as the U.S. Army was kept down to a strength of 25,000 men, Congress allowed the West Pointers to develop it as they wished. Developing the professionalism, including the creation of professional institutions, was not that expensive. "Sherman, for instance, carefully avoided Congress in setting up the School of Application at Leavenworth; he did not wish it to be the subject of legislation." According to Huntington, Sherman repeatedly stressed to Congress that the schools at Leavenworth and Monroe required no extra finding beyond usual garrison expenses.[27]

It is also perplexing that in the late nineteenth century, the U.S. Army embraced the conventional Prussian military system as paragon of professionalism at the same time that the American Army was engaged in the frontier war against the Indians—the most unorthodox of the U.S. Army's nineteenth-century enemies. According to Robert Utley, the regular army was a product of the frontier. In fact, frontier needs prompted the creation of and sustained the justification for a standing army. "Except for two foreign wars and one civil war, frontier needs fixed the principal mission and employment of the Regular Army for a century." Utley considered the frontier employment of the U.S. Army against the Indians to be a paradox: the experience made the U.S. Army unsuited for orthodox war at the same time that its focus on orthodox war made it unsuited for fighting the Indians. The organization of the frontier army in companies and regiments seemed absolutely conventional in the nineteenth-century context. The army's system of border outposts was shaped by the frontier, and it resembled the (conventional) strategic approach used by the British Army in the American War of Independence. Moreover, although most army officers recognized the Indian as master of guerrilla warfare, the Army never institutionalized a counterguerrilla doctrine; nor were there training programs, military schools, or very much professional literature on how to fight Indians. The expert Indian fighters, such as George Crook and Nelson Miles, essentially learned from experience and self-study.[28]

The conventional tactics offered in Upton's, Casey's, and Scott's manuals were sometimes effective, when the Indians were imprudent enough to give battle on the Americans' terms. However, most persistent campaigns of pursuing the Indians simply broke down the horses and made the troops spend as much time trying to keep supplied as they spent fighting Indians. In fact, according to Utley, U.S. Army leaders viewed Indian warfare as an ephemeral nuisance. In 1876, for example, General Winfield Scott Hancock testified before a congressional committee that the army's Indian mission was irrelevant in determining the U.S. Army's composition and organization. The generals were partly driven by their desire to place the army on a more permanent footing than afforded by Indian warfare. They were also sincerely concerned about national defense. Nonetheless, the army they created was designed for the next conventional war rather than the present unconventional one. Even though the army conducted the Indian wars conventionally, it was still unfit for conventional war as evidenced by its less-than-optimal performance in orthodox wars in 1812, 1846, 1861, and 1898. Because its frontier role had the U.S. Army scattered across the continent in small border outposts, units seldom assembled or trained in more than battalion strength.[29]

Utley further asserted that a central component of the U.S. Army's twentieth-century practice can be traced to its frontier mission. The conduct of total war, wherein enemy populations are objects of war, "finds ample precedent in the frontier experience." The practice of total war can be found in the Seminole Wars, but Sherman and Sheridan codified it as a deliberate approach against the Indians after 1865. "With the march across Georgia and the wasting of the Shenandoah Valley as models, they set forth in the two decades after the Civil War to find the enemy in his winter camps, kill or drive him from his lodges, destroy his ponies, food, and shelter, and hound him mercilessly across a frigid landscape until he gave up." Weigley has also testified to this characteristic: as far back as King

Philip's War of 1675–1676, the colonists ensured their military victory was complete by extinguishing the Indians as a military force throughout southeastern New England. Moreover, in the fall of 1868, Sheridan chose a strategy against the Indians that reflected his and Sherman's experiences of "carrying war to the enemy's resources and people." Sheridan waged winter campaigns, "striking when the Indians' grass-fed war ponies were weak from lack of sustenance and the Indians' mobility was at a low ebb." Sheridan would then strike against the enemy's fixed camps where the Indians sheltered against the winter weather.[30]

Thus, essentially every professional officer from Winfield Scott onward—until Schofield, who as commanding general as of 1888 finally eschewed Uptonian prescriptions for civilian subordination to the military and reasserted civilian supremacy by deferring to the secretary of war—was convinced that the only way to solve the civil-military relations issue was for the civilian authorities to yield military policy to the military. "Here was still another pernicious fruit of the divorcement which the professional Army had allowed between itself and civilian America." Separated from the civilians and disdainful of them as soldiers, army officers were not inclined to accept the highest military guidance from citizens whom they perceived to be inept in military matters. Scott, McClellan, Sheridan, and Sherman—all these generals in chief had looked for an Uptonion solution. Moreover, they all helped proselytize among the American officers the dogma that military policy must be left to military men alone. Weigley sums this problem up cogently: "The officer corps had lost sight of the Clausewitzian dictum that war is but an extension of politics by other means." Thus, by the late nineteenth century the U.S. Army exhibited a reluctance to acknowledge that in war, military aims cannot be divorced from political purposes, and that the ultimate decisions rested with the civilian political leaders of the state.[31]

From the turn of the century until World War I, the focus for American military strategy had been twofold: continental defense and the protection of its Pacific possessions. The first focus was traditional, whereas the second part had come about as a result of the U.S. war with Spain in 1898. However, the War Department's plans were based on the army's primary objective of defending the territorial United States. Since the U.S. Navy was the traditional first line of defense and since it was focused on the Pacific, World War I did not really test U.S. strategic doctrine. However, World War I redirected American strategic planning and set important new precedents. According to Maurice Matloff, "The war rooted in the subconscious of the military planners the idea of a major American effort across the Atlantic." Another new strategic principle that emerged from World War I was the "idea that the imbalance of power on the European continent might threaten the long range national security of the United States and require overseas combat operations in Europe." General Pershing's insistence on employing American forces for offensive combat, open warfare, and breakthroughs reflected the traditional American military desire for "sharp and decisive wars." U.S. leaders called for a war of mass and concentration and warned against sideshows. As in earlier wars, the U.S. military's aim from the outset was total victory. Saliently, future World War II U.S. Army leaders received their strategic education in Europe during World War I.[32]

The U.S. Army's participation in World War I was too brief to change the concept of war and strategy that it had developed from the Civil War and that it subsequently nurtured by the study of Civil War campaigns in the interwar period. A concept of war stemming from the final campaigns and results of the Civil War emerged in 1918 when the American military complained about the incompleteness of the destruction of the German Army and the Allied victory. At the strategic level, the U.S. military concluded that World War I testified to the impossibility of fire and maneuver because mass armies were too large to have vulnerable flanks. Most American officers thus concluded that the advent of mass armies left the frontal assault as the only course. As a result, during the years leading up to World War II, America's military culture—one manifest in the military school system that it had borrowed from the Prussians, the instructors at those schools, and the scholarly publications associated with those schools—embraced a concept of war based on the Civil War model. America's strategic aim of completely imposing its political aims upon the vanquished, therefore, would be achieved by applying Grant's method of applying overwhelming combat power to destroy the enemy's armed forces and by applying Sherman's approach of destroying the enemy's economic resources and will to fight.[33]

After World War I, U.S. war planning reverted to a preoccupation with the Pacific and the defense of the continent. "National Policy, the public mood, and starved budgets put constraints on strategic planning and returned it to earlier channels." The color plans, for example, implied a concept of war that was limited in forces, area, and scope. However, the strategic debate in Europe between the defensive school and the offensive school began to resonate in American military thought. Slowly, Matloff explains, "The offensive overtones in European theory came to be seen as reinforcing American experience and began to seep through the constraints imposed on war planning and on the official doctrinal writings." Also, Pershing's victories in France seemed to validate the Clausewitzian principles for total war. The 1923 version of the Field Service Regulations (the antecedent to the current 100–5 series) reflected a model of war focused on annihilation: "The ultimate objective of all military action is the destruction of the enemy's armed forces in battle. Decisive defeat in battle breaks the enemy's will to war and forces him to sue for peace." Borrowed from nineteenth-century European theorists and reinforced by the World War I experience, this model of war remained the American approach to war.[34]

In addition, during the accelerated preparation for war in 1939–1941, new developments began to transform U.S. strategic thought and doctrine. There were four particularly significant developments: the shift from color to rainbow plans; the conceptual shift from continental to hemispheric defense; the adoption of a Europe-first approach; and the emergence of theories on how to defeat Germany. As early as the ABC Conference in 1941, differences between the American and British approaches to strategy began to emerge. Whereas the British argued for an indirect strategy to probe German weaknesses around the periphery of Fortress Europe, the American planners concluded that victory lay in coming to grips with and defeating Germany's ground forces and breaking the German's will to fight. "Vague as they were about preliminary operations," Matloff illumines, "they were already disposed to think in terms of meeting the German armies head on— and the sooner the better." From an institutional perspective, for U.S. strategists World War II was a war of organization, of big planning staffs, and of corporate leadership. The traditional American separation of political and military policy continued throughout the war, and it was buttressed by Roosevelt's focus on unconditional surrender. "No strategic doctrine to relate political and military objectives in a coherent patter," Matloff emphasizes, "emerged before or during the conflict."[35]

America emerged from World War II in a position of uncontested military superiority. According to Henry Kissinger, "The war seemed to have confirmed all traditional American strategic axioms." Notwithstanding its late mobilization, America had in concert with its allies crushed the aggressor; and this victory had been achieved by harnessing and unleashing massive amounts of materiel. However, the onset of the Cold War precipitated a significant and fundamental shift in U.S. strategy and force structure during peacetime. NSC 68, in conjunction with the Korean War, "served as a crucial catalyst for the ultimate implementation of the Army's strategic plans in the early 1950s." Before World War II, the U.S. Army had historically been reduced to minimum strength after wars; and immediately after World War II, the army had again been demobilized in favor of a strategy that relied principally on strategic air power. However, NSC 68 helped the army fulfill its own organizational agenda for the Cold War, "thereby revitalizing more than just its overall force structure, but providing much of the institutional rationale for more men, more money, and more equipment." NSC 68, coupled with the perceived Soviet threat in the context of the North Korean invasion, suppressed rooted American historical and cultural biases against funding and maintaining a large ground force during peacetime. The Cold War army had to support strategic policies that spanned the globe, and it had to be prepared to meet the massive Soviet arsenal in Europe as well as limited wars on the periphery.[36]

World War II had a significant influence on U.S. military culture. Officers in the American Army had been able to prepare themselves for the transition from a small peace-time army in 1940 to the World War II army in part, because the U.S. Army had inherited "the traditions and institutions of one great, European-style war of its own: the American Civil War of 1861–1865." According to Weigley, "The Civil War had molded the American army's conceptions of the nature of full-scale war in ways that would profoundly affect its conduct of the Second World War." However, the Civil War legacy was somewhat incongruous to the frontier-constabulary role that dominated the army's experience until World War I: the experiences on the frontier suggested that mobility was the chief military principle, while the memory of the Civil War pointed to massive force as the chief military principle. Reconciling these two principles to arrive at an appropriate military balance, Weigley asserts, was the main problem of metamorphosing the old U.S. Army of the frontier into the new army of European war.[37]

From the Civil War experience, the U.S. Army inherited a strategic approach that its officers generalized as applicable to all major large-scale wars. Although Grant had continuously tried to turn Lee's flank, the Union Army ultimately destroyed the Army of Northern Virginia by fighting it head-on. Both the Union's superior resources and its aim of unconditional surrender made Grant's strategy of simultaneous offensives on every part of the front an appropriate one. Likewise, in the twentieth century, the United States' confidence in its physical power allowed the armed forces to think about the destruction of enemy militaries not by maneuver but by the head-on use of overwhelming power. America's immense resources and overwhelming power would ensure the annihilation of the enemy's war-making capacity and armed forces. With such vast resources, the U.S. military could all the better attack the enemy everywhere along the front line as Grant's army had done to the Confederate Army.[38]

Subsequently, as the U.S. Army approached World War II, it espoused a clear strategic credo: war is won by destroying the enemy's war-making ability, particularly his armed forces, and maneuver alone will not accomplish this destruction. The destruction was to be accomplished by directly confronting the enemy's main armed forces and overwhelming them with superior power. In the years between the end of World War II and the Korean War, the U.S. Army's doctrine remained essentially as it was during World War II. The advent of nuclear weapons and the postwar strategic environment made it difficult for the army to develop doctrine. However, from the Army's perspective land warfare was not obsolete. "A final victory could still be gained only by rather traditional ground operations, and the World War II experience, especially in the European Theater, remained a valid basis for postwar doctrinal development."[39]

It is disconcerting that an institution with more history and experience fighting irregular conflicts of limited intensity than total wars without limits would have its core culture so profoundly influenced by Sherman, Upton, and the World War II experience. As a result of these factors, the U.S. military culture that emerged is one that ostensibly embraced the Clausewitzian axiom of subordinating military modalities to the political but, in all actuality, was truly Jominian. Instead, the U.S. military, once war breaks out, preferred to fight big conventional wars without limitations and without constraints imposed by its political masters. According to Dunn, the most significant feature of the United States' twelve-year effort in Vietnam is what little impact it has had on strategic thinking in the U.S. Army and Marine Corps. The United States was as unprepared in the 1980s as it was in the 1960s to fight a protracted counterinsurgency campaign. For the army, whose focus had been on the Central Front in Europe, Vietnam was but a large bump on the road to Europe. Many officers say that Vietnam remained unstudied because senior officers felt that in doctrinal terms the Asian experience was irrelevant to Europe.[40]

More recent scholarship also pointed to the U.S. military cultural tendency to divorce the military from the political: "In the United States, one of the basic assumptions of armed force organization at the national level is that war-fighting is an autonomous sphere." In other words, war is an activity that is to be prosecuted by soldiers without significant interference from politicians. "This is an attitude with deep roots in the organizational culture of the Army." Another article that examined the American Army and Vietnam, elucidates that the U.S. Army leaders were unambiguously cognizant of the organization's essence: "Its core competence was defeating conventional armies in frontal combat." The U.S. Army never arrived at a consensus that a change of approach was dictated by the nature of the conflict in Vietnam. "An unshakable belief in the essence of the organization precluded organizational learning and has continued to preclude consensus on the lessons of Vietnam and on required changes in the organization through the present day." Moreover, Cori Dauber argued that "President Bush's pronouncement at the end of the Gulf War that we had finally kicked the Vietnam syndrome was incorrect: the Weinberger Doctrine is its very apotheosis." To clarify, if the Weinberger Doctrine essentially proscribed any type of intervention outside the preferred paradigm of big war and if the U.S. political leadership demanded action outside of the Weinberger script, then the result can be a half-measured intervention that looks a lot like the interventions—Vietnam and Lebanon—that precipitated the Weinberger rules in the first place. In Dauber's own words: "Perhaps paradoxically, the demand to go in with everything or nothing, juxtaposed with a demand to 'do something,' ends up producing precisely the limited forms of military intervention the Weinberger Doctrine was designed to preclude."[41]

PREFERRED PARADIGM FOR WAR

War is death and destruction. The American way of war is particularly violent, deadly and dreadful. We believe in using "things"—artillery, bombs, massive firepower—in order to conserve our soldiers' lives. The enemy, on the other hand, made up for his lack of "things" by expending men instead of machines, and he suffered enormous casualties.[42]

The major risk of a big-war predilection is that the U.S. Army will retain the thinking, infrastructure, and forces appropriate for a large-scale war that may not materialize while failing to properly adapt itself to conduct simultaneous smaller engagements of the type that seem to be occurring with increasing frequency.[43]

The first quote is from the last Military Assistance Command (MACV) in Vietnam, General Fred Weyand, and the second quote is from a 1996 RAND study on American military culture. However, there also is a U.S. national cultural aversion to war that underlies the all-or-nothing approach: "total victory over the enemy in an ideological crusade to make the world safe for democracy, or abstention." The American paradigm for war as it emerged after the world wars focused around a strong strategic and tactical offensive, including full domestic mobilization and use of the full suite of military resources that America can leverage. According to one author, "an effective use of American military force must forge a bond with World War II and its transcendental heroic imagery." Furthermore, a 1996 RAND study identified five very salient U.S. Army cultural characteristics as impediments to planning and innovation. These characteristics were a preference for close-combat maneuver; the centrality of the division; a big-war predilection, a big-army mindset; and defense against all enemies, preferably foreign. In elaborating even further, this RAND study explained that the big-army mindset is a "relatively recent acquisition, since for much of its history the U.S. Army was both small and generally behind European armies technologically and doctrinally." However, before it even became a large army, it exuded a large-army mindset, borrowing technology and doctrine from Europe. It was this predilection that laid the foundation for the development of a big-army mentality during World War II and the Cold War. The U.S. Army became larger and technologically superior to most of its competitors during the Cold War. The army's training and development base expanded and developed advanced training paradigm techniques and doctrine, such as Air Land Battle, that exploited new technologies at least as effectively as any other army in the world. The Persian Gulf War, the RAND authors asserted, simply validated the big-army mindset. However, a culturally embedded big-army mindset, the RAND study concluded, "could represent very expensive impediments to the Army's post–Cold War adjustment."[44]

The RAND study explained that an army that prefers big wars "invests its resources to retain in-depth strength in modern, heavy forces rather than a diversity of one-of-a-kind specialized units." It also focuses its training orientation and doctrine on high-technology, high-intensity warfare against the most capable opponent in the world. World War I was the first opportunity for the U.S. Army to fight against and with the Industrial Age mass armies of Europe, and after that war, the army's focus centered on the equipment and doctrine for fighting a big, conventional war with infantry, armor, and artillery. "The big-war mindset was solidly defined starting with World War II." Although the end of World War II and the advent of the atomic age precipitated a rapid reduction in the size of the Army, the Korean War and, more important, a national strategy of graduated response after 1961 gave the Army a mission confronting the largest land forces in the world. As a result, training and preparation for the "big war" became the principal focus. Moreover, the RAND authors argued that Korea and Vietnam—the only small wars the U.S. Army engaged in during the Cold War—may have only strengthened the big-war preference. Many Army officers were even convinced that those failures stemmed from political constraints on military operations. Both wars thus encouraged the Uptonian biases of the U.S. Army—"what it ought to do was prepare for big wars in which it would have substantial public support and be given the operational freedom necessary to deliver victory."[45]

This RAND study on Army culture concluded that a continued cultural preference for big wars may undermine the Army's ability to develop capabilities for (1) countering insurgencies and terrorism as well as conducting peace operations; (2) suppressing domestic unrest and closing borders effectively; and (3) responding rapidly for small, self-sustaining force elements in crisis situations. Brian Jenkins, another RAND author, commenting on the army's concept of war in 1970, explained that the concept had not changed as a result of the U.S. experience in Vietnam: "War is regarded as a series of conventional battles between two armies in which one side will lose and, accepting this loss as decisive, will sue for peace . . . our Army remains enemy-oriented and casualty-oriented." Jenkins also cogently captured the difficulty that U.S. Army faced by trying to force fit its paradigm for war to Vietnam: "The Army's doctrine, its tactics, its organization, its weapons—its entire repertoire of warfare was designed for conventional war in Europe. In Vietnam, the Army simply performed its repertoire even though it was frequently irrelevant to the situation."[46]

An impediment to changing the approach in Vietnam was the attitude exhibited by many that the war in Vietnam was irrelevant to the *institution*. "Many in the military argue against making drastic organizational changes on the basis of experience in Vietnam, since the war there was regarded by many as an aberration." Higher-echelon positions tended to be dominated by officers with World War II experience whose concept of future war, the one the U.S. Army had to be prepared for, was a European-style general war. "The war in Vietnam is regarded as an exotic interlude between the wars that really count." Thus, transforming the entire organization to fight it was not desirable. With a certain degree of prescience, Jenkins also asserts: "Much more troubling than our apparent failure in Vietnam is our inability to learn and apply lessons from these failures."[47]

In an unprecedented analysis of U.S. covert operations in Vietnam, Richard Shultz affirmed that the American military's preference for conventional wars was a major impediment to developing any meaningful and strategically integrated special operations campaign against North Vietnam. Shultz explained that President Kennedy's demand that the military establish a special warfare capability was an "edict that challenged everything the mainstream military stood for." When Kennedy took office, he perceived incongruity between the changing nature of war and the American way of war. The problem was that if the military continued to embrace conventional war alone, it would be least ready for those conflicts that it was most likely to face. Because the essence of the U.S. armed forces had been significantly shaped by the conventional wars of the twentieth century, it was very resistant to a different model.[48] Shultz offers this succinct explanation of the U.S. armed forces' perspective on war: "They had been victorious in two world wars and successfully prosecuted a limited war in Korea. In each, conventional forces and strategy had been the answer. As a result, the American military developed a conventional mindset. Technological advances in mobility and firepower only reaffirmed this approach."[49]

There is ample research work that demonstrates the U.S. Army's preference for the big, conventional-war paradigm. In 1977, Russell Weigley surveyed the pages of *Military Review*, the U.S. Army's professional journal. For the entire year's (1976) worth of issues, he found almost no critical appraisal of low-intensity conflicts. In contrast, in 1976 there were a preponderance of articles that examined large-scale conventional wars and the World War II paradigm. Likewise, in 1981 and 1982, Weigley also discovered that professional military thought, as reflected in *Military Review* and other professional military journals, pointed to the same conclusion—a focus on World War II—style conflicts with very little critical analysis of Indochina and very little hint at the possibility of small wars in the future. A 1989 survey that examined the 1400 articles published by *Military Review* between 1975 and 1989, discovered only 43 articles dedicated to low-intensity conflicts.[50]

Furthermore, in the late 1970s, the commandant of the U.S. Army War College arranged for Colonel (Ret.) Harry G. Summers to be assigned there. The commandant assigned him to write a book on Vietnam that used the BDM Corporation study. Instead of using the BDM report, Summers used for his theoretical framework Clausewitz's *On War*. Consequently, the perspective Summers argued in his book, *On Strategy: A Critical Analysis of the Vietnam War*, arrived at conclusions that were absolutely obverse to the conclusions of BDM study. Summers concluded that the army failed in Vietnam because it did not focus enough on conventional warfare. In other words, the U.S. Army's problems in Vietnam stemmed from its deviation from the big-war approach and its temporary and very incomplete experiment with counterinsurgency. Not surprisingly, Summer's book was readily embraced by the army culture while the BDM report drifted into obscurity. *On Strategy* has been on the reading lists of the Command and General Staff College (CGSC) and the Army War College and on the official Army professional reading list. However, a 1990 survey of the CGSC class revealed that only six of three hundred ninety-two students in the class had read the BDM study.[51]

Moreover, just as the end of the Cold War was making a conventional war in Europe improbable, the Persian Gulf War occurred. The Gulf War was offered as validation of the American paradigm of war, in contrast to Vietnam. The literature about the Gulf War is replete with the notion that Desert Storm was fundamentally different from Vietnam and that it represented a complete validation of the process of applying lessons learned. According to Dauber, Vietnam became the central metaphor of American foreign policy. General Colin Powell's words to outgoing President Bush also bear testimony: "Mr. President, you have sent us in harm's way when you had to, but never lightly, never hesitantly, never with our hands tied, never without giving us what we needed to do the job." In another chapter, after reflecting on a conversation with General Norman Schwartzkopf, Powell writes, "Go in big and end it quickly." "We could not put the United States through another Vietnam." Powell regarded the Weinberger Doctrine as a set of useful guidelines, derived from the lessons of Vietnam. While serving as chairman of the JCS during the Gulf War, he saw his task as ensuring that victory would be inevitable by applying Weinberger's criteria.[52]

For those who viewed the American way of war as an innate and unalterable manifestation of our strategic culture and national will, Operation Desert Storm served as validation. After Desert Storm, General Powell published a National Military Strategy with a list of strategic principles that included "Decisive Force." Decisive Force is, essentially, an addendum to Weinberger's criteria. It is "the concept of applying decisive force to overwhelm our adversaries and thereby terminate conflicts swiftly with a minimum loss of life." Implicit in decisive force, however, is the notion that long conflicts will cause public dissatisfaction with the military, civilian micromanagement, and a critical media.[53]

> A historical pattern was beginning to work itself out: occasionally the American Army has had to wage a guerrilla war, but guerrilla warfare is so incongruous to the natural methods and habits of a well-to-do society that the American Army has tended to regard it as abnormal and to forget about it whenever possible. Each new experience with irregular warfare has required, then, that appropriate techniques be learned all over again.[54]

As a corollary to the American military's big-war preference, it is important to explain in a few pages how this characteristic had helped marginalize stability and counterinsurgency operations. According to one counterinsurgency expert, low-intensity conflict lies in the category of indirect strategy and thus differs greatly from the view of war and strategy that has dominated U.S. military thinking and experience during the nineteenth and twentieth centuries. The direct application of military force dominated U.S. military thinking during and after World War II and manifested itself in the services' inability to develop strategy and doctrine for the principal type of low-intensity conflict the United States had been involved in—insurgency. The United States has not been very successful in the operations other than war arena. Even though conflicts short of conventional war have become more widespread, the U.S. Army, until now, has had difficulty or had hesitated to develop doctrine for these missions. It has been argued that the U.S. Army never seriously attempted counterinsurgency in Vietnam, its lack of flexibility being summed up in the memorable remark attributed to one American general in Chapter 2: "I will be damned if I will permit the U.S. Army, its institutions, its doctrine, and its traditions to be destroyed just to win this lousy war."[55]

Unfortunately, as a result of the reorganization of the U.S. Army after Vietnam, its lesson learning was replaced by a realignment of responsibilities and functions and no lesson learning function carried over into the new Training and Doctrine Command (TRADOC). TRADOC, "despite having all the essential ingredients for centralized lesson learning within it, it did not inherit any mission for combat processing." Also, a doctrinal shift back toward big conventional operations

(Europe) diminished any residual influence the Vietnam experience-processing system might have exerted. Thus, the U.S. Army, by either default, design, or both, did not institutionalize the lessons from its most recent combat experience in Vietnam. Instead, the army looked to research and analysis, exercises and field tests, and the historical experiences of World War II to prepare it for what it saw as the next war—a high-intensity mechanized war in Europe. Propitiously, the Arab-Israeli War of 1973 served as surrogate laboratory of recent combat experience in the U.S. Army's preferred kind of war. TRADOC studied the lessons of this war very closely and incorporated those lessons into the U.S. Army's doctrine.[56]

Essentially, however, the lesson-learning system and lessons of Vietnam had not been simply forgotten: "The Army cast them aside with the revitalized NATO focus, buried them in the organizational reforms, and considered them unnecessary once the war ended." According to one historian, "The end of American combat in Vietnam by itself would have probably doomed the wartime lesson-learning system, but the Army's postwar organizational and doctrinal changes guaranteed its demise." The war became a concluded event and a matter of history. After January 1973, "Whoever sought lessons from the Vietnam War had to look backwards, historically, with the wisdom and burden of hindsight." The army so diluted the Vietnam experience from its current memory that a 1975 Command and General Staff College version of *Infantry in Battle* included sixty-two case studies from the three most recent U.S. wars: greater than fifty percent were about World War II, almost twenty-five percent were on Korea, and less than ten percent focused on Vietnam.[57]

However, the U.S. Army's first comprehensive examination of the Vietnam war criticized its doctrine and conduct of counterinsurgency in Vietnam. More important, the study reported that the army had ignored the lessons of Vietnam, had failed to study low-intensity conflict, and needed to correct its inability to conduct counterinsurgency. Published by the BDM Corporation in June 1980 for the Army War College, this study concluded that the U.S. Army still did not know how to conduct low-intensity conflict because the strategic lesson the United States learned from Vietnam was that intervention was to be avoided. The report also maintained that the U.S. military's traditional separation between military and political means significantly hindered the effective employment of military force in accomplishing objectives established by the political leadership. It criticized the American paradigm of war aimed at the destruction of enemy forces while ignoring other complex and relevant political factors. According to one expert on counterinsurgency, the BDM report was essentially an indictment of the U.S. Army's conventional and inappropriate approach to Vietnam. However, this study was shunted aside in favor of an assessment more congruous with the U.S. Army's preferred paradigm.[58]

Another study, completed by Kupperman and Associates, Inc., in 1983, examined a conceptual framework for the U.S. Army and low-intensity conflict. It also tried to determine whether the army's organization and doctrine were appropriate for emerging low-intensity missions. The Kupperman study identified a dilemma confronting the U.S. Army: extended high-intensity conventional conflict in Europe dominates the Army's thinking, resource allocation, and doctrine, but it is the conflict least likely to occur. "The low-intensity conflict environment is not one for which the Army is currently prepared." The executive summary of the report asserted that the U.S. Army needed new organization, doctrine, tactics, and equipment "to meet successfully the foreseen challenges at this low end of the violence spectrum." The study also stated that the army must overcome major external and internal barriers in restructuring to meet the focus of the future.[59]

The U.S. Army's response, to be sure a military cultural one, to its failures in Vietnam was not to institutionalize lessons learned there and create a better doctrinal approach to counterinsurgency. Instead, it eschewed such wars and the concomitant doctrine, focusing almost exclusively on the "big war" in Europe after Vietnam. Its institutional solution to the Vietnam imbroglio, therefore, was "we don't do Vietnams." This is all too evident in its responses to post-Vietnam studies trying to answer the question: what went wrong and how can we do these wars better? Downie did a very good job of recapitulating the U.S. Army's response to a host of official and unofficial postmortem analyses. Army Chief of Staff General Creighton Abrams, the first post-Vietnam Chief, directed the Astarita group to conduct a strategic assessment to determine if a conventional strategy was appropriate to the post-Vietnam security environment. Their Astarita Report shifted the U.S. Army's institutional attention away from the frustrations of Vietnam and focused the army on readiness and deterrence issues in Europe. "The Army focused on what it could do well—conventional warfare—as opposed to something the Vietnam War proved that the Army could not do well—counterinsurgency."[60]

In short, Krepinevich and the low-intensity conflict supporters argued that the U.S. Army failed in Vietnam because it fought the war too conventionally, according to its preferred paradigm for war and not according to the principles and tenets of counterinsurgency. They would also agree with the notion that low-intensity conflicts are far more likely to recur and involve U.S. interests than are big wars. According to Krepinevich, "The Army's conduct of the war was a failure, primarily because it never realized that insurgency warfare required basic changes in Army methods to meet the exigencies of the new conflict environment." In attempting to overlay operational methods that were successful in previous wars, the army focused on the attrition of enemy forces instead of denying the enemy access to the population. By focusing on perceived civilian failures and contriving criteria like the Weinberger Doctrine, instead of taking a harder look at its own failures, Krepinevich argues, that the army perpetuated the fiction that its way of war (Concept) remained valid across the spectrum of conflict. On the other hand, low-intensity conflict supporters learned these lessons: overwhelming force does not always work; military operations cannot be divorced from politics; using military force in pursuit of less than vital national interests is feasible; and gaining and maintaining the support of the indigenous population are central to success.[61]

The Kupperman Study of 1983 asserted that low-intensity conflict would be the normal form of conflict in the 1990s. However, the report went on, the U.S. Army was not prepared to conduct low-intensity conflicts and the army would need to develop doctrine and a force structure that would allow it to win in this environment. The Kupperman Study concluded that the Army was least prepared to fight the most likely form of conflict—low-intensity conflict—and best prepared for the least likely form of conflict—conventional war in Europe. In addition, in 1985 the Joint Low Intensity Conflict (JLIC) final report listed four prevalent themes: "As a nation we do not understand low intensity conflict; we respond without unity of effort; we execute our activities poorly; and we lack the ability to sustain operations." It also highlighted two common trends: although low-intensity conflict is the most likely threat, the United States had no coherent strategy for dealing with it; and the U.S. military continually applied conventional solutions to unconventional challenges. The report asserted that the tendency to think and apply the same prescriptions for deterring and fighting conventional wars to the various forms of low-intensity conflicts was the greatest obstacle to developing a low-intensity conflict capability. In other words, an overreliance on the traditional structures and approaches to conventional war impeded the development of low-intensity conflict policy and doctrine.[62]

Of particular salience for this book, however, according to David R. Segal and Dana Eyre, after the Vietnam War, "Peacekeeping became incorporated at the fringes of doctrinal thinking through its inclusion as part of low intensity conflict." Subsuming peacekeeping within low-intensity conflicts had two deleterious results. First, it marginalized peacekeeping along with the theretofore marginalized low-intensity conflict. Second, it defined peacekeeping as a type of conflict rather than conflict resolution or conflict management. This created a skewed perception of peacekeeping and caused the army as an institution to ignore the necessary analysis and confrontation with critical issues, including the role of force in peace operations and the challenges involved in maintaining the linkage between political, diplomatic, and military activities in peace operations. The reasons why low-intensity conflicts, Operations Other than War (OOTW), and, later, Stability Operations, were so marginalized by the American military were summed up best by Dan Bolger: "Americans define war as being waged against a uniformed, disciplined opposing state's armed forces, the sort who will fight fairly, the way the Americans do." Moreover, from 1945 onward, the American military has brutally and successfully annihilated any foe stupid enough to fight it on its terms: force-on-force and tank for tank. For many in the military, TWWRND ("things we would rather not do") would be a more accurate moniker for OOTW. "Desert Storm, a magnificent accomplishment, was a thing we would rather do: war by the American definition." However, the challenges in Iraq and the fact that the U.S. military and its allies are conducting multiple counterinsurgencies began to change all that in 2004–2005. A February 2005 Draft DOD Directive, signed by Ryan

Henry, for coordination, declared stability operations "a core U.S. military mission" and that "stability operations shall be given priority and attention comparable to combat operations."[63]

AN EMPHASIS ON MAXIMUM AND DECISIVE FORCE IN CONVENTIONAL WAR

After Desert Storm, General Colin Powell published a National Military Strategy that included a list of strategic principles that included "Decisive Force," also known as the Powell Corollary to the Weinberger Doctrine. Decisive force is "the concept of applying decisive force to overwhelm our adversaries and thereby terminate conflicts swiftly with a minimum loss of life." Implicit in decisive force, however, is the notion that long conflicts will cause public dissatisfaction with the military, civilian micromanagement, and a critical media. Certainly shaped by his Vietnam experience, Powell declared, "Once a decision for military actions has been made, half-measures and confused objectives extract a severe price in the form of a protracted conflict which can cause needless waste of human lives and material resources, a divided nation at home, and defeat."[64]

In examining trends in our national military strategy, Samuel Huntington explained the reaction to America's experience in Vietnam as "the belief that if we are going to use conventional force in limited engagements abroad, we had better use it in circumstances where we can win quickly and avoid a slow bleed." Huntington also asserts that the U.S. experience in Vietnam has led the military to become the principal and most vociferous opponent to the employment of military force at all. However, the American preference for maximum and decisive force predates Vietnam by a century. According to Russell Weigley, "The Civil War molded the American Army's conceptions of the nature of full-scale war that would profoundly affect its conduct of the Second World War." The conception that the U.S. Army inherited from the Civil War, applied to World War II, and embraced for most of the Cold War was that "overwhelming American power would assure the annihilation of the enemy's strength." The army entered the Vietnam imbroglio with the same maximalist predilection for the use of force and, to be sure, this was incongruent with the nature of counterinsurgency and the winning of hearts and minds.[65]

Krepinevich's analysis arrived at a similar observation—the "Army Concept" comprises two characteristics: a focus on conventional warfare and the reliance on "high volumes of firepower to minimize casualties." However, the U.S. Army's traditional approach to the use of force does not suit it well for low-intensity conflicts, where the emphasis is on minimizing firepower and light infantry formations instead of the massive use of firepower and armored divisions. Weigley asserts that the history of U.S. strategy testifies to an American conception of war that best characterizes American strategists as "strategists of annihilation." In the beginning when America had limited resources, there were some strategists of attrition, but America's wealth and its adoption of unlimited aims in war abrogated that development, "until the strategy of annihilation became characteristic of the American way of war."[66]

Of the post-Vietnam U.S. Army doctrine for counterinsurgency (COIN)/low-intensity conflicts, counterinsurgency expert Thomas Mockaitis observed, "concerning the use of force in COIN: U.S. military doctrine is a curious blend of the British minimum force principle with the American maximalist approach to problem-solving." He paraphrases an excerpt from the 1990 U.S. Army manual for low-intensity conflicts (*FM100-20*): "In COIN, the government should stress the minimum use of violence to maintain order. At times, the best way to minimize violence is to use overwhelming force." However, Mockaitis asserted, "in no case has the application of overwhelming force produced victory in COIN." Mockaitis summed up the U.S. military-strategic cultural problem with the use of force in low-intensity conflicts: "Neither the American political system nor American attitudes are well suited to protracted war. A culture that places great faith in the efficacy of military power to resolve any conflict will have difficulty applying minimum force."[67]

A CULTURAL AND ORGANIZATIONAL AVERSION TO COUNTERINSURGENCY

Until 2004, when the army's new modularity force transformation began, the division was the defining organization of the U.S. Army. It was created on a permanent basis in 1914 subsequent to Army Chief of Staff Leonard Wood's experiment with a maneuver division in San Antonio in 1911. The Stimson Plan, named after Secretary of War Henry Stimson, was the catalyst for the establishment of the three-brigade division in the U.S. Army. Stimson first proposed his plan for four maneuver divisions in 1913 to all the general officers who were stationed within the continental United States. "Some of the older ones still had hesitated before so drastic a departure from what they knew." The 1910 *Field Services Regulations* were revised to reflect the new organization: it defined the division as "a self-contained unit made up of all necessary arms and services, and complete in itself with every requirement for independent action incident to its operations." Robert Doughty's study traces the tactical doctrine of the U.S. Army from 1946 until 1976; it also traces the evolution of the U.S. Army division. And, although strategic requirements, doctrine, and tactics underwent various changes, eliminating the division for the sake of greater dispersion during the "pentomic era," or to more realistically meet the terrain and enemy situations in Vietnam, was almost inconceivable.[68]

Doughty examined the evolution of the army division over thirty years: from the World War II division through the Korean War; the pentomic division for the nuclear battlefield; the ROAD division through the ostensible "counterinsurgency era;" the short-lived TRICAP division (triple capability); back to the conventional division during the post-Vietnam era; and the Army of Excellence (AOE) of the 1980s. As a counterpoint, as early as 1945 Major General Jim Gavin concluded that a nuclear battlefield required widely dispersed and relatively autonomous "battle groups, each one capable of sustained combat on its own." Even though it could be argued that abandoning the division for regiment-sized battle groups would have been a better option, five battle groups came to comprise a redesigned division. Moreover, after World War I, in the interwar period, any reorganization of the division was controversial. John Wilson observes, "Once that organizational structure [the division] became embedded in both the Regular Army and the reserve components, it became exceedingly difficult to alter it in any way."[69]

By the 1980s, the AOE concept introduced the "light infantry division" (LID), even though the Kupperman study had asserted that the army's organizational [divisional] structure would not permit it to win in a low-intensity conflict environment. The study had proposed the creation of regionally oriented light infantry brigades to be trained and equipped under a pilot LID training headquarters. In fact, the LID was being designed to augment heavy forces even though it was originally conceived as a low-intensity conflict organization. One author writing in the mid-1980s argued that the light infantry brigade concept clashed with the U.S. Army's large-unit, division and above emphasis. As a footnote to the centrality of the division, Doughty observed that from 1946 to 1976, the doctrine for the armor and artillery branched seemed almost static. "For most of the period under study, both performed in essentially the same fashion they had in World War II."[70]

"The combat division is the centerpiece of Army war-fighting doctrine and the focus of its operational plans." The RAND study, *Army Culture and Planning in a Time of Great Change*, identified "the centrality of the division" as a distinctive characteristic of U.S. Army culture. This study asserts that the division has long been viewed as the "most prestigious Army assignment and the most sought-after organization in which to command troops." U.S. Army divisions comprise the greater part of its combat power; and to some degree, the army assesses its state of preparedness by the number of divisions it maintains, especially regular army divisions. "As an artifact of the industrial age, the division has remained continually in existence since before World War I." Although the army has periodically redesigned the organization of the division, the division as a concept and an organizing principle remains unaltered. Another author who has argued that the division may no longer be relevant makes this conclusion of the army's post–Cold War "transformation": "Recognizing that the development of American military tactics, doctrine, and war fighting organizations for future conflict has been rendered more difficult because the character of the threat is no longer specified, it is not surprising that the Army's Force XXI program has not resulted in any significant change in the war-fighting structure of Army forces since the Persian Gulf War."[71]

Up until recently, the division was still the dominant U.S. Army organization that trained and fought as a team—the division combined arms team was the centerpiece of the U.S. Army's war-fighting structure and doctrine. Even the creation of Force XXI, a truly innovative and forward-looking concept to fundamentally redesign the army for information-age warfare, implicitly retained the idea of the division as a basic building block. "The very fact that Force XXI testing revolves around brigade, division, and corps operations suggests that test results will explicitly confirm the division's importance." In fact, somewhat ironically, the cultural resistance to move away from the division to a regiment-sized combined battle group or brigade combat team-centric force at the end of the twentieth century was as strong as the army's resistance to transition from regimental operations to divisional operations at the beginning of this century. Macgregor explained how the cultural resistance to eliminating the division can be an obstacle to genuine transformation: "Trained and organized for a style of war that has changed very little since World War II, current Army organizational structures will limit the control and exploitation of superior military technology and human potential in future operations." It was not until 2004, thirteen years after the end of the Cold War and three years into the Global War on Terror, that the Army began to move toward a brigade combat team-centric modular force structure in earnest.[72]

CONCLUSION

> A conventional military force, no matter how bent, twisted, malformed or otherwise 'reorganized' is still one hell of a poor instrument with which to engage insurgents.[73]

The American dilemma of trying to be prepared simultaneously to counter insurgents and wage large-scale conventional war is as follows: "For one kind of task, rapid and agile movement in reaching the scene and in campaigning after arrival was at a premium; the other kind of war demanded heavier formations with a capacity for sustained fighting under severe casualties." However, the U.S. military did not begin to resolve this dilemma conspicuously well until 2003 because an emphasis on European war in doctrine and planning that was redoubled after the Vietnam conflict tended to create an army without appropriate agility for unconventional wars, from operations Eagle Claw to Restore Hope. This examination of American military culture in the twentieth century and earlier arrives at several generalizations. First, although insular geography also afforded the Americans a degree of cheap security, history and geography shaped American military culture much differently than it did the British. Vast land space, hostile indigenous tribes, and a cataclysmic civil war embedded a direct and absolute approach to war. A salient component of this approach was a perceived or real struggle for survival on the new continent dating back to King Philip's War. In addition, as a consequence of the Civil War and of an adulation of first the French and then the Prussian model of war, the U.S. Army became focused on conventional war (alone) and massive firepower. Moreover, Sherman, Upton, and their disciples, as advocates of the conventional Prussian model, fused it with their total-war-of-annihilation approach in the Civil War and imbued it in the profession through institutions and journals. As a result, anything outside of the core paradigm, such as counterinsurgency and peace operations, came to be viewed as aberrant and ephemeral.[74]

In addition, American political culture, vast resources, and values combined to create the view that war is bad and should be waged only as a crusade to achieve victory swiftly and justly. As a result, the notion of war as a last resort but with maximum force evolved. The U.S. Army for most of the twentieth century embraced the combat division as the preferred combat formation; for obvious reasons, the combat division *was* the most appropriate formation for the U.S. Army's favorite kind of war. Also germane, and topical in the context of stability operations, is a U.S. military cultural overreliance on the "silver bullet," or technology. Finally, the aforementioned factors, coupled with the way and context in which the U.S. Army professionalized at the end of the nineteenth century, led to what I have called the "Uptonian Paradox." The contradiction is this: the U.S. military ostensibly worshiped Clausewitz as the principal philosopher/oracle of war on the one hand, but on the other hand it exhibited a Jominian predilection to divorce the political from the military when the shooting starts. U.S. military culture also, while in no way usurping civilian control of the military ultimately, exhibited a proclivity to influence its political masters' views in order to make those views on war congruent with its preferred paradigm for war. Moreover, Vietnam, Harry Summers' book, the Weinberger Doctrine, and Goldwater-Nichols all helped perpetuate and exacerbate this tendency of the military to prescribe to the civilian elite "what kind of wars we do and don't do."

Success in Counterinsurgency

A highly mobile enemy skilled in guerrilla tactics demanded either a highly mobile counter-guerrilla force or a heavy defensive army large enough to erect an impenetrable shield around every settlement and travel route in the West.[1]

Fools say they learn from experience; I prefer to learn from the experience of others.[2]

AMERICAN FORCES, British forces, and to a more circumscribed extent, French forces, along with other coalition partners, are currently prosecuting counter-insurgencies in Afghanistan, Iraq, and elsewhere against internationally networked insurgents who employ terrorist and guerrilla tactics. It is useful to revisit the historical lessons of employing indigenous forces in other counterinsurgencies because leveraging partners and local forces to fight a protracted conflict is a *sine qua non* for ultimate success. It is also imperative to maximize the use of indigenous forces to prosecute counterinsurgency because, when done effectively, it can provide a significant increase in the quantity of troops on the ground, troops whose knowledge of the terrain, culture, and language generally produce an even greater and exponential improvement in actionable intelligence on the insurgents and their infrastructure. Although any operational design for a counterinsurgency campaign must integrate the political, societal, military, economic, legal, informational, and intelligence spheres to fully pacify the population and to establish the legitimacy of the host government, a comprehensive analysis of all these factors is beyond the scope of this chapter-length survey, for the sake of parsimony and clarity. Even still, the realities of the political and strategic context in the foreseeable future, as codified in the corpus of cascading U.S. national and military security charters, also emphasize the imperative to create a credible capacity among our partners and indigenous allies in order to more effectively counter insurgents and terrorists wherever they operate or seek sanctuary.[3]

In the first instance, the September 2002 *National Security Strategy* of the United States directs the U.S. defense establishment to work with other states to defuse regional conflicts. Second, the February 2003 *National Strategy for Combating Terrorism* charges the American national security apparatus to deny further sponsorship, support, and sanctuary to terrorists by ensuring that other states accept their responsibilities in taking action against international threats within their sovereign borders. Third, the March 2005 *National Military Strategic Plan for the War on Terrorism* tasks the American military both to enable partner nations to counter terrorism and to contribute to the establishment of conditions that counter international ideological support for terrorism. Last, in the fall of 2004, the U.S. Army also published a long overdue field manual (interim) that exclusively addresses the doctrine for counterinsurgency. Though this manual is far from perfect due to its relatively rapid production and because of the general dearth of supple thought about counterinsurgency within the U.S. military during the post–Vietnam and post–Cold War eras, it is a start in the right direction. *Field Manual Interim (FMI) 3-07.22* underscores the need to expand and employ capable native forces that must be visibly involved in prosecuting the counterinsurgency to the fullest measure possible. Moreover, this same manual elucidates how the use of indigenous forces can have an impact on all three levels of war: tactically, indigenous forces "eliminate insurgent leadership, cadre, and combatants, through death and capture by co-opting individual members, or by forcing insurgents to leave the area;" operationally such forces help restore government control and legitimacy; and strategically, they "serve as the shield for carrying out reform." Most saliently, this current doctrine prescribes that indigenous security forces operate in concert with American forces wherever practical and assume the major burden in military, paramilitary, and police functions, when capable of doing so. Thus, in their totality, the above prescriptions would seem to provide the rationale for learning how to raise and use local forces effectively.[4]

The introduction to the previous chapter argued that despite the general American military cultural aversion toward small wars and counterinsurgency, the U.S. military has in fact had a host of experiences in counterguerrilla warfare, including some qualified successes with certain aspects of the Vietnam war. Chapter 5 also showed how America's unsuccessful war in the jungles of Vietnam was perceived as a fleeting and unpleasant aberration to the mainstream American military and how lessons learned there about fighting guerrillas were not preserved in the U.S. Army's institutional memory. Even though many lessons exist in the U.S. military's historical experience with small wars, the lessons from Vietnam are the most voluminous. Yet, even as the U.S. military embarked on Operations Enduring Freedom and Iraqi Freedom subsequent to the 11 September 2001 attacks in the United States, these lessons were most likely read little and by few within the U.S. Army. Likewise, the British military and the French Army have

had a host of successful and partially successful experiences with the employment of indigenous forces in the conduct of counterinsurgency. Although the
British military has generally not been as punctilious and consistent in producing myriad doctrinal manuals for fighting every aspect of conventional war, it has
done a better job of codifying its small-war experiences and first principles in
print.[5]

This chapter will cull and synthesize some of the more relevant military
lessons from the American, British, and French military's experiences with the
employment of indigenous forces in counterinsurgencies during the twentieth
century and before. Another goal of this analysis is to show how the prudent
tactical use of indigenous forces can also favorably shape the overall counterinsurgency campaign in the intelligence, societal, and political domains, at both
the operational and strategic levels of war. When generalizing about previous
counter-guerrilla wars it is also important to recognize that in each instance there
were unique ideological, social, political, and geographical factors. Even after
acknowledging this, however, there are still many potentially valuable lessons
to be distilled from those experiences and to be applied to current and future
counterinsurgencies. For example, this framework of analysis will lead to a better
understanding of how to meet the imperatives prescribed in the aforementioned
national security and military doctrines. To distill those prescriptions further,
this chapter will illumine different perspectives on how to work with our state
and non-state partners to counter terrorism and to employ and increase the
number of capable indigenous forces, which must be discernibly active in prosecuting the counterinsurgency, to eliminate insurgents and insurgent infrastructure, to help restore government legitimacy, and to assume the preponderant
burden in military, paramilitary, and police functions. This chapter concludes
with some ideas for organizing and integrating both regular and irregular indigenous forces within both conventional and unconventional American forces
and agencies.

The cases in this chapter vary from the American westward expansion and the
consolidation of its frontiers, to those in which colonial powers strove to pacify
and retain control over colonies acquired by force or treaty, to one in which the
American military aimed to assist the South Vietnamese in preventing a Communist takeover by conventional and guerrilla military means. Prima facie, the
informed reader might wonder if and how it might be conceivable to generalize
useful patterns or principles from these variegated examples. How, for example,
might the cases in this chapter be germane to the ongoing counterinsurgencies in
Afghanistan, Iraq, or elsewhere, where the goals are not to colonize but to democratize? For one thing, even though the U.S. polity may perceive its effort to
democratize Iraq as magnanimous and benign, to be sure, there are Iraqis—Sunnis
and other—that perceive the American invasion and occupation of Iraq no differently than Algerian insurgents may have perceived the French occupation of
Algeria. Given this reality, the effective employment of indigenous forces equally
aids: a benign power trying to guarantee security and implant democracy (U.S. in

Iraq); an embattled and democratically elected government (Rhodesia); or a colonial power attempting to support its own client regime (France in Vietnam) in the face of popular opposition, in that all the governments in question had the similar objectives to maintain some sense of legitimacy and to pacify the populations under their control. All insurgents aim to undermine this legitimacy by demonstrating that the government or regime does not have the capacity to secure the population through the credible use of coercive force, nor the desire to initiate reforms that may assuage the populace's grievances. The recruitment and integration of indigenous forces into regular and irregular roles bring exponential increases in usable intelligence and can contribute to the legitimacy of the campaign, when those forces are disciplined and well trained. Their employment is a necessary component of any sound counterinsurgency strategy.

THE AMERICAN EXPERIENCE

For most of the twentieth century, U.S. military culture has (notwithstanding the Marines' work in small wars) generally embraced the big, conventional-war paradigm and fundamentally eschewed small wars and insurgencies. Thus, instead of learning from our experiences in Vietnam, the Philippines, the Marine Corps' experience in the Banana Wars, and the Indian campaigns, the U.S Army for most of the past one hundred fifty years has viewed these experiences as ephemeral anomalies and aberrations—distractions from preparing to win big wars against other big powers. As a result of marginalizing the counterinsurgencies and small wars that it has spent most of its existence prosecuting, the U.S. military's big-war cultural preferences have impeded it from fully benefiting—studying, distilling, and incorporating into doctrine—from our somewhat extensive lessons in small wars and insurgencies. This section begins starts by briefly examining some of the salient lessons for counterinsurgency from the Indian wars and lists some of the sources for lessons from that war that have been likely forgotten. The remainder of this section examines the American military's historical employment of indigenous forces.

Before Vietnam, both the U.S. Army and the U.S. Marine Corps had much experience fighting guerrilla-style opponents. The army seemed to learn anew for every counterinsurgency, while the Marines codified their corpus of experience in the 1940 *Small Wars Manual*. In fact, the Marines' lessons from leading Nicaraguan Guardia Nacional indigenous patrols in counterguerrilla operations against Sandino's guerrillas served as the basis from which to design their Combined Action Program (CAP) in Vietnam. Nonetheless, there are a host of good works and lessons from the Indian wars, from the Philippine Insurrection, and from the Banana Wars. This section encapsulates some of the common lessons from these wars before it examines some of the salient lessons and methods of employing indigenous forces in Vietnam. The Hukbulahap Rebellion in the Philippines during the post–World War II period is excluded because the U.S. role there was essentially limited to providing money and to the savvy advice of Edward Lansdale.

The Indian Wars and the Apache Scouts

More removed in time and context than the other cases in this chapter, the Indian wars of the nineteenth century nonetheless provide some potential lessons for integrating indigenous forces in contemporary counterinsurgencies. These lessons also demonstrate that the overarching fundamentals for fighting small wars are indeed timeless. With little preserved institutional memory and less codified doctrine for counterinsurgency, the nineteenth century U.S. Army had to adapt on the fly to fight against "a highly mobile enemy skilled in guerrilla tactics" that required either a "highly mobile counter-guerrilla force or a heavy defensive army large enough to erect an impenetrable shield around every settlement and travel route in the West." However, even though the nineteenth century Army may have preferred to focus on the Mexican War or the Civil War as the apotheoses of war, the reality was that for all except a dozen years the Army's principal employment had been set by the requirements of westward expansion and the protection of the frontier population. In fact, hostile Indians were the genesis for the creation of a regular Army in the first place, given the distaste of the Republic's architects for standing armies. The Indian enemies the Army would meet before and after the Civil War differed from the ones it encountered east of the Mississippi before the Mexican War. The Indians of the deserts, plains, and mountains, had learned how to employ the hostile features of their unique environments to military advantage. The horse warriors of the west exhibited the qualities of aggressiveness, physical strength, endurance, courage, mental alertness, stealth, cunning, and knowledge of the terrain. One of the most serious challenges was the western tribes' reluctance to stand and fight, coupled with their exceptional skill at guerrilla tactics.[6]

There was a loose body of principles that emerged from the Indian wars: to ensure the close civil-military coordination of the pacification effort, to provide firm but fair and paternalistic governance, and to reform the economic and educational spheres. Good treatment of prisoners, attention to the Indians' grievances, and the avoidance of killing women and children (learned by trial and error) were also regarded as fundamental to any long-term solution. One of the few manuals published during the era on how to operate on the Plains, *The Prairie Traveler*, is "perhaps the single most important work on the conduct of frontier expeditions published under the aegis of the War Department." In essence, Captain Randolph Marcy's *The Prairie Traveler* was a "how-to" manual for packing, traveling, tracking, and bivouacking on the Plains. More importantly, though, it was also a primer on fighting the Indians. In formulating principles for pacification, Marcy examined his own experiences on the frontier, as well as the French and Turkish experiences conducting pacification operations in North Africa, to arrive at three lessons: over dispersion strips the counterinsurgent force of initiative, increases its vulnerability, and saps its morale; mobility is an imperative (mounting infantry on mules was one way of increasing mobility during that era); and the best way to counter an elusive guerrilla was to employ mobile mounted forces at night to surprise the enemy at dawn. However, *The Prairie Traveler*, in urging soldiers to be adaptive by coupling conventional discipline with the self-reliance, individuality, and rapid mobility of the insurgent, conveys one central message that is still salient and germane today. Because Army leaders viewed fighting Indians as a "fleeting bother," however, the Army never established a formal doctrine for Indian warfare. The absence of a codified doctrine for this type of warfare did not necessarily mean that the Army did not have any officers who were capable of innovative and unconventional thought. For example, General George Crook developed the tactic of inserting small teams from friendly Apache tribes into the sanctuaries of insurgent Apaches to neutralize them, to psychologically unhinge them, and to sap their will.[7]

In George Crook, the U.S. Army found the quintessential counterguerrilla leader because he was resilient, adaptive, and fully knowledgeable about the enemy. As the result of his experience before the Civil War, Crook already knew much about the Indians and he learned much more. He studied them so fervently that one of his aides observed that Crook knew the Indian better than the Indian knew himself. In war, he was ruthless and resolute and in peace, he was considerate and humane. His insisted on fair treatment of the Indians and he never made a promise that he could not honor. Moreover, he consistently got on the trail and he stayed on it until he found and cornered his enemy, despite all obstacles and hardships. His most germane and innovative techniques, methods that were to become his trademark, were his extensive employment of Indians as irregular counterguerrillas to fight Indians and his reliance on pack mules for greatly increased mobility. Crook fully understood the advantages of using friendly Indians as auxiliaries to counter other, unruly Indians. He was not the only advocate of this but his approach was significantly different because instead of allying one tribe against the other, he enlisted fighters from the very tribes against which he was conducting operations. There were three particular merits that derived from this method: it matched the enemy's special skills in irregular warfare; it greatly increased friendly knowledge of the terrain and enemy; and it psychologically unhinged the enemy. As Crook reported himself, "it is not merely a question of catching them with better Indians, but of a broader and more enduring aim—their disintegration."[8]

Crook used scouts as both guides and auxiliaries, normally employing them in some combination with his regular troops, but also using the Indians on independent missions. He used Indian scouts and policemen to apprehend criminals, thus integrating them further into his system of control. He also espoused a divide-and-subjugate strategy in his employment of Indian collaborators to infiltrate hostile tribes with the aim of persuading a portion of the Indians to surrender. Even more ruthlessly, he developed the tactic of inserting small teams from friendly Apache tribes into the sanctuaries of insurgent Apaches to neutralize, psychologically unhinge, and exhaust their will to resist. Part of Crook's success was also attributable to his approach to leadership. He selectively recruited young, aggressive, and adaptive officers who were not so much Indian fighters as they were Indian thinkers. Also, because of the individualistic and personal character of the Indian warrior culture, he demanded that his officers cultivate a personal bond with the Indian scouts. The U.S. military would continue to employ a similarly effective technique essentially in one form or another in the Philippines, in Nicaragua, and in Vietnam. Crook's knowledge and methods of employing irregulars offer lessons for subsequent counterinsurgents in the last century and in this one.[9]

The Philippine Insurrection: The U.S. Army and the Macabebes

During the Philippine insurgency, the American military won a relatively bloodless but unambiguous victory in three and a half years in a way that established the basis for a future friendship between Americans and Filipinos. Anthony James Joes, a scholar on America and guerrilla warfare, succinctly explains why:

> There were no screaming jets accidentally bombing helpless villages, no B-52s, no napalm, no artillery barrages, no collateral damage. Instead, the Americans conducted a decentralized war of small mobile units armed mainly with rifles and aided by native Filipinos, hunting guerrillas who were increasingly isolated both by the indifference or hostility of much of the population and by the concentration of scattered peasant groups into larger settlements.[10]

The Philippine Insurrection lasted from 1899 to 1902 and the U.S. military learned to maximize the employment of indigenous scouts and paramilitary forces to increase and sustain decentralized patrolling. Since the American forces were seriously undermanned, at first they relied on indigenous Filipino help for logistics, then as police and scouts, and ultimately as armed units. The U.S. military was able to enlist auxiliaries during the Philippine insurgency in various ways. The Philippine scouts originated from irregular fighters raised from the Macabebes for employment against the guerrillas in the swamps of central Luzon. In particular, the Army enrolled the Macabebes because the tribe had harbored a long-standing animosity for the Tagalogs, who comprised the majority of the insurgents. On Samar, moreover, the Americans organized a scout force with volunteers from hemp merchant families who opposed the guerrillas because they were losing political and economic power as a result of insurgent actions. In western Mindinao, local Muslim leaders performed so well in suppressing the Catholic guerrillas that the Americans confronted very little resistance there. A combination of religious zeal and self-preservation impelled the sectarian members of the *Guardia de Honor* to join the U.S. cause against the anti-clerical insurgents in La Union province. Lastly, in some instances the town police forces also proved themselves effective in countering guerrillas. In emphasizing the imperative to employ indigenous forces in a counter-insurgent role, one expert on the Philippine Insurrection observed, "We need more Macabebes, and we have to be willing to accept the fact that their behavior will sometimes be motivated by revenge, tribal vendettas, or just bad character."[11]

Max Boot, in his study of America's role in small wars, ascribes American success in the Philippines to its aggressive use of saturation patrolling to locate and subdue the insurgents. Armed principally with rifles, the Americans were only able to successfully prosecute this war of small, dispersed, and very mobile formations with the assistance of indigenous scouts. Combined American forces comprising American soldiers and Filipino scouts hunted insurgents who were "increasingly isolated both by the indifference or hostility of much of the population and by the concentration of scattered peasant groups into larger settlements." One bold and brilliant example of employing the Macabebe scouts effectively to capture guerrilla leaders was Brigadier General Fred Funston's raid and capture of the rebel leader Aguinaldo. Acting on intercepted dispatches, Funston learned of an Aguinaldo request for 400 guerrilla reinforcements at his jungle headquarters and Funston quickly devised a raid on the headquarters based on a ruse that had Macabebe scouts posing as insurgent reinforcements but with five American officers as prisoners (Funston among them). Totaling 89 men, the raiding force comprised a Spanish intelligence officer on the American payroll, four renegade rebels, five U.S. officers, and 79 Macabebe scouts, posing in captured insurgent uniforms. After the force infiltrated through 100 miles of dense jungle, the ruse was so convincing that Aguinaldo's honor guard welcomed the party, right before the Macabebe scouts surrounded Aguinaldo and the Spanish intelligence officer announced that they were Americans.[12]

The U.S. Army prosecuted the Philippine counterinsurgency with some techniques that were similar to the ones it had employed against its irregular opponents during the Indian wars. In fact, 26 of the 30 U.S. generals who served in the Philippines during the insurrection between 1898 and 1902 had also served in the Indian wars. The need for mobility and knowledge about the terrain and enemy led the Army to establish special detachments of mounted scouts and infantry. These detachments were handpicked elite units that performed the preponderance of reconnaissance and strike operations in the counter-guerrilla war. Veterans of the Indian wars appreciated the value of indigenous soldiers who brought the threefold advantage in their knowledge of the people, the terrain, and the language. They also comprehended, as Crook and others did before them that the employment of local forces as auxiliaries or scouts would also contribute to a "divide-and-subjugate" operational campaign. Filipino insurgents also suffered from the deleterious psychological blow of learning that their own people were helping hunt them down. Recruiting Macabebes and similarly distinct indigenous groups accrued the additional value of undermining the unity of the population by exploiting the extant seams in Filipino society. Moreover, the more knowledgeable officers also realized early on that it would be imperative to eliminate or defeat the guerrillas' infrastructure and toward the end of the war, the Army increasingly began to employ Philippine scouts, spies, and informants to gather intelligence on and target the insurgent infrastructure. At the end of the war, the U.S. commanded over fifteen thousand indigenous auxiliary forces, organized into the Philippine scouts, the Philippine Constabulary (paramilitaries), and local police forces. By most accounts, the American Army was successful there because it recognized the twofold imperative to protect the population and to conduct an aggressive counter-guerrilla campaign by leveraging indigenous forces for reconnaissance and intelligence operations.[13]

Nicaragua: The U.S. Marines and the Miskito Indians

The U.S. Marine Corps had much experience fighting guerrilla-style opponents, and they distilled their body of principles and techniques from their small war of experience in the 1940 *Small Wars Manual*. From the Marines' experience in Haiti, the Dominican Republic, and Nicaragua during the first part of the twentieth century, they learned that, unlike conventional war, small war presents no defined or linear battle area and theater of operations. While delay in the use of force may be interpreted as weakness, the manual maintains, the brutal use of force is not appropriate either. "In small wars, tolerance, sympathy, and kindness should be the keynote to our relationship with the mass of the population." Moreover, the *Small Wars Manual of 1940* stressed the importance of focusing on the social, economic, and political development of the people more than simple material destruction. An overarching principle, though, is not to fight small wars with big-war methods—the goal is to gain results with the least application of force and minimum loss of civilian (noncombatant) life. The 1940 *Small Wars Manual* is still the best sources for distilling the Marines' lessons from the Banana Wars and beyond. While the logistical and physical aspects of the 1940 manual have become obsolete, the portions that address the fundamentals and principles of small wars are still quite relevant.[14]

The Marines' lessons from leading Nicaraguan *Guardia Nacional* indigenous patrols in the in actions against Sandino and his guerrilla bands certainly influenced the institutional foundation for their subsequent CAP in Vietnam. The *Small Wars Manual* also urged the Marines to employ as many indigenous troops as practical early on to confer proper responsibility on indigenous agencies for restoring law and order. The manual underscores the importance of aggressive patrolling, population security, and the denial of sanctuary to the insurgents. Because of their relatively small numbers, the Marines in Nicaragua had to adapt on a shoestring, almost always coupling their leaders to some type of indigenous element. The most effective tactics were found to be sustained small-unit mobile patrols that comprised about twenty men that could cover up to 30 miles a day. The most notable *Guardia Nacional* formation was the one that Lewis

(Chesty) Burwell Puller led on the hunt for Sandino—Company M, Mobile Company.[15]

Notwithstanding the greater publicity of Puller's exploits, the east coast of Nicaragua witnessed another group of Marines, working with very limited manpower, who successfully used local Indians to achieve Washington's counterinsurgency goals. Captain "Red Mike" Edson established a very useful alliance with the indigenous Miskito tribe in efforts to patrol the strategic Coco River area. This area presented a potentially important guerrilla sanctuary since the northern part of the zone was contiguous to two major areas of guerrilla operations. Establishing a forward operating base in this inhospitable area, which was essentially Sandino's strategic rear area, enabled combined Marine and indigenous patrols to potentially throw the guerrillas off balance. This eastern area of Nicaragua had few Spanish-speaking Nicaraguans and the Miskito tribe, who had hated Hispanic Nicaraguans ever since the colonial period, preponderated in the region. However, not only did Edson need to establish cordial relations with them to win their hearts and minds, he could not navigate the treacherous Coco River without the help of the Miskitos' special boat skills. Native canoes (*pitpans*) were the only means of transportation along most of the river and the Miskitos were one of the tribes who knew how to maneuver them. Thus, mastery of the river, enabled by the skills of the Miskitos, gave Edson the capacity to conduct long-range patrols into the enemy's sanctuaries. On one such raid in August 1928, Edson's combined Marine-Miskito element culminated in the capture of Sandino's headquarters in Poteca, disrupting the enemy guerrillas prior to the fall 1928 U.S.-supervised elections.[16]

Vietnam: CORDS (Civil Operations and Revolutionary [Later Rural] Development and Support), Combined Action Program (CAP), and Irregulars

If and when most Americans think about Vietnam, they probably think of General William C. Westmoreland, the Americanization of the war that was engendered by the big-unit battles of attrition, and the Tet Offensive of 1968. However, there was another war—counterinsurgency and pacification—where many Special Forces (SF), Marines, and other advisers employed small-war methods with some success. Moreover, when General Creighton Abrams became the commander of the war in Vietnam in 1968, he put an end to the two-war approach by adopting a one-war focus on pacification. Although too late to regain the political support for the war that was irrevocably squandered during the Westmoreland years, Abrams' unified strategy to clear and hold the countryside by pacifying and securing the population met with much success. Abrams based his approach on a study prepared by the Army staff in 1966 that was entitled *A Program for the Pacification and Long-Term Development of South Vietnam (PROVN Study)*. Abrams' PROVN study–based expansion of the Civil

Operations and Revolutionary (later Rural) Development and Support (CORDS) pacification effort under Military Assistance Command Vietnam (MACV), the Marines' CAP, and the experiences of the SF in organizing Civilian Irregular Defense Groups (CIDGs) all offer some valuable lessons for current and future counterinsurgencies.[17]

Although CORDS was integrated under MACV when Abrams was still the Deputy Commander and when Robert Komer was still the Director in 1967, it was Abrams and William Colby, as Komer's successor and director of CORDS, who expanded and invested CORDS with more and better people and resources. Under the one-war strategy, CORDS was established as the organization under MACV to unify and provide single oversight of the pacification effort. After 1968, Abrams and Colby made CORDS and pacification the main effort. An invigorated civil and rural development program, thus, provided increased support, advisers, and funding to the police and territorial forces (regional forces and popular forces). Essentially, this rural development allowed military and civilian U.S. Agency for International Development (USAID) advisers to work with their Vietnamese counterparts at the province and village level to improve local security and develop infrastructure. Identifying and eliminating the Vietcong Infrastructure (VCI) was a critical part of the new focus on pacification and Colby's approach—the Accelerated Pacification Campaign—included the Phuong Hoang program, or Phoenix, in English. Although the Phoenix program received some negative attention in the instances when it was abused, its use of former Vietcong and indigenous Provincial Reconnaissance Units (PRUs) to root out the enemy's shadow government proved effective. The Accelerated Pacification Campaign focused on territorial security, neutralizing VCI, supporting programs for self-defense, and self-government at the local level.[18]

Begun in November 1968, the Accelerated Pacification Campaign called for the employment of former Vietcong who had been turned to fight for the government under the Chieu Hoi program. Because of their specialized knowledge of the enemy, the Chieu Hoi cadre was particularly useful in the elimination of the VCI. This cadre provided indigenous manning for PRUs whose tasks were to root out the enemy's secret underground network—they were very effective. Interestingly enough, the year after the Tet Offensive—1969—witnessed an all-time high in Chieu Hoi recruitment with 47,087 enemy cadre and troops electing to change sides and serve the Government of Vietnam (GVN), evidently as a result of setbacks during and after Tet. By late 1970, the Accelerated Pacification Campaign helped the government of Vietnam control most of the countryside. "Four million members of the People's Self-Defense Force, armed with some 600,000 weapons" were an example of the commitment of the population in support of the government of Vietnam and in opposition to the enemy. Though an imprecise and flawed instrument, the Hamlet Evaluation System (HES) as a measure of pacification did indicate that from 1969 to 1970, 2600 hamlets (three million people) had become secured. Other more practical measures of the

Accelerated Pacification Campaign's success were a reduction in the extortion of taxes by the Vietcong, a reduction in recruiting by the enemy in South Vietnam, and a decrease in enemy food provisions taken from the villagers. However, there were certainly other factors that contributed to better government control of the countryside by that time: The enemy's Tet Offensive in January 1968 and Mini-Tet in May 1968 resulted in devastating losses to Vietcong forces in the south and the Vietcong's brutality during Tet helped create a willingness to accept the more aggressive conscription required to expand the forces in the South.[19]

Another program that greatly improved the U.S. military's capacity to secure the population and to acquire better tactical intelligence was the U.S. Marine Corps CAP. The CAP was a local innovation with potentially strategic impact—it coupled a Marine rifle squad with a platoon of local indigenous forces and positioned this combined action platoon in the village of those local forces. This combined Marine/indigenous platoon trained, patrolled, defended, and lived in the village together. The mission of the CAP was to destroy the VCI within the village or hamlet area of responsibility; protect public security and help maintain law and order; protect friendly infrastructure; protect bases and communications within the villages and hamlets; organize indigenous intelligence nets; participate in civic action; and conduct propaganda against the Vietcong. Civic action played an important role in efforts to destroy the Vietcong as it brought important intelligence about enemy activity from the local population. Because of the combined action platoon's proximity to the people and because it protected the people from reprisals, it was ideal for acquiring intelligence from the locals. The Marines' emphasis on pacifying the highly populated areas prevented the guerrillas from coercing the local population into providing rice, intelligence, and sanctuary to the enemy. The Marines would clear and hold a village(s) in this way and then expand the secured area. The CAP units accounted for 7.6 percent of the enemy killed while representing only 1.5 percent of the Marines in Vietnam. The lessons from CAP provide one model for protracted counterinsurgencies because it employed U.S. troops and leadership in an economy of force while maximizing indigenous troops. In this way, a modest investment of U.S. forces at the village level or local level can yield major improvements in local security and intelligence.[20]

For much of the Vietnam War, the 5th Special Forces Group also trained and led CIDG Mobile Strike Forces (Mike Forces) and reconnaissance companies that were manned by indigenous ethnic minority tribes from the mountain and border regions. These Strike Forces conducted reconnaissance by employing small unit patrols and they also defended their home bases in the border areas, denying them to the Vietcong and North Vietnamese regular units. The rationale for creating the CIDG was twofold: the U.S. mission in Saigon wanted a paramilitary force raised from the minority groups of Vietnam to strengthen and broaden the counterinsurgency effort; to prevent the Vietcong from recruiting them first with their propaganda because, as malcontented minorities, the Montagnards and other minority groups were prime targets for such efforts. There was also a geographic-strategic imperative for establishing the CIDG program—the government was failing to assert sovereignty and security over the tribal-minority-populated areas of the highlands and the remote lowland districts of the Mekong Delta, and as a result the government was not exploiting the area as a buffer for early warning intelligence against Vietcong infiltration. As early as December 1961, the Special Forces were training indigenous paramilitaries as mountain commandos. Later called mountain scouts, these troops conducted long-range reconnaissance in remote mountain and jungle areas to establish a presence and to collect intelligence. Another early CIDG program witnessed Special Forces cadre training indigenous trail watchers, whose mission was to identify, locate, and report Vietcong movements near the border. The trail watcher program was significant in that it was the precursor to the border surveillance program, where area development and border surveillance combined to create one of the more valuable components of the CIDG program.[21]

In 1963, the area development program grew and shifted toward the western borders of Vietnam. In 1964, these irregular indigenous forces also took on other roles, assuming missions that involved operations against Vietcong safe havens and operations to interdict Vietcong infiltration routes into Vietnam. In the beginning, the U.S. Special Forces and the civilian irregulars were not hunting the Vietcong. However, following the buildup of U.S. conventional forces in 1965, the next stage in the evolution of the CIDG program began, casting the Special Forces and the irregulars in an offensive role as hunters with the mission of finding and eliminating the enemy. By 1967 Project Delta, which had first become operational in December 1964, expanded to sixteen reconnaissance teams comprising two Special Forces members, four Vietnamese members, eight road-runner teams, and a reaction force of six companies. Initially, their operations involved the infiltration and the reconnaissance of Vietcong-controlled areas but these teams were subsequently authorized to attack targets small enough for them to handle without help. One other irregular force of note was the Apache Force, which saw combined forces of indigenous troops and Special Forces orienting American battalions prior to their commitment against Vietcong or North Vietnamese Army forces. During 1966–1967 American field commanders also increasingly employed Special Forces-led indigenous Mike Forces in long-range reconnaissance missions or as economy-of-force security elements in support of regular units. Other CIDG-type forces, called mobile guerrilla forces, raided enemy base areas and employed hit-and-run guerrilla tactics against regular enemy units. To be sure, the CIDG program provided a significant contribution to the war effort. The approximately 2,500 soldiers assigned to the 5th SF Group essentially raised and led an army of 50,000 tribal fighters to operate in some of the most difficult and dangerous terrain in Vietnam. CIDG patrolling of border infiltration areas also provided reliable tactical intelligence and the CIDG did provide a degree of security for populations in austere areas that might have been otherwise conceded to the enemy. In the end, the use of indigenous tribes and Vietnamese troops across a range of irregular and regular roles, increased the quantity of security forces, provided a good amount of useful intelligence, and established a pro-government presence in remote areas where otherwise there would not have been one.[22]

THE BRITISH-ANGLO EXPERIENCE

The British military has a thread of continuity in its use of indigenous irregulars for counterinsurgency operations dating back at least to the eighteenth century when it employed local American Indian tribes like the Iroquois against the French in the French and Indian War and later against the revolutionary American colonists in their war for independence. This legacy of experience remained in the British Army and its Commonwealth descendents throughout the nineteenth-century period of Empire and it also continued within the British military tradition and institutional culture to the post–World War II period. In this modern era, the United Kingdom has employed a number of indigenous irregulars to augment various counterinsurgency campaigns. Moreover, a prominent feature of the British experience was the use of turned insurgents for the conduct of counterinsurgency operations. This rather unique model goes beyond the mere use of native forces in stability operations. These "pseudo-gangs" not only provided the standard advantages of knowledge of the people, the terrain, the culture, and the language; but they also supplied a group of fighters who had truly been in the mind of the insurgent, knew his organization and tactics, and could exploit both the tactical and psychological aspects of this intimate relationship. The use of turned insurgents as a countermeasure could also offer a positive benefit for the U.S. Army in its current counterinsurgency campaigns and is an idea that merits consideration. This section examines the British experience during the Malayan emergency and the white's government Rhodesian war to maintain its independence. Although the former was successful and the latter ended in a loss, both counterinsurgencies illuminate lessons for the employment of indigenous forces.[23]

Malaya and Indigenous Tribesmen

In the aftermath of World War II, the United Kingdom had to reexert control over a number of colonial possessions. Malaya was no exception to this challenge, but local power politics had changed, and presented challenges for British rule. By March 1950, the Malayan Communists were conducting a terrorist campaign from their jungle bases that challenged stability in the region. During the Malayan emergency, European soldiers were at first unskilled in the ways of the jungle. To overcome this handicap, the British imported, from nearby North Borneo and Sarawak, a number of Dyak tribesmen as trackers and scouts for government patrols. These men, members of headhunting tribes, were able to read such signs as bent twigs and turned leaves—things that were meaningless to the European unfamiliar with the jungle. Regardless of the topography, this local ability to read the "signs" provided a powerful tool for counterinsurgency forces to avoid being ambushed, to close with, and to destroy the insurgents. The effectiveness of well-supported native irregulars, however, goes beyond mere reconnaissance and tracking, and their close combat skills should not be underestimated. For example, certain Malayan jungle tribes had been much exploited by the Malayan Communist Party during the Japanese occupation and early stages of the emergency, so that when contacted by the government they became willing allies. Jungle forts with small airstrips for short take-off and landing (STOL) aircraft were established in these tribes' areas to facilitate their logistical support. As a native force, for example, the Senoi Pr'ak, numbering not more than three hundred, many of them armed only with their traditional blowpipes, managed to kill more guerrillas in the last two years of the emergency than did all the rest of the security forces combined.[24]

The best guides, however, were ex-guerrillas, who often led patrols into jungle camps they knew. With the exception of a very few hard-core communists, whom the government either executed, banished, or imprisoned, guerrillas who surrendered, known as surrendered enemy personnel (SEP) or captured enemy personnel (CEP), were rehabilitated in special schools. The majority of these guerrillas had become involved in the communist movement through force of circumstance rather than through any deep political conviction. Many of the SEPs joined the government's Special Operational Volunteer Force (SOVF), where they received the pay of a lower-grade policeman and participated in patrols against their former comrades in the jungle. The SEPs proved invaluable to the government, both as sources of intelligence and as agents of psychological warfare. After some eighteen months' service in the volunteer forces, SEPs were released unconditionally to return to civilian life. This use of pseudo-gangs in Malaya followed initial prototypes that had been developed by the British during the Mau-Mau terror campaign in Kenya. In this counterinsurgency, captured insurgents were used extensively in "counter-gangs." These had started initially as groups of loyal blacks led by suitably-resilient white officers and non-commissioned officers, who went into the forests posing as Mau-Mau gangs. Their aim was to use the enemy's methods to contact and eliminate him. This concept developed further by taking turned terrorists on-board for the operations. Many surrendered rebels willingly operated against their former colleagues. This paradigm for employing indigenous forces, however, reached its apogee during the Rhodesian counterinsurgency campaign.[25]

Rhodesia and the Selous Scouts

What started out in the 1960s as a low-grade and containable insurgency grew so that by 1971–1973 the complexion of the war began to change. The insurgent activity developed to a point that demanded the total commitment of the security forces. Ultimately, the government faced two different major insurgent groups:

The Zimbabwe African People's Union (ZAPU), together with its military arm, the Zimbabwe People's Revolutionary Army (ZIPRA); and the Zimbabwe African National Union (ZANU), with its military wing, the Zimbabwe National Liberation Army (ZANLA). These two groups, largely tribal based, used two very different strategies—ZIPRA focused on conventional Soviet-style operations, while ZANLA operated under a Maoist rural strategy. Neither group cooperated with the other; in fact, there were clashes between the two. Initially, the Rhodesian Army was able to isolate the war to the northern border region with Zambia. However, as the Portuguese failures in Mozambique became more apparent, the basis for support and sanctuary operations for the Rhodesian black terrorists began to increase and spread into Mozambique. This expansion, when linked to a larger and better trained insurgent element, resulted in several guerrilla military successes throughout 1973. These tactics resulted in very few white casualties. The primary victims were the local blacks who supported the European-owned farms. There is little evidence that the majority of the Rhodesian black population supported the nationalist cause, but it also was not an enthusiastic supporter of the white minority government. Throughout this stage of escalation, the brutalization of the black tribesmen by the insurgents may have increased their sympathies for the minority government, but it also undermined their confidence in that government's ability to protect them. From 1973 to 1975, both sides in this conflict began to learn the lessons of unconventional warfare. The guerrillas received a higher degree of training and demonstrated the discipline required to wage an effective campaign to "win the hearts and minds" of the populace. The Rhodesian security forces, in turn, developed the counterinsurgency tactics that would bring them so much favorable recognition in the following years.[26]

Every war produces its elite and special unit, and the Rhodesian War was no exception. Because of the unfavorable balance between the government and insurgent forces—a one-to-one ratio at the height of the conflict, the Rhodesian security forces had to rely on small-unit tactics, innovation, and special operations to prosecute counterinsurgency successfully. The concept of pseudo-counterinsurgency eventually emerged as a useful approach after overcoming initial bureaucratic resistance from the Rhodesian Army. The conditions on the ground required troops who could pose as terrorists, pass themselves off among the local population, and be convincing enough to deceive the enemy themselves. The role of the pseudo gangs was to gather intelligence, locate insurgent groups, and, when the time was right, to eliminate the insurgent leaders. Also, they could simply stir things up and set one group of nationalists against another. These requirements impelled the formation of the Selous Scouts (named after Rhodesia's most famous big game hunter), soldiers who were predominantly black and which conducted a highly successful and clandestine war against the guerrillas by posing and fighting as guerrillas themselves. The Selous Scouts were initially charged to gather intelligence and to provide tactical information on guerrilla movement and strength. However, their skills soon evolved and migrated beyond these tasks to direct strike operations against the terrorists. Their unrivalled tracking, survival, reconnaissance, and counterinsurgency techniques made the Selous Scouts one of the most feared and despised of the Rhodesian army counterinsurgent units among the insurgents.[27]

The purpose of the Selous Scouts was the clandestine elimination of the African terrorists without regard to international borders. The unit incorporated the same tactics that the British had initiated in Malaya and Kenya. It was defined as a pseudo-gang concept. Captured insurgents were "turned" and used against their former comrades. The turning of terrorists was carried out with much skill. After an engagement, captured or wounded terrorists would be made the "offer" to turn coat and after receiving good treatment at the hands of the security forces, the captives would have a one-to-one discussion with an insurgent who had already switched sides, who would inform the captive of his alternatives—death at the gallows or a chance for redemption, with service for the government's forces. If placed back in operations, the new counterinsurgent had to successfully convince his Selous Scout comrades of his good faith. In operations, a team of four to ten men was deployed into an operational area. All other friendly forces in that region were withdrawn. The team was dressed in insurgent uniforms, carried communist weapons, and gave the appearance of being a guerrilla force down to all details. It was essential that these scouts were better trained and more disciplined than the terrorists. Once they ascertained the presence of an insurgent force, the the Selous Scouts would begin to stalk them. They were proficient at remaining undetected throughout this phase. This gave them the advantage of initiating contact with the insurgents at their discretion. A further advantage was that the local populace would also perceive them to be real terrorists and, depending on how far an area had been infiltrated, supply them with all types of supplies and intelligence. This support allowed civil and military police measures to be expanded and improved within these heretofore lost zones. The Selous Scouts achieved remarkable results by carrying the war directly to the guerrillas. The professional reputation of the Rhodesian security force was solid but the skills of the Selous Scouts were extraordinary. During the war the Scouts were credited with the deaths of 68 percent of the insurgents killed within the borders of Rhodesia. Furthermore, the example and the limited success of the Selous Scouts represent one essential component of an effective counterinsurgency campaign—using indigenous forces with knowledge of the terrain, the culture, and the enemy to defeat the guerrilla within its own paradigm. The Selous Scouts were simply much better at guerrilla warfare than were their opponents.[28]

THE FRENCH EXPERIENCE

The French Expeditionary Corps in Indochina and the French armed forces in Algeria fought two consecutive wars that likewise witnessed the employment of indigenous forces and colonial forces in the conduct of counterinsurgency operations, first against the Viet Minh and later against the Algerian National

Liberation Army (ALN). In their war in Indochina, the French suffered a humiliating and unambiguous political and military defeat; General Giap prosecuted a strategy that combined both insurgent operations and human-wave conventional attacks, culminating with the Vietnamese victory at Dien Bien Phu. In their war in Algeria, however, the French adopted some effective and some very ruthless counterinsurgency methods within the military sphere, but they failed to link their military methods to the political exigencies of that war. In fact, the French Army's use of torture itself, while proving expedient at the tactical level, essentially undermined their efforts at the operational and strategic levels. However, in Indochina, and to a greater extent in Algeria, the French armed forces employed indigenous forces in a counterinsurgent role, with some degree of success. To be certain, these experiences are salient in the context of twenty-first century counterinsurgency in that they offer some ideas that might help overcome the challenges that Western forces face in their efforts to train and employ indigenous forces. Indeed, there are some parallels to be discerned between the counterinsurgency in Algeria and the U.S. counterinsurgency in Iraq.[29]

Indochina and the Composite Airborne Commando Group

By the end of the war in Indochina, the French Expeditionary Force, in airborne units alone, comprised six European battalions, including two airborne legionnaire battalions (BEP), six Vietnamese battalions, one battalion each from Cambodia and Laos, plus a miscellany of support units, all of which necessitated the creation of a separate Airborne Forces Command Indochina. The *groupe mobile* was another formation that was heterogeneous in composition and it was designed particularly for offensive operations. These mobile groups comprised three partially motorized battalions from different origins—Legion, Senegalese, North African, or Vietnamese, and they also included either an artillery battalion or a heavy mortar battalion. By the end of the war, the French Expeditionary Corps included eighteen *groupes mobiles*, to include Vietnamese formations. The mobile groups performed well as intervention forces, particularly during General Giap's offensives in the Tonkin Delta in 1951, but they did not constitute a formula that could help the French win the war because they were road bound and their effectiveness was essentially limited to those areas, like the Tonkin Delta, where developed road networks existed.[30]

Although exact figures for the entire indigenous troop strength serving with the French remain elusive, one study states that approximately 325,000 of the total of 500,000 French forces in Indochina were Indochinese. Almost all of these soldiers were employed in conventional formations. However, the French did form mobile counterguerrilla groups comprising indigenous tribes. Later renamed the Groupement Mixte d'Intervention (GMI), they were initially called the Groupement de Commandos Mixtes Aéroportés (Composite Airborne Commando Group or GCMA). The aim of these organizations was to prosecute mobile and disruptive counterguerrilla operations in the rear areas of the Viet Minh. Some

GCMA operations began to take on strategic importance by the end of 1953. One of the most successful GCMA operations was a combined assault against Lao-Kay in Vietnam and Coc-Leu in China, sister cities on the Sino-Vietnamese border that served as an important enemy logistics hub. With the support of a French paratroop platoon that dropped in directly over the target, six hundred Meo and T'ai tribesmen raided Coc-Leu on 3 October 1953, with the support of a B-26 aerial bombardment. The raiding force completely surprised the enemy and destroyed important supply depots, inflicting about one hundred fifty Communist casualties before it safely withdrew into the mountains. In the end, however, the GCMA operations had both proponents and opponents. One expert on the French war in Indochina concluded that the Composite Airborne Commando Groups "were designed for a mission of guerrilla warfare which they performed well, but not for one of raiding against well organized forces, which would have required a level of tactical training and coordination that could not reasonably be expected from primitive tribesmen." As a footnote, another heterogeneous unit that performed extremely well in Indochina was the Bataillon de Marche Indochinois (BMI), a composite unit comprising Europeans, resilient Vietnamese mountaineers, and Cambodians, which was among one of the best infantry battalions of the war.[31]

By far the greatest challenge to the adaptability of the Legion forces in Indochina was the *jaunissement*, or literally "the yellowing process," which was the French term for the effort to increase their force strength by the increased incorporation and employment of Vietnamese forces with French forces. Thirty thousand Vietnamese regulars and thirty-five thousand auxiliaries, or *supplétifs*, were serving along with French forces in early 1951. One year after that, the number of Vietnamese serving for the French had increased to 54,000 regulars and 58,000 *supplétifs*, with another 15,000 Vietnamese in training. Training this many indigenous forces was indeed the crux of the challenge for the French, and four hundred French officers and noncommissioned officers were dedicated to these fledgling Vietnamese formations from French Army units that were already extended to the limits of their manpower. Additionally, the French command ordered the Legion to form composite battalions with a foundation of five hundred thirty-four legionnaire officers and noncommissioned officers and two hundred ninety-two indigenous recruits. Each Legion regiment incorporated a composite battalion, in some cases two, and every Legion battalion attached a mixed company under its command and control. This experiment definitely increased the amount of troops available to the French to prosecute the war and many Vietnamese formations acquitted an honorable military performance. Although the Viet Minh did infiltrate some of these units, desertions and betrayals were not entirely common.[32]

Thus, the French effort to form heterogeneous units composed of legionnaires and Vietnamese troops was generally successful but not without its flaws. In the 5th Foreign Legion regiment, French leaders found that the Vietnamese troops performed well in combat but they did not take well to the building of defensive posts. The 5th regiment also declared that its Vietnamese battalions had experienced fewer desertion problems than did other units. In May 1953, the French command in central Vietnam transformed the 4th battalion of the 2nd Foreign Legion regiment into a composite battalion because of the challenges in recruiting sufficient numbers of legionnaires. Moreover, the Regiment Étranger Coloniale (REC) converted its armored amphibious units (also called crab units given their role) into composite units comprising up to fifty percent Vietnamese troops, after the regiment discovered that these vehicles could transport more of the smaller Vietnamese than they could transport Europeans, thereby increasing the regiment's combat forces on operations. These indigenous troops were also more effective in searching local villages. A case could be made, therefore, that the employment of increasing numbers of Vietnamese soldiers helped mitigate the French manpower shortages and improved their effectiveness as well. Other Vietnamese paratrooper formations also performed very credibly during the Battle of Dien Bien Phu.[33]

The problems with mixed Vietnamese and Legion units were threefold. First, even though there was a sufficient pool of available men for recruiting purposes, there was not a sufficient pool of quality Vietnamese cadres because Bao Dai did not call up the middle class students who continued to avoid the war in university classrooms. Second, the effort to increase the amount of indigenous Vietnamese forces lacked political direction and motivation. Indeed, the French high command was convinced that the Viet Minh had already skimmed off the cream of the recruitment pool, collecting the most politically motivated and physically fit, thus leaving the flotsam for French recruiting efforts. Additionally, the recruitment effort, and consequently the Vietnamese formations that stemmed therewith, simply lacked legitimacy because the French refused to make the political concessions to the Bao Dai government that would have conferred to it genuine status and autonomy in the eyes of the Vietnamese people. Last, because the French Army trained them and the American Army at least partially equipped them, the Vietnamese formations were not nearly as adapted to the conditions of guerrilla warfare in Indochina as were their Viet Minh adversaries. In addition, the French tended to misuse these indigenous forces, particularly the auxiliaries, or *supplétifs*, by positioning them and their families in isolated outposts with the hope that they would fight relentlessly to defend them. However, this war of posts stimulated less zeal and enthusiasm among the Vietnamese than it had even among French soldiers. The war of the posts was extremely tedious because the side that did not have the support of the population was required to be constantly vigilant and continuously ready for action. The proliferation of posts, moreover, made them increasingly vulnerable to attack because of the smaller size of their contingents and because the Viet Minh adapted their tactics and their weaponry faster than the French forces could adapt their defensive measures.[34]

An important postscript to the French defeat in Indochina was how it traumatized the French Army in general and how it influenced the French Army's approach in Algeria in the formulation of its concept of revolutionary war (*guerre révolutionnaire*), in particular. The French defeat in Indochina was the proximate genesis for their revolutionary war doctrine, which became a decisive element for the French national military policy in Algeria. The defeat brought groups within the army to the recognition that conventional methods of colonial suppression were inadequate to confront a politically sophisticated enemy fighting on his native territory. To many army professionals, the loss of Indochina to the Communists had clearly proved that *esprit de corps* and conventional patriotism were insufficient weapons against revolutionary élan, especially so if their claim that the government neither sufficiently supported nor understood the nature of the fighting was true. The revolutionary warfare theorists came to understand that the insurgents in Algeria fought for a cause—they could label the rebel ideology pan-Arabism or Communism, but a precise analysis of this moniker was not as salient to them as the imperative to create an equally effective counterideology. These theorists insisted that the French Army would fight the next war under different conditions. They called for two changes: that the nation and the government must give the fullest support to the armed forces and that the French forces themselves had to undergo revolutionary changes in their tactics as well as in their concept of a duty ethic.[35]

This group of French Army theorists would profess that the prerequisite for the successful prosecution of a counterinsurgency in Algeria was a code of combative values that were strong enough to animate and unite national energies in order to "regenerate the moral fiber of metropolitan France." This quest for a counterideology thereby became intimately linked to a sense of mission. In addition to saving Algeria from pan-Arabism, the war in Algeria was to be part of a larger crusade to save France itself from corruption and inefficiency and to transform it into a disciplined and progressive power to preserve its national future. The war in Algeria provided the French Army with one final chance to renew its reputation and to regain its confidence. A key tenet of this revolutionary warfare theory was the idea that the Army must guide its methods in Algeria as much by psychological and political considerations as by purely military ones. These officer-theorists intended to inspire their tactics by guerrilla warfare and to exploit every success with psychological operations directed at demoralizing the enemy. Thus, the doctrine of *guerre révolutionnaire*, or *guerre subversive*, as subsequently manifested in Algeria, described a conflict waged within a state, a type of conflict that one student of the French military distilled down to the following formula: partisan warfare, plus psychological warfare, equals revolutionary warfare.[36]

The Algerian War and the *Harkas*

In Algeria, the French High Command recognized the imperative of recruiting and employing the largest number of Muslims possible, but it also understood the shortcomings that inhered in such an effort—in a poor and overpopulated country, many of the indigenous troops simply served for money and a meal;

Algerian forces complicated the operational context; and the loyalty and the reliability of these forces were often suspect, sometimes enabling FLN infiltration.
The total contribution of the indigenous Muslim troops to the French counterinsurgency effort for the duration of the war was significant, approaching 150,000
regulars and auxiliaries. In addition to the village defense forces, the French employed three principal types of indigenous forces. The *harkas*, squad-sized sup-
plementary forces that French officers and senior noncommissioned officers
commanded, were the most significant of these and they conducted *quadrillage*
and mobile operations either as commandos or as part of a regular company or
platoon. The *makhzan* were recruited guards, orderlies, and messengers who
supplemented the French Army's civil affairs teams. Last, the civil administration
also employed thousands of Muslims as auxiliary policemen and in the Mobile
Security Groups (Groupes Mobiles de Securité), including the *paras bleus*, which
comprised former FLN guerrillas and terrorists.[37]

One example of a French innovation in Algeria that met with some success,
both in winning hearts and minds and in harnessing the support of indigenous
elements, was the creation of an entirely news corps called the Sections Ad-
ministratives Specialisées, or SAS. The French authorities in Algeria created
some four hundred SAS detachments, each under the command of an army captain
or lieutenant who was an expert in Arab affairs and Arabic, trained to handle
every possible aspect of civil-military administration, from building houses and
administering justice to health, teaching, and agronomy. In some respects, the
SAS seem to have been the logical forebears to the Civil Operations and Rural
Development Support (CORDS) teams who served well later during the U.S. war
in Vietnam and perhaps to have been the harbingers of the Provincial Reconstruction Teams (PRT) who now operate in Afghanistan. The SAS were affec-
tionately called the blue caps (*képis bleus*), and they were a selflessly dedicated
and tenacious group of very qualified men whom the local populaces came to
love and whom the ALN came to target often because of their effectiveness and
because of the concomitant threat they posed to the insurgent cause. They consequently suffered the highest casualties of any category of administrator. By
1957 and 1958, the excellent and crucial service that the SAS detachments
performed had begun to have some effect in restoring the indigenous confidence
in the French presence in broad areas of Algeria. For example, the French Army
had tripled the number of primary schools that it had opened between April 1956
and August 1957; and the number of Muslim functionaries in French service
had increased from about 6850 to almost 10,000. It was a notable improvement
but it was not sufficient. With the myriad qualifications required for work in the
SAS, there, unfortunately, were too few SAS to bring about the effect intended
throughout Algeria in its totality.[38]

The thinking of the French Army planners also increasingly turned to concepts for employing special operations to help counter the insurgents. In addition
to the black commandos (*commandos noirs*), lightly armed detachments of
guerrilla-like troops assigned the role of roaming with the Muslim populations in

the countryside, 1957 witnessed the serious development of *harkas* forces that comprised what the French considered loyal Algerians. In one example, French ethnologist Jean Servier had been granted permission to create light companies from some thousand trustworthy and able-bodied defectors, former enemy combatants (*anciens combatants*) from the FLN. Because every Muslim soldier away from his family was potentially vulnerable to a threatening letter from the FLN, Servier insisted that his *harkas* units be located near their homes. Servier's *harkas* quickly proved very resilient in hunting down the ALN, partly because they were familiar with every path in their local areas. News of the *harkas'* good conditions and good pay quickly spread and precipitated a concomitant increase in these quasi-private armies. For example, during the two years beginning in January 1957, the quantity of *harkas* self-defense villages increased from 18 to 385, with their total manpower ultimately reaching 60,000. However, the steadfastness and the quality of these *harkas* formations varied widely, in many instances, in direct proportion to the quality of the SAS administrator within whose purview they operated.[39]

Another example of French special operations in Algeria that employed turncoat indigenous forces in an irregular role was the "blue operations." The name for these operations, in fact, derived from an initial plan to employ turned ALN or FLN members that went badly awry. The French name for this prototypical special operation was *Operation Oiseau Bleu* (Operation Blue Bird) and it originally involved exploiting the ancient enmity between the Kabyles and Arabs in Kabylia. Known as "Force K," this anti-FLN guerrilla group comprising Kabyle separatists grew to over 1000 men and requested more effective arms, with responsibility for its operations subsequently passing to the French Army. Unfortunately, the FLN was able to infiltrate the leadership of Force K and it perpetrated acts of perfidy, including the ambush of a French unit. The French terminated Force K and liquidated about one hundred thirty of its members, turning the Force K effort into a stain known as Affaire K. Nonetheless, out of this debacle emerged a very effective counterinsurgent operation known only as Léger's bleus, named after its founder, Captain Christian Léger, a shadowy Zouave and intelligence officer who had worked for Colonel Roger Trinquier during the Battle of Algiers as the head of a top secret organization called the *Groupement de Renseignement et d'Exploitation* (GRE). The GRE had established a network of Muslim agent informers who, unbeknownst to the FLN, had been turned at the French *paras'* interrogation centers. After the Battle of Algiers, seeing the value of these *bleu* double agents, Captain Léger quite effectively expanded and exploited this network of *bleu* agents to fully infiltrate the FLN infrastructure that was to reestablish itself in Algiers after the battle. Essentially, in command and control of the FLN apparatus without the insurgent leadership's knowledge, the GRE's *bleu* agents were able to deceive and capture the equivalent of the FLN general staff in the Algiers operational zone in January 1958. This neutralization was so thorough that the FLN was never able to recreate its infrastructure in Algiers until the closing months of the war.[40]

Such a large portion of Algerian soldiers—over twenty-five percent of the ground forces—serving under the French tricolor added some credibility to the French claim that it was not fighting against Algeria but for Algeria. Many local troops in fact distinguished themselves in combat, but the French inclined to use them for reconnaissance, guard, transport, and supply functions. However, their recruitment often included a guarantee for the security of the *harkas'* immediate families, and thus the French Army in some instances had to pay to build protected compounds for the dependents of these forces. Indeed, if the French had implemented a more effective political program with an integrated military component with flexible counterinsurgency tactics that did not alienate the population and the French public, they might have achieved a more favorable outcome. Even the French officers who readily embraced the theory of *guerre révolutionnaire* had to concede that it would have been impossible to prosecute to the fullest measure within the context of a liberal and multiparty metropolitan France. The nature of their operational techniques posed one of many problems with the French's almost exclusively military approach in Algeria. The requirement to impose on the French polity a policy of full support for the war was incompatible with the proper notion of subordinating the military instrument to civilian policy. Victory would have required employing the totality of the elements of national power, not just military power alone.[41]

MEASURING SUCCESS IN COUNTERINSURGENCY

There was something faddish about the writings of Clausewitz and Jomini, because they used geometry and Newtonian physics to describe Napoleonic warfare in terms of mass, space, and time. Clausewitz observed conventional land warfare between large armies within defined theaters of operations and used the analogy of popular physical and mathematical theory to describe what he saw.[42]

Training and mental habits had formed in McNamara a man of implicit belief that, given the necessary material resources and equipment and the correct statistical analysis of relative factors, the job—any job—could be accomplished.[43]

Western military tradition, especially the American military tradition, has continued to almost exclusively rely on the military theory of its favorite oracle of true war, Carl von Clausewitz. The problem that inheres in such a philosophical dependence in this age of information dominance and global insurgents, prima facie, is that Clausewitz theorized about war in a context that is two paradigms out of date. Having derived and contrived his precepts in an era when the Cartesian and Newtonian paradigms predominated, Clausewitz's theory on war was very mechanistically, quantitatively, and linearly oriented. Clausewitz's cognitive construct stemmed from back in the sixteenth and seventeenth centuries when a scientific revolution associated with the names of Descartes and Newton, among others, brought about new discoveries in mathematics, physics, and astronomy that replaced the notion of the world as a living and organic universe, with the metaphor of the world as a machine. Qualitative analyses were subsequently banned from science, which was limited to the study of phenomena that could be measured and quantified. Descartes himself promulgated a method of analytic thinking that broke down complex phenomena into smaller pieces in order to better understand the behavior of the whole by understanding the properties of its parts. However, Descartes only laid the conceptual foundations—precise mathematical laws governing the world as a perfect machine—that enabled Isaac Newton to synthesize all of this in his Newtonian mechanics, the culminating achievement of the seventeenth century.[44]

In the military domain, the linear and quantitative nature of the Newtonian metaphor was most manifest in the American way of war of the twentieth century. The U.S. Army as an institution was a paragon of conventionality and linearity— a large hierarchical and bureaucratic organization with an almost exclusive emphasis on attaining victory in the context of big conventional force-on-force wars, achieved through maneuver, technology, and superior firepower, lots of firepower. This institutional culture fused the geometry of Jomini with the annihilatory propensities of Clausewitz to arrive at a doctrinal and cultural approach to war replete with terms like "lines of operations," "decisive points," and "centers of gravity." In big, conventional wars, militaries employed maneuver, shock, and firepower and measured victory by phase lines crossed, objectives seized, bombs dropped, and enemy destroyed. However, during the U.S. military's biggest and most unsuccessful foray into counterinsurgency in the twentieth century, employing these types of metrics in the jungles of Vietnam did not work. In fact, the ubiquitous body count, the quintessential quantitative "metric" and the logical result of overlaying McNamara's mindset on the American way of war, became one symbol of what had gone awry with the Vietnam war. Now that the U.S. military and its allies are prosecuting multiple counterinsurgencies in different regions, and are arguably waging a global counterinsurgency against the forces of radical fundamentalist jihad, a survey of how to measure effectiveness of operations in the context of counterinsurgency might offer some value. The following section recapitulates some of the challenges that face military cultures trying to change and adapt to counterinsurgency. It also offers a distillation of some lessons of those measures that were useful in the past and some other proposed measures from the present that might inform today's counterinsurgencies.

OURSELVES: ROME'S LEGIONS, QUO VADIS?

> We wage a global war on terror—a confusing array of threats—while we continue to concentrate on future conventional wars with hypothetical, nation-state foes. We still consign all lesser contingencies to the other war as opposed real war. We still tend to view the enemy through the narrow bores and restricted optics of our existing national security structure.[45]

The early twenty-first century security environment engenders a contradiction between military cultures and the essence of modern war that presents traditional Western military institutions with a dilemma. Enemies of the West solve the dilemma by eliminating the culture of order. The members of al Qaeda and the terrorist groups associated with it do not wear uniforms, dawn formal ranks, conduct drill, or render salutes. It is quite possible that the global insurgents who wage war against Western tradition in Afghanistan, Iraq, and elsewhere have or are developing a military culture that is congruous with the unruly character of modern war. The broader non-Western culture from whence many of these terrorists hail is a variable that may facilitate this development. To be certain, today the United States and its allies face a panoply of enemies whose various aims are best achieved by avoiding or mitigating U.S. military superiority, attacking Western cities, and disrupting commerce. This type of war is not the preferred paradigm for a military culture that has exhibited a nearly exclusive predilection for conventional war in the past. Preferred wars are ones that are consistent with preplanned templates; fourth generation–like wars are also least preferred because they tend to mitigate the West's obvious advantages in firepower and technology. The current and emerging enemies of the United States will wage wars "that compel us to rethink our assumptions, to reconfigure our forces, and to reinvigorate our alliances."[46]

Some have asserted that a distinctively Western way of warfare can be traced through the history of American and Western military history all the way back to the Greeks and Romans. The Greeks, who had established a new kind of warfare for themselves that emphasized the purpose of battle as a decisive action, "fought within the dramatic unities of time, place, and action and dedicated to securing victory, even at the risk of suffering bloody defeat, in a single test of skill and courage." Rome's legions adopted and improved upon the Greeks' methods. The Roman legions were without peer on the conventional battlefield, but the German barbarians attacked them in wooded and hilly terrain. Arminius' Germanic guerrillas ambushed and harassed Varus' three legions. Inept leadership, inclement weather, rigid tactics, unfavorable terrain, and a cunning and imaginative opponent vitiated the Roman advantages in discipline, technology, and training. The legions maintained their unit cohesion as best as they could but ultimately succumbed to exhaustion and attrition. The survivors were taken prisoner and crucified, buried alive, or offered as living sacrifices to the pagan gods. Three legions vanished in the Teutoburg forest, and Arminius had the heads of key Roman leaders nailed to the trees as a warning to Rome. The German barbarians also ripped apart the half-burned corpse of Varus, cut off his head, and delivered it to the Emperor Augustus, who subsequently decided that the barbarian lands in northern Germany were too tough for his legions to colonize and occupy.[47]

During the years leading up to World War II, officers in the American military had been able to prepare themselves for the transition from a small peacetime army in 1940 to the enormous World War II army in part because the U.S. Army had embraced the traditions of the only big, European-style war in its history—the American Civil War. America's strategic aim of completely imposing its political aims upon the vanquished would thus be achieved by applying overwhelming and decisive combat power to destroy the enemy's armed forces and by destroying the enemy's economic resources and will to fight. World War II further shaped U.S. military culture because it validated and further embedded the cultural predilections for big conventional wars. One military policy expert noted that "the Civil War had molded the American army's conceptions of the nature of full-scale war in ways that would profoundly affect its conduct of the Second World War." The remembered memory of the Civil War pointed to massive force as the principal military principle. Competition between powerful European and Eurasian states in the military sphere before and after World War II produced a homogeneity of military thinking and doctrine that emphasized conventional battles aimed at the annihilation of the similarly predisposed adversaries with similar aims.[48]

One can postulate that this homogenization emerged in different regions according to two cultural patterns—the blitzkrieg pattern and the guerrilla warfare pattern. On the one hand, the measure of success in the blitzkrieg pattern was the capacity to employ large armored and mechanized formations designed to destroy a similarly manned and armed opponent. On the other hand, the measure of success in the guerrilla warfare pattern was the capacity to wage a protracted war against a technologically superior opponent. The blitzkrieg preference emphasizes a direct strategic approach, whereas the guerrilla warfare preference emphasizes an indirect strategic approach. Throughout the previous century, Western militaries, especially the American military, were surprisingly consistent in how they waged war. They had developed an unusual ability to translate national treasure, an industrial base capacity, and technological innovation into a conventional battlefield overmatch. However, the composition and character of non-Western military entities are changing as they develop concepts for defeating the firepower-centric methods engendered by the American way of war. The imperative to remain effective and to survive against overwhelming firepower is compelling enemies to disperse and hide, while adapting or eliminating the cumbersome logistics and transportation tails that still afflict the Western way of war.[49]

In fact, the gravest mistake the U.S. military leadership committed in Vietnam was attempting to wage a guerrilla enemy the same way it had fought the German army in World War II. U.S. forces staged large-unit operational sweeps with sexy names like Junction City, and one had the historically ironic moniker of "Operation Francis Marion." U.S. airplanes also dropped more than seven million tons of bombs, exceeding three hundred times the explosive power of the atomic bombs they dropped on Japan in World War II. Neither the big-unit sweeps nor the 'bomb-them-into-the-Stone-Age' method had much effect on a guerrilla enemy who hid in the jungles and then emerged when he chose to ambush American soldiers. Moreover, the paucity of knowledge about how best to win the support of the population was at the center of the American military's doctrinal challenges in Vietnam. The U.S. Army's doctrine for operations against insurgent forces, prescribed then by its capstone manual *FM 100-5, Operations,* emphasized the destruction of the guerrilla units. "Despite the intimation that elimination of the guerrillas might not solve the country's problems, *Operations*, with its aggressively offensive nature, pointed the advisors squarely at the PLAF guerrillas as their objectives and not the South Vietnamese people." What the U.S. military in general learned from Vietnam was only that it did not want to get involved in limited but inherently protracted counterinsurgencies. Moreover, much of the United States military's interpretation of transformation also remains focused on decisive and orthodox battles, instead of small wars and insurgencies. As a consequence, according to two military experts, the U.S. armed forces neither dedicated adequate resources to thinking about protracted counterinsurgencies nor did they establish the doctrine, training, and equipment to prosecute small wars effectively.[50]

PAST AS PROLOGUE: PROVN AND A FRAMEWORK FOR PACIFICATION

A Program for the Pacification and Long-Term Development of South Vietnam (PROVN Study), which was the genesis for a more unified and deliberate approach to pacification in the Abrams years in Vietnam, found it essential to develop and execute a positive program that assisted the indigenous government in establishing an attractive environment that would foster the genesis and the growth of the population's firm commitment to the government. This study also identified five major problem areas that were preventing the United States and the South Vietnamese from achieving success in the counterinsurgency: a well-led and adequately supported political network; an ineffective and inefficient government that was neither representative of nor responsive to the people; inappropriate methods and poor interagency coordination that undermined U.S. efforts; the paucity of indigenous resources, communication infrastructure, or skills required to sustain the escalating conflict; and deeply ingrained traditional values that impeded social change.[51] In response to the aforementioned challenges, the PROVN Study delineated five major short-range objectives that were established to provide a foundation for gaining the initiative in the Vietnam War. The first objective was to defeat the Vietcong and to reduce the Vietcong infrastructure. The second objective was to develop government institutional practices and leadership that was capable of advancing the nation-building program. The third objective was to establish a civil-military integrated organization and methodology that would ensure the execution of U.S. government of Vietnam programs in South Vietnam. The fourth objective was to establish the initial basis for economic growth and to establish a war-supporting economic infrastructure. The last short-range objective was to develop an allegiance among the South Vietnamese population to their government.[52]

Among the long-range objectives that the PROVN Study proposed was to develop a society that had the benefit of internal social cohesion, a viable government, a maturing and diversifying economy, and a sufficient security posture. The stated goal for South Vietnam was a basically democratic government with well-established political institutions that were capable of allowing for the peaceful and legal transfer of political power. In the military sphere, PROVN proposed that a "somewhat smaller, well-equipped and well-trained military establishment, backed by regional and international security guarantees, should be able to ensure national security." Moreover, the U.S. presence was to be minimal throughout this long-range period. The most discerning statements that appeared in this part of the PROVN Study were ones that addressed the measures of success, or effectiveness. It stated that the most dependable measures of progress were the qualitative assessments that U.S. representatives and competent Vietnamese officials, with a direct involvement with the area concerned, had reported. Moreover, PROVN posited that even though statistical metrics were being maintained on "nearly every measurable aspect of the conflict, from casualty ratios to VC propaganda incidents," many of the more important measures of progress, such as those germane to the nonmilitary aspects of pacification, were not precisely quantifiable.[53]

The PROVN Study also delineated a number of actions, thrusts, and objectives, some of which would seem to provide relevant context for trying to measure success or progress in counterinsurgencies in general. Two ostensibly germane actions that it recommended were to vitalize the Chieu Hoi Program, including the amnesty program, and to employ American influence to achieve political and social reform. Toward the aim of establishing a capacity to defeat subversion and maintain stability, moreover, this study called for the provision of a sufficient degree of security for the lines of communication—in other words, major roads and highways—to allow routine use and the commencement of a positive program to survey, and to selectively clear and secure the country's borders. Another stated objective and measure of success to be found in the PROVN Study was the reduction of regional and popular forces in the pacified provinces, to be accompanied by a commensurate increase in national police forces and nation building organizations. As some other examples of objectives that a counterinsurgent campaign ought to seek, and to possibly measure or evaluate, the following actions appeared among the many short-range thrusts and specific actions in the PROVN Study: establish popular allegiance to the government as a principal objective; establish a Director for Rural Construction and Development (DRCD); place all in-country U.S. agencies under the DRCD; establish outlets for political expression; integrate minority group participation in government; achieve unity of command and effort at the provincial level; selectively shift resources to support districts showing progress; through civic action, involve military forces with the population; curtail troop misconduct toward noncombatants; orient national police against the VCI; employ minority and sectarian forces in native areas under territorial control; and take military and diplomatic actions against external safe havens.[54]

The old Indochina hand and counterinsurgency expert Bernard Fall, who died in 1967 on the same Vietnamese Highway 1 (Colonial Route 1) after which he entitled his 1961 book *A Street Without Joy*, also had some helpful ideas on measures of effectiveness. In a reprinted chapter from 1965, Fall maintained that the killing of village chiefs, among other things, was a measure of ineffectiveness or effectiveness in counterinsurgency, depending on whether the killings were increasing or decreasing, respectively. Another measure was the degree to which a province was paying taxes—if an area was no longer paying taxes, this indicated a loss in government control and an increase in insurgent control. Likewise, in the Vietnamese case anyway, Fall found that since the government of Vietnam centrally assigned school teachers, where the school teachers were teaching without impediment or without being killed, was a measure or indicator that the counterinsurgency campaign was effective in that particular area. However, whether it was taxes, village chiefs, or schoolteachers, the measures were not precise in a quantitative way per se. It was more a matter of a qualitative pattern analysis of clusters of overlapping indicators of progress or lack of progress. If a province indicated an overlapping increase in the murders of schoolteachers and village chiefs, with an attendant decrease in tax receipts, for example, this would indicate failure on the part of the counterinsurgent forces. Taking one further step back in the Vietnam experience, there also exist the official French lessons for their war in Indochina, which offer a few germane observations on the indicators of success in counterinsurgency. The elimination of all manifestations of hostility on the part of the people and the proliferation of quality self-defense organizations in a preponderance of the populated areas were two fundamental indicators of progress in that report. On the other hand, the abandonment of populated areas to the guerrillas would be a measure of failure. One additional indicator that things are moving in the right direction is when the population itself increasingly reports accurately on the location of insurgents that reside among it.[55]

SOME CURRENT THOUGHTS ON MEASURES OF EFFECTIVENESS

Every quantitative measurement we have shows we are winning this war."—Robert Strange McNamara on the Vietnam War[56]

We have a room here, the Iraq Room, where we track a whole series of metrics."—Donald Henry Rumsfeld on the Iraq War[57]

One very cogent research project at the U.S. Army War College describes the four fundamental thrusts that lead to success in counterinsurgency as: (1) the creation of a secure environment, (2) the prevention of external support to the insurgents, (2) the initiation and establishment of a political process to address local aspirations, and (4) the management of information operations to shape the desired perceptions of all internal and external governmental and non-governmental players. According to this study, some very broad measures of a "secure environment" would be the following—the absence of fear from the insurgent's or terrorist's gun; the change of the environment to one where order and law can be enforced by the civil administration by means of the police; the smooth functioning of government institutions, and the return to normalcy where the population can pursue prosperity with freedom and human dignity. The same study postulated the following indicators for success when assessing the indigenous military as it pacifies the countryside and "wins the hearts and minds" of the population—the number of insurgents or terrorists killed, surrendered, or apprehended based on actionable intelligence, the number of insurgent supporters neutralized, the population's stance toward the military, the successful administration of local government agencies, the scope of malign media reporting, decrease in alleged human rights violations, and the response of the local population to the neutralization of insurgents and insurgent infrastructure.[58]

Another study from the U.S. Navy War College offers some salient recommended measures of effectiveness in two categories. The following would measure how well the Joint Force Command (JFC) is isolating its counterinsurgency area of operations from external infiltration from sanctuary: frequency and scope of combat operations along the border regions; increase or decrease in the number of friendly forces engaged in border security; proportional decreases in insurgent activity in areas with ongoing operations; and indicators of a change in insurgent weaponry, training, size of elements, and tactics. This same report also offers measures for how well the force is improving or establishing security in the area: access and relatively unimpeded use of main supply routes, lines of communications, water sources and fuel storage sites; expansion of friendly operations into territory influenced by insurgents; expansion of friendly operations into territory controlled by the insurgents; increase in the quantity of indigenous military and police; increase in the quality of indigenous military and police; and increase in friendly ability to deny insurgent capacity to disrupt friendly support base operations.[59]

In terms of measuring reconstruction and development, a collaborative project begun in the last five years between the Association of the U.S. Army and the Center for Strategic and International Studies (CSIS) identified and described four major pillars or issue areas—security, justice and reconciliation, social and economic well-being, and governance and participation. This study further defined security as the establishment of "a safe and secure environment and development of legitimate and stable security institutions." *Security* is the precondition for successfully accomplishing tasks within the other three pillars. *Justice and reconciliation* is defined as the establishment of effective law enforcement, fair laws, and open judicial process, humane corrections facilities, and mechanisms for resolving disputes and grievances stemming from the conflict. *Economic and social well-being* comprise restoring essential services to the people, establishing the foundation for a sufficient economy, and starting a sustainable and inclusive development program. The last pillar, *governance and participation*, addresses the requirement for effective and legitimate political and administrative institutions. This essentially translates to establishing a representative constitutional structure, ensuring the open participation of civil society in the formulation of government policies, and strengthening public sector administration.[60]

One other measure is when the number of groups that were previously identified as insurgents or terrorists adopting nonviolent political means increases. In the context of development and postconflict reconstruction, some indicators of progress might be a reduction in the number of refugees, an increase in the number of people moving back into their homes, and an increase in the presence of NGOs. Resuming full service and operations at hospitals, public utilities, factories, and government buildings are indicators of progress. Indicators that point to a decrease in the level and types of violent crimes may also be interpreted as a measure of progress. In addition, a general election with the requisite preceding voter registration is a measure of success. Other measures of the counterinsurgency and reconstruction campaign's effectiveness would be a decrease in the effectiveness of the insurgents and a decrease in casualties caused by improvised explosive devices and unexploded ordnance.[61]

CONCLUSION

The Army was hampered by severe manpower deficiencies which greatly impeded both cordon and search and search and destroy efforts. It took better ideas for the Army to finally win.[62]

Only if the government has the opportunity and the boldness to recruit unusual personnel—former insurgents, for example—and permits them to fight in an unorthodox political framework, does there seem any prospect for success.[63]

Although the quotes above describe the American Army in the Indian wars and the French-led indigenous guerrilla counter-guerrilla operations during the Algerian War, they could just as easily describe any of the examples surveyed in this chapter. Two ostensible truisms that can be logically inferred from this short survey on the employment of indigenous forces in a counterinsurgent role are that (1) heterogeneity of formation is better than the obverse and (2) operating on a shoestring compels innovation and adaptation. In all of these cases, government forces coupled with indigenous elements and, as result, achieved an exponential increase in the forces available to prosecute counterinsurgency, better knowledge of the terrain and environment, and more actionable intelligence about the enemy and enemy sanctuaries. In most of these examples, American, British, Rhodesian, and French forces were very not heavily armed and were relatively thinly manned vis-à-vis the insurgents. This chapter has examined some of the more relevant military lessons from the American, British, and French experiences with the employment of indigenous forces during those counterinsurgencies. It has elucidated examples where these militaries employed indigenous forces in regular and irregular roles to increase the number of capable indigenous forces, to eliminate insurgents and insurgent infrastructure, to help restore government legitimacy, and to assume a larger burden of military, paramilitary, and police functions.

In the American cases, the employment of Apaches, Macabebe scouts, and Chieu Hoi former Vietcong, as irregular scouts to hunt down and eliminate the insurgent leadership worked somewhat effectively and offered the additional value of undermining the enemy's morale. One of Crook's most germane methods was his extensive employment of Indians as irregular counter-guerrillas to fight enemy Indians. One that was particularly effective was his tactic of inserting small teams from friendly Apache tribes into the sanctuaries of insurgent Apaches to neutralize them and to psychologically unhinge them. There were two merits that derived from this approach: he matched the enemy's special skills in irregular warfare and he greatly increased friendly knowledge of the terrain and of the enemy. In addition, the Marines' technique of combining Marines with indigenous fighters proved moderately successful on long-range patrols with the Guardia Nacional and the Miskitos in Nicaragua, and in Vietnam, with the Combined Action Program's progress in the pacification of a portion of the countryside. Because of their relatively small numbers, the Marines in Nicaragua had to adapt on a shoestring, almost always coupling their leaders to some type of indigenous element. Finally, for a decade in Vietnam U.S. Special Forces trained and led indigenous tribal groups on conventional and special operations in some of the most inhospitable border areas of western Vietnam, with some degree of success. They ultimately led Roadrunner teams, Mike Forces, and mobile counter-guerrilla forces to locate and target the Vietcong in its own sanctuaries.

In the British examples, moreover, first in Malaya they innovated by importing Dyak tribesmen as trackers and scouts whose tracking skills helped the counterinsurgency campaign by avoiding ambushes and locating the insurgents for destruction. In particular, in the last two years of the counterinsurgency, a force of 300 Senoi Pr'ak tribesmen was able to track and kill more insurgents than all the rest of the security forces combined. More saliently, ex-guerrillas, known as Surrendered Enemy Personnel (SEP) or Captured Enemy Personnel (CEP), were employed very effectively as guides and counterinsurgents who were able to lead combat patrols into the jungle camps they knew well from their service on the insurgent side. Many of these turned guerrillas ultimately joined the government's Special Operational Volunteer Force where they proved their worth to the government, both as intelligence sources and as psychological warfare agents. This approach was further developed by then incorporating the turn-coat insurgents into counterinsurgent forces. Second, in Rhodesia, the security forces employed pseudo gangs was to gather intelligence, to locate insurgent groups and also to eliminate the insurgent leaders. The Selous Scouts, a group that was predominantly black, conducted a successful secret war against the guerrillas by posing and fighting as guerrillas themselves. The Selous Scouts, whose skills in tracking, survival, reconnaissance, and counterinsurgency were unequaled, became a lethal instrument and they instilled fear in the hearts and minds of the guerrillas.

The role of the Selous Scouts was to eliminate the African insurgents and their leadership, without any compunction about crossing international boundaries. The Selous Scouts achieved extraordinary results and were credited with killing 68% of the insurgents that were killed within the borders of Rhodesia.

For the French cases examined in this survey, there was very limited success in Indochina with the employment of indigenous troops. By the end of the war, the French had eighteen mobile groups who performed reasonably well as intervention formations but they did not really help with the overall war aims simply because they were road bound, limiting their effectiveness to areas outside the guerrilla dominated jungles and mountains. However, the French did develop mobile counter-guerrilla groups that consisted of indigenous tribes. These composite airborne commando groups, or GCMA, had the role of mobile counter-guerrilla forces operating in the rear areas of the Viet Minh. While they did carry out some successful raids against the enemy rear areas, they were not effective for raids against well organized forces. While the employment of Vietnamese soldiers did help the French address their manpower shortages and did improve the effectiveness of their counterinsurgency effort to a degree, there was not a sufficient number of quality Vietnamese cadres to make a significant difference in the end. For the purposes of this chapter, the French implementation of new concepts for counterinsurgency in Algeria is more insightful. While the cadre of the SAS were French, and not indigenous, the creation of 400 SAS detachments whose officers were experts in Arabic and Arab affairs met with some success in both winning hearts and minds, and in harnessing the support of indigenous elements. By 1957 and 1958, the services that the SAS detachments performed had begun to have some effect in restoring the population's confidence in the French. One last and germane example of the French use of indigenous irregulars in a special operations role was the "blue operations." Although their first attempt with the Force K ended in a debacle, out of it emerged *Léger's bleus*, a group of turned insurgents who Captain Léger effectively expanded and employed as a double-agent network that was subsequently able to fully infiltrate and neutralize the FLN infrastructure—the equivalent of the FLN general staff—in the Algiers operational zone by January 1958.

The French employment of SAS detachments to integrate security and development was certainly a sound concept but the challenges it engendered for raising a sufficient quantity of qualified detachments to cover all the regions in Algeria also remain an even more daunting reality for the U.S. military and its partners running the Provincial Reconstruction Teams (PRT) in Afghanistan, as well as for any future efforts to implement a similar model in Iraq. Moreover, the similarities between the French approach and the effectiveness of the GRE *bleu* operations to eliminate FLN infrastructure in Algeria, the Rhodesian Selous Scouts operations to eliminate ZANLA and ZIPRA networks, and the U.S. Phoenix Program's PRU operations to eliminate Vietcong infrastructure, point to the potential continued utility of this model on the Pakistani border and in Iraq. CORDS, CAP, and CIDG also met with success in prosecuting key aspects of the counterinsurgency in Vietnam. Each program expanded the quality and quantity of the forces conducting pacification and counterinsurgency, improved the capacity for dispersed small unit patrolling, and consequently improved the scope and content of actionable intelligence. The lessons and successes of these programs are salient today because both in Afghanistan and Iraq, improving the quantity and capabilities of indigenous forces, ensuring that there is an integrated and unified civil-military approach, and increasing the security of the population, all continue to be central goals toward a successful outcome.

One caveat lies in the fact that many of the examples described in this chapter also include flaws and drawbacks. Any use of indigenous forces in regular or irregular roles demands a scrupulous screening to ensure reliability. As was the case with the Miskitos and with other non-Hispanic populations on the Coco River, when the United States pulled the Marines out of the Coco River area in 1929–1930, the local population was abandoned to suffer the retribution inflicted by the Sandinistas when they recaptured key parts of the area in 1931. All three of the Vietnam-era programs, however, also exhibited some significant problem areas. The CIDG program was plagued by two persistent problems. First, continuous hostility between the South Vietnamese and the ethnic minority groups who comprised CIDG Strike Forces impeded the U.S. efforts to have RVN SF take over the CIDG program. Second, partly as a consequence of the aforementioned, 5th SF Group failed to develop an effective indigenous counterpart organization to lead the CIDG since the Republic of Vietnam SF continued to prove ineffective in this role. Moreover, Marines, who have written studies that generally laud the benefits of the CAP model, also reveal that the combined action platoons were not all completely effective. In some instances, the effects of CAP "were transitory at best" because the villagers became dependent on the Marines for security. In other instances, especially before Abrams ushered a new emphasis on training popular forces, the local militia's poor equipment and training made them miserably incapable of defending the villages without the Marines.[64]

Nevertheless, the benefits and leverage that indigenous forces give to the lead country in a counterinsurgency, whether as auxiliaries, pseudo gangs, or integrated troops, have merit. One enduring lesson that all the military efforts described here seem to show, over and over again, is that the early and deliberate employment of indigenous forces in a counterinsurgent role can be a very effective method in helping to achieve a desirable outcome within the context of the overall strategy. This chapter concludes below with two general proposals for organizing and integrating both regular and irregular indigenous forces with both conventional and unconventional American forces and agencies. One proposal for the U.S. Army would be the use of pseudo formations. Pseudo operations units, which formed part of the British and Rhodesian experience, could be integrated with U.S. special operations forces (SOF) or CIA covert units. For counterinsurgency operations in Iraq or Afghanistan, these could prove useful in collecting human intelligence for action by conventional force units. In fact, it might be one way to overcome the deficiency of human intelligence noted in Iraq. A successful counterinsurgency construct requires an extremely capable intelligence infrastructure endowed with human sources and deep cultural knowledge. Useable intelligence is crucial and in fact, the Commanding General of the U.S. Army's 1st Armored Division in Iraq, Major General Martin Dempsey, observed in November 2003, "fundamentally, here in Baghdad we do two things: we're either fighting for intelligence or we're fighting based on that intelligence." Despite the improvements in military intelligence since 2001, the United States does not seem to have the depth and breadth required in the human intelligence and cultural intelligence arenas—it lacks Arabic linguists, in uniform or otherwise. The Undersecretary of Defense for Intelligence, Stephen Cambone, in discussing intelligence shortcomings documented in an internal report, might have understated the problem, when he admitted, "We're a little short on the humint [human intelligence] side; there's no denying it."[65]

Another design for the organization and integration of indigenous forces in counterinsurgency, across the spectrum of special and conventional missions, might be a two-star equivalent joint and combined interagency counterinsurgency task force headquarters that integrates elements from the armed services conventional forces, SOF, CIA, Department of State, and indigenous intelligence elements. This joint and combined special and conventional interagency task force might then include three subordinate components that would build on the lessons in this chapter: (1) a composite special reconnaissance and direct action unit that would comprise turn-coat indigenous former insurgents or friendly tribes, special mission units, and other government assets (CIA and others) with the role of gathering intelligence, locating enemy infrastructure, and eliminating insurgent leadership; (2) a combined action force that would build on the CAP model, consisting of combined coalition and indigenous conventional elements, with the roles of area denial and saturation patrolling within the entire task force area of operations; and (3) a composite reserve or decisive action force postured over the shoulder for helicopter or fixed wing insertion, building on the Apache Force concept from Vietnam by comprising conventional coalition mobile groups that include SOF-led attachments of turned insurgent or friendly tribes, with the role of responding to developing actions or battles that are beyond the means of the combined action force. A task force that organizes and integrates special, conventional, and indigenous forces in this way, leveraging the best counterinsurgency practices surveyed here, would be able to carry out the full range of counterinsurgency requirements within an autonomous are of operation. It would obviously require control over and support by both conventional and special rotary-wing and fixed wing assets.

To prosecute an effective counterinsurgency on a global scale, future operations and campaigns in this long war against al Qaeda and associated terrorist and insurgent groups, then, are more likely to meet with success if they subscribe to the "less-is-better" axiom. The Combined Joint Task Force–Horn of Africa (CJTF-HOA) offers an excellent example of a successful and economical counterinsurgency, employing small numbers of special operations forces, coupled with indigenous forces, to establish security, to build clinics, and to pacify the population. Combined Joint Task Force–Horn of Africa (CJTF-HOA) is the quintessence of a twenty-first century paradigm of how to win against the global insurgents. It consists of little groups of warriors conducting dispersive security, counter-terrorism, and humanitarian operations along with indigenous forces in traditional areas of terrorist sanctuary and bad governance, operating on a shoestring. Its roles encompass the entire range of stability-type operations— successful theater security cooperation initiatives, civil affairs, interagency cooperation, intelligence gathering, and even tracking, and on occasion, neutralizing. The new paradigm will center on dispersive and adaptive teams operating on the "fringes." Smaller will indeed be better when it comes to operating within the arc of chaos: well-trained little groups of warriors, with linguistic skills and cultural knowledge, operating in a dispersive fashion, leveraging indigenous ties and forces, will be more effective than the converse.[66]

As a final postscript, there are no magic and inherently quantifiable "metrics" that we can slap on a Power Point matrix with green and amber gumballs, ones that might precisely measure our path to victory in counterinsurgency. This type of warfare is much more complex and qualitative because much of it deals with the population's perception of both the guerrillas' and the government's legitimacy and credible capacity to coerce. The credible capacity to coerce, with restraint, and the security that this brings, is also inexorably linked to the people's perception of the government's legitimacy. These two fundamental requirements, the credible capacity to coerce and legitimacy, moreover, will help drive and underpin the notions of sovereignty, justice, human security, freedom, liberty, and popular support. Notwithstanding whether all of these are measurable, either qualitatively or quantitatively, in any counterinsurgency it is important to ensure that the counterinsurgent forces are adhering to the following imperatives, derived over time, from every time the U.S. has engaged in counterinsurgency: employ force minimally but credibly and persuasively; ensure there is a unified and joint civil-military interagency approach; take all measures to enhance the perceived legitimacy of the government; co-opt and include the political opposition, to include the former insurgent infrastructure, into the legitimate political process; and maximize the employment of indigenous forces early, in both regular and irregular roles.[67]

Notes

Chapter 1

1. The term "World War X" is from John B. Alexander, "The Evolution of Conflict Through 2020: Demands on Personnel, Machines, and Equipment," an unpublished Joint Special Operations University Paper prepared for the Conference on "The Changing Nature of Warfare" in support of the "Global Trends 2020" Project of the U.S. National Intelligence Council, May 2004, 1. There are two very good current works—John Mackinlay, *Defeating Complex Insurgency*, Whitehall Paper 64 (London: RUSI, 2005) and David Kilcullen, "Countering Global Insurgency," unpublished paper, Canberra, Australia, November 2004—that identify this war as a global insurgency that must be countered. However, both of these studies strongly state the difference between the regional and local insurgencies of the twentieth century vis-à-vis the globally dispersed, information-enabled, and radical-fundamental *jihadist* insurgency of this century. This book and this author acknowledge that there are differences between the new global insurgency and the national/transnational insurgencies of the twentieth century (transnational examples included, among others, external support from Cambodia and Pakistan for the Vietcong and the mujahideen, respectively.) But, this author would also emphasize the continued utility of those methods that proved effective in countering national insurgencies, methods that should now be adapted and applied both locally and globally, to counter the insurgencies in Iraq, Afghanistan, and elsewhere in Asia; and to counter the global and networked insurgency that is animated by a radical interpretive version of jihad.

2. Robert Taber, *The War of the Flea: Guerrilla Warfare in Theory and Practice* (New York: Lyle Stuart, Inc., 1965), 180.

3. D. Robert Worley, *Waging Ancient War: Limits on Preemptive Force* (Carlisle, PA: U.S. Army Strategic Studies Institute, 2003), 9.

4. Richard H. Shultz, Douglas Farah, and Itamara V. Lochard, *Armed Groups: A Tier-One Security Priority*, INSS Occasional Paper 57 (USAF, CO: Institute for National

Security Studies, 2004), 35–36 and 41–42. For elaboration on either Zarqawi's role in Iraq or the influence of Hezbollah, see Arnaud de Borchgave, "Iran's Strategy," *Washington Times*, 18 August 2005, 14; Steven Coll and Susan B. Glasser, "The Web as Weapon," *Washington Post*, 9 August 2005, 1; or Michael Ware, "Inside Iran's Secret War for Iraq," *Time*, 22 August 2005, 26.

5. John Keegan, *A History of Warfare* (New York: Vintage Books, 1993), 387.

6. The Bismarck quote is cited in Colonel Samuel B. Griffith II, "Guerrilla, Part I," *Marine Corps Gazette*, July 1950, 43.

7. Mao Tse-Tung, *On Guerrilla Warfare*, trans., Samuel B. Griffith II (Champaign, IL: University of Illinois Press, 2000), 68.

8. Rohan Gunaratna, *Inside al Qaeda: Global Network of Terror* (New York: Berkley Books, 2002), 72–73.

9. Gunaratna, 76; Bruce Hoffman, "Redefining Counterterrorism: The Terrorist Leader as CEO," *RAND Review*, 28 (Spring 2004), 15.

10. Brian Michael Jenkins, "Redefining the Enemy: The World Has Changed, but Our Mindset Has Not," *RAND Review*, 28 (Spring 2004), 21; Worley, 8–9.

11. John Mackinlay, *Globalization and Insurgency*, Adelphi Paper 352 (London: The International Institute for Strategic Studies, 2002), 79 and 82–83.

12. Bernard Lewis, "The Revolt of Islam," *The New Yorker*, 19 November 2001, Online Archives, 3; and Michael Vlahos, *Terror's Mask: The Insurgency Within Islam* (Laurel, MD: Johns Hopkins University Press, 2001), 1, cited in Grant R. Highland, "New Century, Old Problems: The Global Insurgency Within Islam and the Nature of the Terror War," in *Essays 2003* (Washington, DC: NDU Press, 2003), 20. Youssef H. Aboul-Enein and Sherifa Zuhur, *Islamic Rulings on Warfare* (Carlisle, PA: U.S. Army War College Strategic Studies Institute, 2004), 4, 30.

13. Aboul-Enein and Zuhur, 11–12; Highland, 21.

14. Jenkins, "Redefining the Enemy," 21.

15. Highland, 18–19, 20–21; Osama bin Laden, cited in Bernard Lewis, "License to Kill: Osama bin Laden's Declaration of Jihad," *Foreign Affairs* (November–December 1998), 15.

16. Cheryl Bernard, "Five Pillars of Democracy: How the West Can Promote an Islamic Transformation," *RAND Review*, 28 (Spring 2004), 10–11.

17. Brian Michael Jenkins, *Countering al Qaeda: An Appreciation of the Situation and Suggestions for Strategy* (Santa Monica, CA: RAND Corporation, 2002), 4.

18. Bernard Lewis, "The Revolt of Islam," *The New Yorker*, 19 November 2001, Online Archives, 13.

19. Mackinlay, 87; Worley, 9–10; and Lewis, "The Revolt of Islam," 13.

20. Keegan, 388; Ralph Peters, "The New Warrior Class," *Parameters*, 24 (Summer 1994), 16; and David Tucker, "Fighting Barbarians," *Parameters*, 28 (Summer 1998), 70.

21. Bruce Hoffman, *Al Qaeda, Trends in Terrorism and Future Potentialities: An Assessment* (Santa Monica, CA: RAND Corporation, 2003), 5 and 9; Joseph Joffe, unpublished presentation at the Conference on Religion and Terrorism, Harvard University, 21 November 2002, 7; William S. Lind, et al., "The Changing Face of War: Into the Fourth Generation," abridged, *Marine Corps Gazette*, October 1989, 25–26.

22. Colonel Thomas X. Hammes, USMC, "4th Generation Warfare: Our Enemies Play to Their Strengths," *Armed Forces Journal* (November 2004), 42.

23. Jenkins, "Redefining the Enemy," 16.

24. The strategic paradox concept is from Russell F. Weigley, *The American Way of War: A History of United States Military Strategy and Policy* (Bloomington, IN: Indiana University Press, 1973), 18; Highland, 22; Worley, vii; and Hoffman, 6.

25. Worley, viii; Michael Ignatieff, "The Challenges of American Imperial Power," *Naval War College Review* (Spring 2003): 53–54; Mackinlay, 79; and Hoffman, 5–7.

26. *FMI (Field Manual Interim) 3–07.22, Counterinsurgency Operations* (Washington, DC: Department of the Army, October 2004), 1–1 and 1–8; and Steven Metz and Raymond Millen, *Insurgency and Counterinsurgency in the 21st Century: Reconceptualizing Threat and Response* (Carlisle, PA: U.S. Army Strategic Studies Institute, 8 November 2004), 7.

27. Metz and Millen, 13–14.

28. Paul Moorcraft, "Can Al Qaeda Be Defeated?," *Armed Forces Journal* (July 2004): 30 and 33; and Anthony Cordesman, "The West Is Mired in a Losing Battle," *London Financial Times*, 22 July 2004.

29. Stephen Gale, "Terrorism 2005: Overcoming the Failure of Imagination," Foreign Policy Research Institute, E-Notes, 16 August 2005, 2–4. Michael F. Morris, "Al Qaeda as Insurgency," unpublished paper, U.S. Army War College, Carlisle, PA, March 2005, 2–3, 6–7, 11, 14.

30. Worley, 9; Highland, 25; Lind et al., 1 and 3; Major General (ret.) Robert Scales, quoted in Stephen P. Hedges, "Military Voices Say Blame Isn't All on Civilians," *Chicago Tribune*, 15 August 2004.

31. Highland, 23–24.

32. C. J. Chivers and Steven Lee Myers, "Chechen Rebels Mainly Driven by Nationalism," *The New York Times*, 12 September 2004.

33. Anthony James Joes, *America and Guerrilla Warfare* (Lexington, KY: University Press of Kentucky, 2000), 328.

34. Ahmed S. Hashim, "The World According to Osama Bin Laden," *Naval War College Review* (Autumn 2001), online archives, 4; Steven Metz, "Insurgency and Counterinsurgency in Iraq," *The Washington Quarterly*, 27 (Winter 2003–2004), 28; and Highland, 25–26.

35. Thomas P. M. Barnett, "The Pentagon's New Map," *Esquire*, March 2003, 174.

36. Metz and Millen, 23–24; Highland, 28–29.

37. Bernard, 12–13; Aboul-Enein and Zuhur, 31–32.

38. Aboul-Enein and Zuhur, 32.

39. The British Army, *Army Field Manual, Volume V, Operations Other Than War* (London: Chief of the General Staff, 1995), 3–1 and 3–2. For a concise survey of some valuable American military lessons in effective counterinsurgency methods, see Robert M. Cassidy, "Winning the War of the Flea: Lessons From Guerrilla Warfare," *Military Review* (September–October 2004), 41–46.

Chapter 2

1. This quote, attributed to an anonymous U.S. Army general, is from Brian M. Jenkins, *The Unchangeable War*, RM-6278-ARPA (Santa Monica, CA: RAND Corporation, 1970), 3.

2. Harvey M. Sapolsky, "On the Theory of Military Innovation," *Breakthroughs* (Spring 2000), 35 and 38.

3. To win, or to be effective, in the context of counterinsurgency or stability operations is subjective and relative. However, although diverse missions comprise the realm of stability operations, a general corpus of principles has emerged from a legacy of experiences in operations short of war. To be effective, doctrine in this area should help promote two central aims: (1) to integrate military, political, economic, and social objectives, moving them toward the desired strategic outcome; and (2) to gain and maintain support of the indigenous population.

4. Based on Andrew Mack, "Why Big Powers Lose Small Wars: The Politics of Asymmetric Conflict" in *Power, Strategy, and Security: A World Politics Reader*, ed. Klaus Knorr (Princeton, NJ: Princeton University Press, 1983), 126–51. This implies a qualitative and quantitative superiority by empirical conventional measures of military capabilities, only.

5. These battles witnessed European armies handily and brutally defeating their non-European adversaries because the latter chose, imprudently, to fight the former symmetrically. See Winston S. Churchill, *The River War* (London: Prion, 1997), 191–225 and Daniel P. Bolger, "The Ghosts of Omdurman," *Parameters* (Autumn 1991), 34, for an analysis of the Battle of Omdurman. Mao Tse-Tung, *On Protracted Warfare* (Peking: Foreign Language Press, 1967), 9–10.

6. Once again, inferior connotes a weakness in conventional measures of military might, not necessarily in strategy, tactics, and warrior skills. Asymmetric conflict was also the norm during the Cold War and for most of the history of the United States. During the Cold War, the threat of nuclear escalation precluded a symmetric conflict between the two superpowers.

7. The term "asymmetric conflict" first appeared in Andrew Mack, "The Concept of Power and Its Uses in Explaining Asymmetric Conflict" (London: Richardson Institute for Conflict and Peace Research, 1974). See John F. Antal, "The Conquest of Malaya and Singapore 1941–1942," *Army* 50 (February 2000): 70 for a description of the Japanese invasion of Singapore as an asymmetric attack.

8. Henry Kissinger, "The Vietnam Negotiations," *Foreign Affairs* (January 1969), 214.

9. Mack, "Why Big Powers Lose Small Wars," 132.

10. B. H. Liddell Hart, *Strategy*, 2nd ed. (New York: Praeger, 1967), 26–27. The term "Fabian" connotes an indirect strategic use of force and stems from the Roman general Quintus Fabius Maximus, who protracted the war against Hannibal in the Second Punic War by the avoidance of decisive battles.

11. Russell F. Weigley, "American Strategy from its Beginnings through the First World War" in *Makers of Modern Strategy*, ed. Peter Paret (Princeton, NJ: Princeton University Press, 1986), 410–12; and Weigley, *The American Way of War*, 5, 15, 18–19. Mack, "Why Big Powers Lose Small Wars," 145–46.

12. Weigley, "American Strategy From its Beginnings," 410–11; and Weigley, *The American Way of War*, 18, 23–24, 26, 29.

13. Sean J. A. Edwards, *Mars Unmasked: The Changing Face of Urban Operations* (Santa Monica, CA: RAND Corporation, 2000), 28.

14. Mack, "Why Big Powers Lose Small Wars," 128 and 133.

15. Timothy Thomas, "The Caucasus Conflict and Russian Security: The Russian Armed Forces Confront Chechnya, Part III (Fort Leavenworth, KS: Foreign Military Studies Office, hereafter, FMSO, 1997), 6; Raymond Finch, "Why the Russian Military Failed in Chechnya" (Fort Leavenworth, KS: FMSO, 1997), 4–7; Gregory J. Celestan,

"Wounded Bear: The Ongoing Russian Military Operation in Chechnya" (Fort Leavenworth, KS: FMSO, 1996), 4.

16. Lester W. Grau, *Changing Russian Tactics: The Aftermath of the Battle of Grozny*, Strategic Forum Number 38 (Washington, DC: INSS, 1995), 5; and Thomas, 9 and 22–23.

17. Finch, 5–6, and Celestan, 5. Wiping out the noncombatant population is not the preferred solution in counterinsurgency. In order to counter Mao's approach, in which the people in a guerrilla war are "likened to water" and the guerrillas are likened "to the fish who inhabit it," most counterinsurgency experts would assert the necessity of separating the fish from the water by winning the hearts and minds of the population. For Mao's fish and water simile, see Mao Tse-Tung, *On Guerrilla Warfare*, trans., Samuel B. Griffith, II (Champaign, IL: University of Illinois Press, 2000), 93.

18. Lester W. Grau, "Bashing the Laser Range Finder With a Rock" (Fort Leavenworth, KS: FMSO, 1997), 4.

19. Edward N. Luttwak, "Toward Post-Heroic Warfare," *Foreign Affairs* (May/June 1995), 116.

20. Samuel B. Griffith II, "Introduction" in Mao Tse-Tung, *On Guerrilla Warfare*, 7.

21. Francis Ford Coppola, *Gardens of Stone*, produced by Columbia TriStar Home Video, 111 minutes, 1987, videocassette.

22. Jenkins, 4.

23. Mack, "Why Big Powers Lose Small Wars," 128, 130, and 132–33.

24. Ibid., 136–39. This is not the case in Afghanistan where the U.S. military is trying to eradicate al Qaeda in order to prevent future attacks against the U.S. homeland. However, the lack of a direct threat to the security of the great power is germane to the Vietnam war as well as the other historical cases in this article.

25. Ibid., 129–30, and Mao Tse-Tung, *On Guerrilla Warfare*, 90. For tons of bombs dropped on Vietnam, see John G. Stoessinger, *Why Nations Go to War*, 5th ed. (New York: St Martin's Press, 1990), 111–12.

26. Anonymous American senator cited by Edward Foster in *NATO's Military in the Age of Crisis Management* (London: Royal United Services Institute for Defence Studies, 1995), 13.

27. For casualty figures, see Susan Rosegrant and Michael D. Watkins, *A Seamless Transition: United States and United Nations Operations in Somalia 1992–1993 (B)* (Cambridge, MA: Harvard University, 1996), 12–16 and Rick Atkinson, "Night of a Thousand Casualties," *Washington Post*, 31 January 1994, A01. Don M. Snider, John A. Nagl, and Tony Pfaff, *Army Professionalism, the Military Ethic, and Officers in the 21st Century* (Carlisle, PA: Strategic Studies Institute, 1999), 23. This is not necessarily true in Afghanistan, however, where the American public and political elite seem to be more patient and tolerant toward casualties because the war is against an unambiguous and direct threat to U.S. security.

28. Colin S. Gray, "National Style in Strategy: The American Example," *International Security* (Fall 1981), 38.

29. Karl W. Eikenberry, "Take No Casualties," *Parameters* (Summer 1996), 113–15; See James Gentry, "Military Force in an Age of National Cowardice," *Washington Quarterly* (Autumn 1998), 181–82; and *National Military Strategy of the United States* (Washington, DC: U.S. Department of Defense, 1995), 10.

30. Snider, Nagl, and Pfaff, 24–25. The zero-casualties syndrome is not manifest in Afghanistan because the U.S. military is prosecuting a war against an enemy who has attacked and continues to threaten the U.S. citizenry in its homeland. Moreover, there

seems to be a high degree of resolve and consensus among both the U.S. political elite and the public to see the war against al Qaeda through to a successful conclusion. It is also important to note that minimizing casualties is not necessarily a bad thing—it is prudent for any democracy with vast resources to leverage technology to limit casualties so long as minimizing casualties does not become more important than mission accomplishment.

31. Eric V. Larsen, *Casualties and Consensus: The Historical Role of Casualties in Domestic Support for U.S. Military Operations* (Santa Monica, CA: RAND Corporation, 1996), 50–51. While there are similarities between Somalia and Afghanistan, the key difference is that the U.S. has compelling and vital interests at stake in Afghanistan—the elimination of al Qaeda.

32. Charles A. Stevenson, "The Evolving Clinton Doctrine on the Use of Force, *Armed Forces and Society* (Summer 1996), 511–25; and *National Security Strategy of Engagement and Enlargement* (Washington, DC: The White House, Februrary 1995), 12–13.

33. For a discussion of the professionalization and homogenization of Western militaries, see Samuel P. Huntington, *The Soldier and the State: The Theory and Politics of Civil-Military Relations* (Cambridge, MA: The Belknap Press, 1957), 46–65. Some would argue that A. A. Svechin and V. K. Triandafillov are the true-faith apostles of operational art and maneuver warfare. However, Sigismund von Schlichting and Helmuth von Moltke the elder, two Germans, were among the first military thinkers to recognize the shift away from the Napoleonic (Clausewitzian) paradigm that the American Civil War had signaled. See James J. Schneider, *The Structure of Strategic Revolution* (Novato, CA: Presidio Press, 1994), 168–77.

34. Scott E. McIntosh, "Leading With the Chin: Using Svechin to Analyze the Soviet Incursion Into Afghanistan, 1979–1989," *The Journal of Slavic Military Studies* (June 1995), 420.

35. Olivier Roy, *The Lessons of the Soviet/Afghan War*, Adelphi Paper 259 (London: International Institute for Strategic Studies, 1991), 16 and 18. It is hard to miss the similarity, and the concomitant irony, between the names Pavlovsky and Pavlov. In some manner, the Soviet Army in Afghanistan acted like Pavlov's dogs in that it exhibited a previously conditioned response, however inappropriate.

36. Ibid., 18 and 19; and Bernard Expedit, "Les Sovietiques en Afghanistan," in *Strategies de la guerilla: Guerres Revolutionaires et Contre-Insurrections*, Gerard Chaliand (Paris: Gallimard, 1984), 327–29.

37. Daniel P. Bolger, *Savage Peace: Americans at War in the 1990s* (Novato, CA: Presidio Press, 1995), 69.

38. Bolger, "The Ghosts of Omdurman," 28–29.

39. Russell F. Weigley, *The History of the United States Army* (New York: MacMillan Publishing Company, 1967), 161.

40. Sam C. Sarkesian, "The Myth of U.S. Capability in Unconventional Conflicts," *Military Review* (September 1988), 5–8; and Jenkins, 3;

41. Rick Atkinson, *The Long Gray Line* (Boston, MA: Houghton Mifflin Company, 1989), 82; and Peter M. Dunn, "The American Army: The Vietnam War, 1965–1973" in *Armed Forces and Modern Counter-Insurgency*, eds. Ian F. W. Beckett and John Pimlot (New York: St. Martin's Press, Inc., 1985), 84–85.

42. Elliot A. Cohen, "Constraint's on America's Conduct of Small Wars," *International Security* (Fall 1984), 165–68.

43. Andrew F. Krepinevich, *The Army and Vietnam* (Baltimore, MD: Johns Hopkins University Press, 1986), 5. LIC changed to Operations Other Than War (OOTW) in 1993 and the most current doctrinal manuals subsume counterinsurgency and peace operations under the rubric of SOSO. This author finds it ironic that, finally after many years of marginalization by the mainstream army, these types of missions now have an acronym that is descriptive of their perceived value. See Weigley, *The American Way of War*, xxi.

44. Daniel P. Bolger, *Savage Peace*, 69; and Jeffrey Record, *Beyond Military Reform* (New York: Pergamon-Brassey's, 1988), 81. The play on acronyms is from *Savage Peace*.

45. Record, 84–85.

46. General Eric Shinseki, Interview, 14 January 1999, in Howard Olsen and John Davis, "Training U.S. Army Officers for Peace Operations," *Special Report* (Washington, DC: United States Institute of Peace, 1999), 2. Edith B. Wilkie and Beth C. DeGrasse, *A Force for Peace: U.S. Commanders' Views of the Military's Role in Peace Operations* (Washington, DC: Peace Through Law Education Fund, 1999), 40.

Chapter 3

1. Mao Tse-Tung, *On Protracted Warfare* (Peking: Foreign Language Press, 1967), 97.

2. Clifford Geertz, *The Interpretation of Cultures* (New York: Basic Books, 1973), 5, 11, 14, 363.

3. Lucien W. Pye and Sydney Verba, eds., *Political Culture and Political Development* (Princeton, NJ: Princeton University Press, 1965), 8–10, 550.

4. Edgar Schein, "Organizational Culture," *American Psychologist* 45 (February 1990): 111.

5. Jeffrey W. Legro, "Culture and Preferences in the International Cooperation Two-Step," *American Political Science Review* 90 (March 1996): 127; Alan Macmillan, "Strategic Culture and National Ways in Warfare: The British Case," *RUSI Journal* 140 (October 1995): 33 (33–38); and James M. Smith. *USAF Culture and Cohesion: Building an Air Force and Space Force for the 21st* Century, INSS Occasional Paper 19 (Colorado Springs, CO: USAF INSS, 1996), 11–12.

6. Smith, 11–12.

7. James Dewar, et al., *Army Culture and Planning in a Time of Great Change* (Santa Monica, CA: RAND Corporation, 1996), 2–3, 8, 42.

8. Williamson Murray, "Armored Warfare" and "Innovation: Past and Future" in *Military Innovation in the Inter-War Period*, eds. Williamson Murray and Alan R. Millett (New York: Cambridge University Press, 1996), 23 [footnote], 309, and 313.

9. Russell F. Weigley, *The American Way of War* (Bloomington: Indiana University Press, 1973), xvii; Legro, "Military Culture and Inadvertent Escalation in World War II," 112; Schein, 111; Kier, 66; Klein, 5–6, 10, 13; Legro, "Culture and Preferences in the International Cooperation Two-Step," 118, 121; MacMillan, 33; and Lord, 273–74.

10. Henry Kissinger, Landon Lecture, Kansas State University, 29 April 1996.

11. Vernon V. Aspaturian, "Soviet Foreign Policy," in *Foreign Policy in World Politics,* 7th ed. ed. Roy C. Macridis (Englewood Cliffs, NJ: Prentice Hall, 1989), 194–95.

12. Richard Pipes, "Is Russia Still an Enemy?" *Foreign Affairs* 76 (September/October 1997): 68; and Aspaturian, 194.

13. Anthony Clayton, *The End of Empire: The Experience of Britain, France, and the Soviet Union/Russia Compared*, Occasional Number 17 (Camberley, UK: Strategic and

Combat Studies Institute, 1996), 3–4; Paul Kennedy, *The Rise and Fall of the Great Powers* (New York: Random House, 1987), 15–16; Aspaturian, 195; and Pipes, 68.

14. George F. Kennan, "The Sources of Soviet Conduct," *Foreign Affairs* 66 (Summer 1987): 855–56.

15. Kennedy, 93; Henry Kissinger, *Diplomacy* (New York: Simon and Schuster), 173–74.

16. Patrick Brunot and Viatcheslav Avioutski, *La Tchétchenie* (Paris: Presses Universitaires de France, 1998), 11.

17. Robert F. Baumann, *Russian-Soviet Unconventional Wars in the Caucasus, Central Asia, and Afghanistan*, Leavenworth Paper Number 20 (Fort Leavenworth, KS: Combat Studies Institute, 1993), 19.

18. Baumann, 5, 19–22.

19. Baumann, 25, 35–36.

20. Jack L. Snyder, *The Soviet Strategic Culture: Implications for Limited Nuclear Operations* (Santa Monica, CA: RAND Corporation, 1977), 28–31.

21. Snyder, 28–31.

22. David R. Jones, "Soviet Strategic Culture," in *Strategic Power USA/USSR* ed. Carl G. Jacobsen (New York: St. Martin's Press, 1990), 36.

23. Pipes, 68; and Clayton, 6 and 30.

24. William E. Odom and Robert Dujarric, *Commonwealth or Empire?* (Indianapolis: Hudson Institute, 1995), 166–67.

25. Odom and Dujarric, 168–69.

26. Kissinger, *Diplomacy*, 176.

27. Aymeric Chauprade, *Introduction à l'analyse géopolitique* (Paris: Ellipses, 1999), 59–68; Aspaturian, 195. Jean-Christophe Romer, Lecture, French Joint Defense College, 22 January 2001; Kissinger, *Diplomacy*, 174.

28. Condoleezza Rice, "The Making of Soviet Strategy," in *Makers of Modern Strategy*, ed. Peter Paret (Princeton, NJ: Princeton University Press, 1986), 674–75; Aspaturian, 196.

29. Milan Hauner, *The Soviet War in Afghanistan: Patterns of Russian Imperialism* (Philadelphia, PA: University Press of America, 1991), 51–52; Kissinger, *Diplomacy*, 142–43.

30. Halford Mackinder, "The Geographical Pivot of History," *The Geographical Journal* 23 (1904): 423 and 436, cited in Hauner, 11–12. Hauner, 17–18.

31. Kissinger, *Diplomacy*, 140–141, 143–144, 398, 432.

32. Ibid., 172.

33. Baumann, 1; Hauner, 83–84.

34. Andrei P. Tsygankov, "Hardline Eurasianism and Russia's Contending Geopolitical Perspectives," *Eastern European Quarterly* 32 (Fall 1998): 317–20.

35. Walter Pintner, "Russian Military Thought: The Western Model and the Shadow of Suvorov," in *Makers of Modern Stategy*, ed. Peter Paret (Princeton, NJ: Princeton University Press, 1986), 356.

36. Rice, 674.

37. For a discussion of the evolution of war in Europe, see Michael Howard, *War in European History* (New York: Oxford University Press, 1977).

38. Rice, 655, 658, 674, 676.

39. Carl Van Dyke, "Kabul to Grozny: A Critique of Soviet (Russian) Counter-Insurgency Doctrine," *The Journal of Slavic Military Studies* 9 (December 1996): 690–91.

40. John Erickson, "The Development of Soviet Military Doctrine," in *The Origins of Contemporary Doctrine*, ed. John Gooch, Occasional Number 30 (Camberley, UK: Strategic and Combat Studies Institute, 1997), 88–89, 91.

41. Ibid., 81, 88–89, 98–100, 101–103, 105.

42. Scott R. McMichael, "The Soviet Army, Counter-Insurgency, and the Afghan War," *Parameters* 19 (December 1989): 21–22; Olivier Roy, *The Lessons of the Soviet/Afghan War*. Adelphi Paper 259. (London: International Institute for Strategic Studies, 1991), 51–52.

43. Van Dyke, 695–96.

44. Sherman W. Garnett, "Russia and Its Borderlands: A Geography of Violence," *Parameters* 27 (Spring 1997): 6–7.

45. Andrew Mack, "Why Big Powers Lose Small Wars: The Politics of Asymmetric Conflict," in *Power, Strategy, and Security: A World Politics Reader*, ed. Klaus Knorr (Princeton, NJ: Princeton University Press, 1983), 132.

46. B. H. Liddell Hart, *Strategy*, 2nd ed. (New York: Praeger, 1967), 26–27. Also see B. H. Liddell Hart, *The British Way in Warfare* (New York: The Macmillan Company, 1933), 97.

47. Cited in Frontinus, *Strategems and Aqueducts of Rome*, trans. Charles E. Bennett (Cambridge, MA: Harvard University Press, 1997), 67–68.

48. Baumann, 135.

49. Alex Alexiev, *The War in Afghanistan: Soviet Strategy and the State of the Resistance* (Santa Monica, CA: RAND Corporation, 1984), 2–3.

50. Scott E. McIntosh, "Leading With the Chin: Using Svechin to Analyze the Soviet Incursion Into Afghanistan," *The Journal of Slavic Military Studies* 8 (June 1995): 429; Stephen J. Blank, *Afghanistan and Beyond: Reflections on the Future of Warfare* (Carlisle Barracks, PA: Strategic Studies Institute, 1993), 1. Henry Kissinger, "The Vietnam Negotiations," *Foreign Affairs* 47 (January 1969): 214.

51. Gregory J. Celestan, *Wounded Bear: The Ongoing Military Operation in Chechnya* (Fort Leavenworth, KS: Foreign Military Studies Office, 1996), 6. Foreign Military Studies Office hereafter appears as FMSO.

52. Russell F. Weigley, "American Strategy from its Beginnings through the First World War" in *Makers of Modern Strategy*, ed. Peter Paret (Princeton, NJ: Princeton University Press, 1986), 410–11. Ibid., 410–12; and Weigley, *The American Way of War*, 5, 15, 18–19.

53. This explanation is based on Weigley, *The American Way of War*, 34. Weigley discusses this contradiction in the context of another asymmetric conflict—the American Revolution.

54. Mack, 128 and 133; Lester W. Grau, *The Bear Went Over the Mountain: Soviet Combat Tactics in Afghanistan* (Washington, DC: NDU Press, 1996), 205.

55. Grau, *The Bear Went Over the Mountain*, 205–06.

56. McMichael, 31.

57. Joseph W. Collins, "The Soviet-Afghan War: The First Four Years," *Parameters* 14 (Summer 1984): 50–51.

58. Bernard Expedit, "Les Sovietiques en Afghanistan" in *Strategies de la guerilla: Guerres Revolutionaires et Contre-Insurrections*, Gerard Chaliand (Paris: Gallimard, 1984), 327.

59. Robert S. Litwak, "The Soviet Union in Afghanistan" in *Foreign Military Intervention: The Dynamics of Protracted Conflict*, eds. Aeriel E. Levite, Bruce W. Jentleson, and Larry Berman (New York: Columbia University Press, 1992), 84.

60. Roy, 53; Litwak, 84; and Grau, *The Bear Went Over the Mountain*, xix.

61. Mack, 128, 130, 132–33, and 136–39.

62. Roy, 32–33.

63. Mack, 129–30 and Mao, 90.

64. Roy, 15 and 17.

65. Roy, 20 and 32.

66. Ibid., 33.

67. Douglas A. Borer, *Superpowers Defeated: Vietnam and Afghanistan Compared* (London: Frank Cass, 1999), 234–35.

68. Sean J. A. Edwards, *Mars Unmasked: The Changing Face of Urban Operations* (Santa Monica, CA: RAND Corporation, 2000), 73.

69. Anatol Lieven, *Chechnya: Tombstone of Russian Power* (New Haven, CT: Yale University Press, 1999), 324–25 and 336.

70. Timothy Thomas, "The Battle of Grozny: Deadly Classroom for Urban Combat," *Parameters* 29 (Summer 1999): 89–90.

71. Thomas, "Deadly Classroom for Urban Combat," 90; and Edwards, 72–73.

72. Edwards, 73.

73. Patrick Brunot and Viatcheslav Avioutski, *La Tchétchenie* (Paris: Presses Universitaires de France, 1998), 11.

74. Borer, 230–31.

75. Thomas, "Deadly Classroom for Urban Contact," 88, 90–91.

76. Thomas, "Deadly Classroom for Urban Combat," 91.

77. Stasys Knezys and Romanas Sedlickas, *The War in Chechnya* (College Station, TX: Texas University Press, 1999), 116–19.

78. Knezys and Sedlickas, 120; and Edwards, 83, footnote 132.

79. Sean J. A. Edwards, 83; and Knezys and Sedlickas, 106–07.

80. Mao Tse-Tung, *On Protracted Warfare* (Peking: Foreign Language Press, 1967), 65.

81. Liddell Hart, *Strategy*, 365.

82. Mack, "Why Big Nations Lose Small Wars," 138–39.

83. Mao Tse-Tung, *On Guerrilla Warfare*, trans. Samuel B. Griffith (Champaign, IL: University of Illinois Press, 1961), 98; Mack, 138–39; and Liddell Hart, *Strategy*, 366.

84. Mao, *On Guerrilla Warfare*, 68.

85. Baumann, 136, 139, and 149.

86. McMichael, 22.

87. Baumann, 149–50, and 164; Hauner, 92–93.

88. Sun Tzu, *The Art of War*, tran. Samuel B. Griffith (New York: Oxford University Press, 1982), 98.

89. Knezys and Sedlickas, 108.

90. Thomas, "Deadly Classroom for Urban Combat," 95; Lieven, 113–18.

91. Lieven, 114.

92. Knezys and Sedickas, 158–60.

93. Edwards, 73–74.

94. Lieven, 125, 138–41.

95. Ibid., 142.

96. Luttwak, 121–22.

97. Ibid., 121.

98. Thomas, "Deadly Classroom for Urban Combat," 89.

99. John B. Dunlop, *Russia Confronts Chechnya: Roots of a Separatist Conflict* (Cambridge, UK: Cambridge University Press, 1998), 222.

100. Pipes, 71, 74.

101. Lester W. Grau, "Technology and the Second Chechen Campaign: Not All New and Not That Much" in *The Second Chechen War*, ed. Anne Aldis, Occasional Number 40 (London: SCSI, 2000), 101–07.

102. Jeffrey Record, *Beyond Military Reform: American Defense Dilemmas* (New York: Pergamon-Brassey's, 1988), 84–85.

103. Knezys et Sedlickas, 211.

Chapter 4

1. Thomas R. Mockaitis, *British Counterinsurgency, 1919–60* (New York: St. Martin's Press, 1990), 146.

2. Russell F. Weigley, *The American Way of War: A History of United States Military Strategy and Policy* (Bloomington, IN: Indiana University Press, 1973), 5–15 and 18–34. See B. H. Liddell Hart, *The British Way in Warfare* (New York: The Macmillan Company, 1933), 97; and David French, *The British Way in Warfare: 1688–2000* (London: Unwin-Hyman, 1990), 96–97; 116–18.

3. J. Bowyer Bell, "Revolts Against the Crown: The British Response to Imperial Insurgency," *Parameters* 4 (1974): 31, 40–41.

4. Correlli Barnett, *Britain and Her Army: 1509–1970* (New York: William Morrow and Company, 1970, xix; David Chandler and Ian Beckett, eds., *The Oxford History of the British Army* (New York: Oxford University Press, 1996), xv; and Hew Strachan, "The British Way in Warfare," in *The Oxford History of the British Army*, 408.

5. Jock Haswell, *The British Army: A Concise History* (London: Book Club Associates, 1977), 9.

6. Michael Howard, *The Continental Commitment* (Bristol, Great Britain: Western Printing Services Ltd., 1972), 9; Michael Yardley and Dennis Sewell, *A New Model Army* (London: W. H. Allen and Co., 1989), 13–15.

7. Harold R. Winton, *To Change an Army* (Lawrence, KS: University Press of Kansas, 1988), 9–10.

8. French, 133, 138–40.

9. Winton, 9–10 and 232; Colin McInnes, *Hot War, Cold War: The British Army's Way in Warfare 1945–1995* (Washington, DC: Brassey's, 1996), 115; French, 133, 138–41, 144; and Peter Burroughs, "An Unreformed Army," in *The Oxford History of the British Army*, 185.

10. French, 141–43.

11. Ibid. and Daniel P. Bolger, "The Ghosts of Omdurman," *Parameters* 21 (Autumn 1991): 28–31.

12. Bolger, 31; and Kitchener's quotation is from Hew Strachan, *European Armies and the Conduct of War* (London: George Allen and Unwin, 1983), 84, quoted in "The Ghosts of Omdurman," 31.

13. Lyttleton is quoted in Winton's *To Change an Army*, 11.

14. Barnett, 359–61, 367.

15. Yardley and Sewell, 17–20.

16. Williamson Murray, "Armored Warfare: The British, French, and German Experiences" in *Military Innovation in the Interwar Period*, eds. Williamson Murray and Allan R. Millet (New York: Cambridge University Press, 1996), 9–11.

17. Ibid., 9–10.

18. Williamson Murray, "Armored Warfare: The British, French, and German Experiences" in *Military Innovation in the Interwar Period*, eds. Williamson Murray and Allan R. Millet (New York: Cambridge University Press, 1996), 9–12; Winton, 225–26, 229–30.

19. Ibid., 9 and 232; McInnes, 115; David French, 133, 138–41; and Peter Burroughs, "An Unreformed Army," in *The Oxford History of the British Army*, 185.

20. Winton, 174 and 230. In 1931 British Army Chief of the Imperial General Staff Milne authorized the creation of the First Brigade, Royal Tank Corps by joining up the only four tank battalions in the British Army. This sole British armored brigade's purpose was to test tank maneuver concepts and became known as the Tank Brigade.

21. See Winton, French, Chandler and Beckett, Liddell Hart, *When Britain Goes to War: Adaptability and Mobility;* and B. H. Liddell Hart, *The British Way in Warfare* (New York: The Macmillan Company, 1933).

22. Howard, *The Continental Commitment*, 146. McInnes, 4. Michael Dewar, *Brushfire Wars: Minor Campaigns of the British Army Since 1945* (London: Robert Hale, 1990), 15.

23. McInnes, 30.

24. Ibid., 49.

25. Ibid., 49–50.

26. Alun Gwynne Jones, "Training and Doctrine in the British Army Since 1945," in *The Theory and Practice of War*, 315–16, 318.

27. Ibid., 319 and 325.

28. Ibid., 325–26.

29. Keith Jeffrey, "Colonial Warfare 1900–39," in *Warfare in the Twentieth Century: Theory and Practice*, eds. Colin McInnes and G. D. Sheffield (Winchester, MA: Unwin Hyman, Inc., 1988), 31.

30. McInnes, 74–75.

31. Ibid., 111–12.

32. Ibid., 4.

33. Thomas R. Mockaitis, "Low-Intensity Conflict: The British Experience," *Conflict Quarterly* (Winter 1993): 14.

34. David Gates, "The Transformation of the Army 1783–1815," in *The Oxford History of the British Army*, 157–158; and B. H. Liddell Hart, *Strategy*, 2nd ed. (New York: Praeger, 1967), 26–27, 110–11, 115–17.

35. Liddell Hart, *Strategy*, 110–11 and 114–17; and French, 111.

36. French, 111–13; and Liddell Hart, *Strategy*, 110–11 and 115–17.

37. Burroughs, 161–62.

38. Strachan, "The British Way in Warfare," 403–04.

39. Barnett, 324.

40. Cohen, 172–73.

41. Strachan, "The British Way in Warfare," 404–05.

42. Anthony Verrier, *An Army for the Sixties* (London: Secker and Warburg, 1966), 61–62.

43. John Pimlott, "The British Army: The Dhofar Campaign, 1970–1975," in *Armed Forces and Modern Counter-Insurgency*, eds. Ian F. W. Beckett and John Pimlott (New York: St. Martin's Press, Inc., 1985), 16–19.

44. Ibid., 19 and 24.

45. McInnes, 182.

46. Mockaitis, 8 and 10; and Thomas R. Mockaitis, "A New Era of Counter-Insurgency," *The RUSI Journal* 136 (Spring 1991): 75.

47. Mockaitis, "Low-Intensity Conflict: The British Experience," 11; and Ian Beckett, "The Study of Counter-Insurgency: A British Perspective," *Small Wars and Insurgencies* 1 (April 1990): 47–48.

48. Beckett, 48–49.

49. Dewar, 180–81.

50. Barnett, 487–89, 484–85.

51. Dewar, 43–44.

52. Dewar, 15; and John Stone, email correspondence, London, King's College, 26 July 1999.

53. John Strawson, "The Thirty Years Peace," in *The Oxford History of the British Army*, 350–52.

54. McInnis, 149–50; Gavin Bulloch, "Military Doctrine and Counter-Insurgency: A British Perspective," *Parameters* 26 (Summer 1996): 4 ; and Mockaitis, "A New Era of Counter-Insurgency," 75–76.

55. Hew Strachan, "The British Way in Warfare," 408–09; and Strawson, 348.

56. Thomas R. Mockaitis, "A New Era of Counter-Insurgency," 75.

57. Tim Travers, "The Army and the Challenge of War 1914–1918," in *The Oxford History of the British Army*, 210, 212–13; Peter Simkins, "The Four Armies 1914–1918," in *The Oxford History of the British Army*, 236.

58. Dewar, 181–82.

59. Mockaitis, "Low-Intensity Conflict: The British Experience," 10–11; and Mockaitis, "A New Era of Counter-Insurgency," 75.

60. Hew Strachan, *The Politics of the British Army* (New York: Oxford University Press, 1997), 166–71.

61. Bulloch, "The Development of Doctrine for Counter-Insurgency—the British Experience," 21; and John Shy and Thomas W. Collier, "Revolutionary War" in *Makers of Modern Strategy*, ed. Peter Paret (Princeton, NJ: Princeton University Press, 1986), 845.

62. Yardley and Sewell, 37; Winton, 10.

63. Yardley and Sewell, 38–39, 42–43.

64. Strachan, "The British Way in Warfare," 414–15; and Hew Strachan, *The Politics of the British Army*, 196–97.

65. Strachan, *The Politics of the British Army*, 208–09.

66. Strachan, *The Politics of the British Army*, 211–12; McInnes, 49; Murray, 23.

67. Strachan, *The Politics of the British Army*, 214–18 and 223.

68. Strachan, "The British Way in Warfare," 411–14; Strachan, *The Politics of the British Army*, 225–26; and Douglas A. Macgregor, *Breaking the Phalanx: A New Design for Landpower in the 21st Century* (Westport, CT: Praeger, 1997), 89.

69. Murray, 26–28; and Strachan, *The Politics of the British Army*, 232–33.

Chapter 5

1. Anthony James Joes, *America and Guerrilla Warfare* (Lexington, KY: University Press of Kentucky, 2000), 325.

2. For an explanation of this rebirth, see Robert M. Cassidy, "Prophets or Praetorians: The Uptonian Paradox and the Powell Corollary, *Parameters* (Autumn 2003), 132–33.

3. Russell F. Weigley, *Towards an American Army: Military Thought From Washington to Marshall* (New York: Columbia University Press, 1962), viii-ix.

4. Russell F. Weigley, "Reflections on Lessons From Vietnam," in *Vietnam as History*, ed. Peter Braestrup (Washington, DC: University Press of America, 1984), 116.

5. Carl Builder, *The Masks of War: American Military Styles in Strategy and Analysis* (Baltimore, MD: Johns Hopkins University Press, 1989), 38, 185–86; and Weigley, "Reflections on Lessons From Vietnam," 115.

6. Builder, 186–87; and Daniel P. Bolger, "The Ghosts of Omdurman," *Parameters* 21 (Autumn 1991): 34. Bolger refers to the Battle of Omdurman in the Sudan in 1898 as an analogy for the American-led victory against Iraq in 1991. The Battle of Omdurman saw the British handily and brutally defeat their Dervish adversary because the Dervishes decided, as imprudently as Saddam Hussein decided, to fight a European-style conventional war against a European-style army.

7. Daniel P. Bolger, *Savage Peace: Americans at War in the 1990s* (Novato, CA: Presidio Press, 1995), 69–70; Eliot Cohen, "Constraints on America's Conduct of Small Wars," *International Security* 9 (Fall 1984): 167–68.

8. Cohen, 168; and Michael Vlahos, "The End of America's Postwar Ethos," *Foreign Affairs* 66 (Summer 1988): 1101–02, 1105; Weigley, *History of the U.S. Army*, 558, 589.

9. Weigley, "Reflections on Lessons From Vietnam," 115; and Paul H. Herbert, *Deciding What Has to Be Done": General William E. Depuy and the 1976 Edition of FM 100–5, Operations*, Leavenworth Paper, No. 16 (Fort Leavenworth, KS: Combat Studies Institute, U.S. Army CGSC, 1988), 21 and 99.

10. Hugh M. Arnold, "Official Justifications for America's Role in Indochina, 1949–67," *Asian Affairs* (September/October 1975): 31 in Harry G. Summers, Jr., *On Strategy: A Critical Analysis of the Vietnam War* (Novato, CA: Presidio Press, 1982), 98; and Stephen J. Mariano, "Peacekeepers Attend the Never Again School," (unpublished master's thesis, Naval Postgraduate School, 1995), 2, 6, 50–51; and Casper Weinberger, "The Uses of Military Power," News Release 609–84 (Washington, DC: Office of the Assistant Secretary of Defense for Public Affairs, November 1984). Mariano explains the "Never Again School" as the core of the post-Vietnam army culture although it stems from the Korean War experience. It describes the actions that political and military leaders should never again take in the conduct of war and foreign policy—essentially those actions that prevent the military from using overwhelming force in the pursuit of decisive victory, in other words, the World War II model.

11. Loren B. Thompson, ed., *Low-Intensity Conflict: The Pattern of Warfare in the Modern World* (Lexington, MA: Lexington Books, 1989), x; John Nagl, "Learning to Eat Soup With a Knife: British and American Counterinsurgency During the Malayan Emergency and the Vietnam War, Ph.D. dissertation, Oxford University, 1997, 252; and Richard Duncan Downie, *Learning from Conflict: The U.S. Military in Vietnam, El Salvador, and the Drug War* (Westport, CT: Praeger, 1998), 167.

12. William Head and Earl H. Tilford, Jr., eds., *The Eagle in the Desert* (Westport, CT: Praeger, 1996), 5, 11; Nagl, 253; and Cori Dauber, "Poisoning the Well: The Weinberger Doctrine and Public Argument Over Military Intervention" (unpublished paper, UNC Chapel Hill, 1998), 7–8, 23.

13. Russell F. Weigley, "American Strategy From Its Beginnings Through the First World War" in *Makers of Modern Strategy*, ed. Peter Paret (Princeton, NJ: Princeton University Press, 1986), 408.

14. Ibid., 409.

15. Ibid., 410–12; and Russell F. Weigley, *The American Way of War: A History of United States Military Strategy and Policy* (Bloomington, IN: Indiana University Press, 1973), 5, 15, 18–19.

16. Weigley, "American Strategy From Its Beginnings Through the First World War," 411; and Weigley, *The American Way of War*, 36.

17. Weigley, *The History of the United States Army*, 160–61.

18. Weigley, *Towards an American Army*, 78 and 47.

19. Weigley, *Towards an American Army*, 78 and 101; John Winthrop Hackett, *The Profession of Arms* (London: The Times Publishing House, 1962), 38.

20. Samuel P. Huntington, *The Soldier and the State* (Cambridge, MA: The Belknap Press, 1957), 232–35.

21. Ibid., 235; and Weigley, *History of the United States Army*, 272–73.

22. Weigley, *History of the United States Army*, 273–75.

23. Ibid., 278–81.

24. Huntington, 232–34; and Stephen F. Ambrose, *Upton and the Army* (Baton Rouge, LA: Louisiana State University Press, 1964), 96 and 122.

25. Emory Upton, *The Military Policy of the United States* (Washington: 1904), 305, 318 and Alvin Brown, *The Armor of Organization* (New York: 1953), 191–92 in *Upton and the Army*, 131–32.

26. Deborah D. Avant, *Political Institutions and Military Change: Lessons From Peripheral Wars* (Ithaca, NY: Cornell University Press, 1994), 27.

27. Ibid, 28–29; Huntington, 226–34.

28. Robert M. Utley, "The Contribution of the Frontier to the American Military Tradition," *The Harmon Memorial Lecture Series Number 19* (Colorado Springs, CO: USAF Academy, 1977), 3–5.

29. Ibid., 5–6.

30. Ibid., 8–10; and Weigley, *The American Way of War*, 19, 159.

31. Weigley, *Towards An American Army*, 167–71.

32. Maurice Matloff, "The American Approach to War: 1919–1945," in *The Theory and Practice of War*, ed. Michael Howard (New York: Praeger, 1966), 215–17.

33. Russell F. Weigley, *Eisenhower's Lieutenants, Volume I* (Baltimore: Johns Hopkins University Press, 1981), 4 and 7.

34. Matloff, 219 and 223.

35. Ibid., 230, 234–35.

36. Henry Kissinger, "American Strategic Doctrine and Diplomacy," in *The Theory and Practice of War*, ed. Michael Howard (New York: Praeger, 1966), 279; and David T. Fautua, "The Long Pull Army: NSC 68, the Korean War, and the Creation of the Cold War U.S. Army," *The Journal of Military History* 61 (January 1997): 95–98.

37. Weigley, *Eisenhower's Lieutenants, Volume I*, 2–3.

38. Weigley, *Eisenhower's Lieutenants, Volume I*, 4–5 and 7.

39. Ibid., 9–10; and Robert A. Doughty, *The Evolution of U.S. Army Tactical Doctrine, 1946–76*, Leavenworth Paper No. 1 (Ft Leavenworth, KS: U.S. Army CGSC, 1979), 2.

40. Bernard, *Brodie, War and Politics* (New York: Macmillan Publishing Company, 1973), 10; and Michael I. Handel, *Masters of War: Sun Tzu, Clausewitz, and Jomini* (Portland, OR: Frank Cass and Co. Ltd., 1992), 161. According to Handel, a Jominian approach separates politics and strategy, which are viewed as independent fields of activity. This approach is manifest in U.S. Army, *The Principles of Strategy for an Independent Corps or Army in a Theater of Operations* (Fort Leavenworth, KS: Command and General Staff School, 1936), 19. In an explanation of politics and the conduct of war, this manual explains: "Policy and strategy are radically and fundamentally things apart." It also maintains that strategy starts where politics stops. "All that soldiers ask is that once the policy is settled, strategy and command shall be regarded as being in a sphere apart from politics." Peter M. Dunn, "The American Army: The Vietnam War, 1965–1973" in *Armed Forces and Modern Counter-Insurgency*, eds. Ian Beckett and John Pimlott (New York: St. Martin's Press, Inc., 1985), 99.

41. Thomas K. Adams, "Military Doctrine and the Organization Culture of the U.S. Army" (Ph.D. dissertation, Syracuse University, 1990), 27; John Nagl, "Learning to Eat Soup With a Knife," *World Affairs* 161 (Spring 1999): 195; and Dauber, 41–43.

42. General Fred C. Weyand and LTC Harry G. Summers, Jr., "Vietnam Myths and American Realities," *CDRS CALL* (Ft Leavenworth, KS: U.S. Army CGSC, July–August 1976), 3.

43. James Dewar, Debra August, Carl Builder, et al., *Army Culture and Planning in a Time of Great Change* (Santa Monica, CA: RAND Corporation, 1996), 28.

44. James B. Motley, "U.S. Unconventional Conflict Policy and Strategy," *Military Review* 70 (January 1990): 10; Cohen, 168–71; Vlahos, 1105; and Dewar, August, Builder, et al., 16, 23–25.

45. Dewar, August, Builder, et al., 26–28.

46. Dewar, August, Builder, et al., 28; and Brian M. Jenkins, *The Unchangeable War* RM-6278-2-ARPA (Santa Monica, CA: RAND Corporation, 1970), 3–4.

47. Jenkins, 2, 6–7.

48. Richard H. Shultz, Jr., *The Secret War Against Hanoi* (New York: HarperCollins Publishers, Inc., 1999), 269–70.

49. Ibid., 269.

50. Weigley, "Reflections on Lessons From Vietnam," 115; and Michael J. Brady, "The Army and the Strategic Military Legacy of Vietnam," master's thesis, U.S. Army CGSC, 1990, 110.

51. The BDM study concluded that the U.S. Army still did not know how to do low-intensity conflict because the strategic lesson the United States learned from Vietnam was that intervention was to be avoided. The report also maintained that the U.S. military's traditional separation between military and political means significantly hindered the effective employment of military force in accomplishing objectives established by the political leadership. It criticized the American paradigm of war aimed at the destruction of enemy forces while ignoring other complex and relevant political factors. See The BDM Corporation, *A Study of the Strategic Lessons in Vietnam, Volume III Results of the War* (Washington, DC: Defense Technical Information Center, 1981), Executive

Summary, 4-3-4-14, and 4–22; Downie, 73; Brady, 250–91; and Department of History, *Officer's Professional Reading Guide* (West Point, NY: United States Military Academy, 1996), 28.

52. Dauber, 7 and 23; Colin Powell, *My American Journey* (New York, Random House, 1995), 567–68, 487; and Rick Atkinson, *Crusade: The Untold Story of the Persian Gulf War* (New York: Houghton Mifflin Company, 1993), 122.

53. Dauber, 7, 23; Powell, 567–68, 487; Atkinson, 122; Colin Powell, "National Military Strategy of the United States" (Washington, DC: United States Department of Defense, 1992), 10; and F. G. Hoffman, *Decisive Force: The New American Way of War* (Westport, CT: Praeger, 1996), xii.

54. Weigley, *The History of the United States Army*, 161.

55. Richard H. Shultz, Jr., "Doctrine and Forces for Low Intensity Conflict" in *The United States Army: Challenges and Missions for the 1990s*, eds. Robert L. Pfaltzgraff and Richard H. Shultz, Jr. (Lexington, MA: Lexington Books, 1991), 119–20 and 127; Ian Beckett and John Pimlott, eds., *Armed Forces and Modern Counter-Insurgency* (New York: St. Martin's Press, Inc., 1985), 7. The quote attributed to the anonymous general is attributed to C. B. Currey, *Self-Destruction: The Disintegration and Decay of the U.S. Army During the Vietnam War* (New York: W. W. Norton, 1981), 60. This is also quoted in *The Unchangeable War*, 3.

56. Dennis J. Vetock, *Lessons Learned: A History of U.S. Army Lesson Learning* (Carlisle Barracks, PA: U.S. Army Military History Institute, 1988), 119–20.

57. Ibid., 120.

58. Downie, 71–73.

59. Robert H. Kupperman and Associates, Inc., *Low Intensity Conflict, Vol. 1, Main Report*, AD-A 137260 (Fort Monroe, VA: U.S. Army TRADOC, 1983), iv, vi-vii.

60. Downie, 70.

61. Andrew F. Krepinievich, *The Army and Vietnam* (Baltimore, MD: Johns Hopkins Univeristy Press, 1986), 259 and 271; and Mariano, 2.

62. Kupperman and Associates, Inc., Executive Summary; and Downie, 75 and 78.

63. David R. Segal and Dana P. Eyre, "The U.S. Army in Peace Operations at the Dawn of the Twenty-First Century," Report (Draft) prepared for the U.S. Army Research Institute for the Behavioral and Social Sciences, 1994, 63–64; Bolger, *Savage Peace*, 69. Department of Defense Directive Number 3000.ccE, ASD (SO/LIC), Draft, Washington, DC, 28 February 2005, 2.

64. Dauber, 7, 23; Powell, *My American Journey*, 567–68, 487; Atkinson, *Crusade* 122; Powell, "National Military Strategy of the United States," 10; and F. G. Hoffman, *Decisive Force: The New American Way of War* (Westport, CT: Praeger, 1996), xii.

65. Samuel P. Huntington, "The Evolution of U.S. National Strategy" in *U.S. National Security Strategy for the 1990s*, eds. Daniel J. Kaufman, David S. Clark, and Kevin P. Sheehan (Baltimore: Johns Hopkins University Press, 1991), 17; and Weigley, *Eisenhower's Lieutenants, Volume 1*, 3–4 and 6–7.

66. Krepinevich, 5; and Weigley, *The American Way of War*, xxi.

67. Thomas R. Mockaitis, "A New Era of COIN," *The RUSI Journal* 136 (September 1991): 77–78. Although Mockaitis' endnote 23 references this excerpt as being from page 2–19, it is actually on page 2–10 of the 1990 manual. See *Field Manual 100–20: Military Operations in Low Intensity Conflict* (Washington, DC: U.S. Army and U.S. Air Force, 1990), 2–10.

68. Weigley, *History of the United States Army*, 334–35; John B. Wilson, *Maneuver and Firepower: The Evolution of Divisions and Separate Brigades* (Washington, DC: U.S. Army Center of Military History, 1998), 33–34; and Doughty, 1.

69. Doughty, 16; and Wilson, 415.

70. Kupperman and Associates, Inc., 47; Downie, 75–77; John L. Romjue, *The Army of Excellence: The Development of the 1980s Army* (Fort Monroe, VA: U.S. Army TRADOC Military History Office, 1997), 119; Peter N. Kafkalas, "The Light Infantry Divisions and Low Intensity Conflict: Are They Losing Sight of Each Other?" *Military Review* 66 (January 1986): 18–27 in *The Army of Excellence*, 119; and Doughty, 48.

71. Dewar, August, Builder, et al., 16 and 28–29; Weigley, *The History of the United States Army*, 330–40; and Douglas A. Macgregor, *Breaking the Phalanx: A New Design for Landpower in the 21st Century* (Westport, CT: Praeger, 1997), 50.

72. Dewar, August, Builder, et al., 16 and 28–29; and Macgregor, 62 and 227.

73. Attributed to an anonymous U.S. general, cited in Jenkins, *The Unchangeable War*, 6.

74. Weigley, *The History of the United States Army*, 589.

Chapter 6

1. Robert M. Utley, *Frontiersmen in Blue* (New York: Macmillan Company, 1967), 8.

2. Attributed to Otto von Bismarck and cited in Colonel Samuel B. Griffith, II, "Guerrilla, Part I," *Marine Corps Gazette* (July 1950), 43.

3. The use of the word indigenous herein simply connotes forces comprising troops from the native populations of the region. In cases, where the state or region is multi-ethnic or multi-tribal, this term applies to all those local people who offer the potential to serve as trained auxiliaries to the government forces, their supporting allies, or with the occupation forces.

4. *FMI (Field Manual Interim) 3–07.22, Counterinsurgency Operations* (Washington, D.C.: Department of the Army, October 2004), 1–10 and 3–8.

5. For example, two of the more prominent British works were Charles C. E. Callwell's *Small Wars: Their Principles and Practice* (London: His Majesty's Stationary Office, 1896) and Sir Charles W. Gwynn's *Imperial Policing* (London: Macmillan and Company, 193. On French counterinsurgency theory, *Modern Warfare: a French View of Counterinsurgency* (London: Pall Mall Press Ltd., 1964), by Roger Trinquier, a French counterinsurgency theorist and veteran of both Indochina and Algeria, was republished and is available online at the Combat Studies Institute site at Fort Leavenworth, home of the U.S. Army Command and General Staff College.

6. Utley, *Frontiersmen in Blue*, 2, and 6–8.

7. Andrew J. Birtle, *U.S. Army Counterinsurgency and Contingency Operations Doctrine 1860–1941* (Washington, D.C.: U.S. Army Center of Military History, 1998), 63–66, 69–70, and 83–85; and Robert M. Utley, *The Contribution of the Frontier to the American Military Tradition*, The Harmon Memorial Lecture Series in Military History Number 19 (Colorado: U.S. Air Force Academy, 1977), 6–7.

8. Robert M. Utley, *Frontier Regulars: The United States Army and the Indian, 1866–1890* (New York: Macmillan Publishing Co., Inc., 1973), 53–55 and 185.

9. Birtle, 68–69 and 83–85.

10. Anthony James Joes, *America and Guerrilla Warfare* (Lexington, KY: University Press of Kentucky, 2000), 120–23.

11. Brian McAllister Linn, "The U.S. Army and Nation Building and Pacification in the Philippines," in *Armed Diplomacy: Two Centuries of American Campaigning* (Fort Leavenworth, KS: U.S. Army TRADOC and the Combat Studies Institute, 2003), 84–87.

12. Max Boot, *Savage Wars of Peace: Small Wars and the Rise of American Power* (New York: Basic Books, 2003), 118–19 and 126–28; and Joes, 123.

13. Birtle, 114–17 and Boot, 127–28.

14. U.S. Marine Corps, *Small Wars Manual* (Washington, DC: Government Printing Office, 1940), 1-1-1-31; and Max Boot, "A Century of Small Wars Shows They Can be Won," *New York Times Week in Review*, 6 July 2003.

15. 1940 *Small Wars Manual*, 1-1-1-31; Max Boot, "A Century of Small Wars;" Joes, 141–42; and Boot, *Savage Wars of Peace*, 244–46. See James Donovan, "Combined Action Program: Marines' Alternative to Search and Destroy," *Vietnam Magazine*, August 2004, page 30, for an explanation of how the Marines' experience in Haiti, the Dominican Republic, and Nicaragua served as the conceptual basis for CAP.

16. David C. Brooks, "U.S. Marines, Miskitos and the Hunt for Sandino: The Rio Coco Patrol in 1928," *Journal of Latin American Studies* 21 (May 1989), 311, 316, 318, 323, and 338; Harold H. Utley, "An Introduction to the Tactics and Techniques of Small Wars," *The Marine Corps Gazette* 18 (August 1933), 45–46; and David C. Brooks, "U.S. Marines and Miskito Indians: The Rio Coco Patrol of 1928," *Marine Corps Gazette* 80 (November 1996), 67–68.

17. *A Program for the Pacification and Long-Term Development of South Vietnam* (Washington, DC: Department of the Army, 1966), 1–9, hereafter, *PROVN*. Lewis Sorley, *A Better War* (New York: Harcourt Brace & Company, 1999), 10–125.

18. Sorley, 22–23 and 64–67.

19. Tran Dinh Tho, *Pacification* (Washington, DC: U.S. Army Center of Military History, 1997), 70 and 135. The "Chieu Hoi," or "Open Arms," Program was a psychological operation in Vietnam with two objectives: to induce Viet Cong defections and to increase the solidarity of South Vietnam's citizens in support of the government. Also, see Sorley, 22–23, 64–67, 72–73, and 217–24.

20. Frank Pelli, "Insurgency, Counterinsurgency, and the Marines in Vietnam," unpublished paper, USMC Command and Staff College, Quantico, VA, 1990, 13–16; and Brooks R. Brewington, "Combined Action Platoons: A Strategy for Peace Enforcement," unpublished paper, USMC Command and Staff College, Quantico, VA, 1996, 13–19.

21. Jeffrey J. Clarke, *Advice and Support: The Final Years* (Washington: U.S. Army Center of Military History, 1988), 196 and 203–206; and Francis J. Kelley, *U.S. Army Special Forces 1961–1971* (Washington, D.C.: Department of the Army, 2004), 19, 32–33.

22. Clarke, *Advice and Support, 203–06*; and Kelley, *U.S. Army Special Forces 1961–1971*, 14, 35, 46, 90, and 137. Project Delta was the first special operations unit that combined Special Forces and irregulars. Roadrunner teams conducted long-distance reconnaissance over enemy trail networks.

23. Kevin Stringer, Ph.D., contributed this section on the Anglo experience.

24. Bert H. Cooper, Jr., Chapter 2 "Malaya (1948–1960)" in *History of Revolutionary Warfare, Volume IV,* eds. H. M. Hannon, R. S. Ballagh, and J. A. Cope (West Point, NY: United States Military Academy Department of History, 1984), 2–23; Sir Robert Thompson, "Emergency in Malaya" in *War in Peace; Conventional and Guerrilla Warfare since 1945,* ed. Sir Robert Thompson (New York: Harmony Books, 1982), 89.

25. Cooper, "Malaya" in *History of Revolutionary Warfare,* 2-27-2-28. See H. P. Willmott, "Mau Mau Terror" in *War in Peace: Conventional and Guerrilla Warfare since 1945,* 113.

26. Lawrence E. Cline, *Pseudo Operations and Counterinsurgency: Lessons from Other Countries* (Carlisle, PA: Strategic Studied Institute, 2005), 8–11.

27. Barbara Cole, *The Elite: The Story of the Rhodesian Special Air Service* (Transkei, South Africa: Three Knights, 1985), 89–90. See Bruce Hoffmann, Jennifer Taw, and David Arnold, *Lessons for Contemporary Counterinsurgencies: The Rhodesian Experience* (Santa Monica: RAND Corporation, 1991), 47; The definitive book on the Selous Scouts is by their founder and commander Lieutenant Colonel Ron Reid-Daly. R. F. Reid-Daly, *Pamwe Chete: The Legend of the Selous Scouts* (Weltevreden Park, South Africa: Covos-Day Books, 1999).

28. Lt.Col. Ron Reid-Daly, *Selous Scouts, Top Secret War* (Galago, RSA, 1982), 175–81; See Robin Moore, Rhodesia (New York: Condor, 1977), 127; and R. F. Reid-Daly, *The Legend of the Selous Scouts,* ii. Also, see Captain James K. Bruton, Jr., USA, "Counterinsurgency in Rhodesia," *Military Review* 59 (March 1979), 26–39.

29. The ALN acronym is from the Francophone term *Armée de Libération Nationale.* The FLN, or the *Front de Libération Nationale,* was the Francophone term for the National Liberation Front, which was the political entity that directed the Algerian insurgents' operations.

30. Douglas Porch, *The French Foreign Legion* (New York: Harper Collins Publishers, 1991), 525 and 546–47. BEP is the French Foreign Legion acronym for *bataillon étranger de parachutistes.*

31. Lawrence E. Cline, *Pseudo Operations and Counterinsurgency: Lessons From Other Countries* (Carlisle, PA: Strategic Studied Institute, 2005), 6–7; Bernard B. Fall, *Street Without Joy* (New York: Schocken Books, 1961), 275–79 and 97.

32. Porch, 550–51.

33. Ibid., 553–54.

34. Ibid., 551–54 and 543.

35. Peter Paret, *French Revolutionary Warfare from Indochina to Algeria* (New York: Praeger, 1964), 100–02 and 26–27. On pages 23–32, Paret offers a lucid and distilled explanation of the French doctrine of *guerre révolutionnaire.*

36. Ibid., 28–30, 23, and 9–10.

37. Ibid., 35 and 40–41. Harka is from the Arabic word for troop or band of warriors and was the generic Algerian term for Muslim Algerians serving as auxiliaries with the French Army during the Algerian War. Since Algerian independence, the term 'Harki' has been used as a derogatory term for collaborator. The term 'Harka' is used throughout Peter Paret's 1964 *French Revolutionary Warfare from Indochina to Algeria. Quadrillage* was the French Army term for their system of checkerboard garrisons and fortified posts, designed to impose a network of close territorial control in the greater part of Algeria north of the Sahara. It derived from the French verb *quadriller,* which means to mark out in squares and to keep under tight control. The term makhzan was the Moroccon term for the

Sultan's administration and it stems from the French policy in Morocco during the Lyautey era that distinguished between those under government control—makhzan—and those who were not. It came to mean collaborators or colonial (indigenous) soldiers in the Algerian context.

38. Alistair Horne, *A Savage War of Peace* (London: Macmillan London Limited, 1977), 108–09 and 220.

39. Ibid., 251–61.

40. Ibid., 255–61. In English, the GRE translates into the Intelligence and Exploitation Group.

41. Paret, *French Revolutionary Warfare*, 27–28 and 40–41.

42. Gordon M. Wells, *The Center of Gravity Fad: Consequence of the Absence of an Overarching American Theory of* War, Landpower Essay Number 01-01 (Arlington, VA: AUSA Institute of Land Warfare, March 2001), 3.

43. Barbara Tuchman, *The March of Folly: From Troy to Vietnam* (New York: Ballantine Books, 1984), 297.

44. The two paradigmatic changes in warfare since Clausewitz were (1) the emergence of the operational art with its attendant distributed maneuver of formations in time and space during the last year of the American Civil War; and (2) the diminished salience of industrial era conventional war and the concomitant increase in transnational insurgency by globally networked actors since the end of the Cold War. For a more complete explanation of the influence of Newton and Descartes, see Fritjof Capra, *The Web of Life* (New York: Anchor Books, 1996): 19–20.

45. Brian Michael Jenkins, "Redefining the Enemy: The World Has Changed, but Our Mindset Has Not," *RAND Review*, 28 (Spring 2004), 16.

46. William S. Lind, et al., "The Changing Face of War: Into the Fourth Generation," abridged, *Marine Corps Gazette*, October 1989, 25–26; Jenkins, "Redefining the Enemy," 23.

47. John Keegan, A *History of Warfare* (New York: Vintage Books, 1993), 244; David Tucker, "Fighting Barbarians," *Parameters*, 28 (Summer 1998), 69; and Hans Delbruck, *The Barbarian Invasions*, trans., Walter J. Renfroe, Jr. (Lincoln: University of Nebraska Press, 1980), 95.

48. Russell F. Weigley, *Eisenhower's Lieutenants, Volume I* (Baltimore: Johns Hopkins University Press, 1981), 2–3, 4 and 7.

49. Ivan Arreguin-Toft, "How the Weak Win Wars: A Theory of Asymmetric Conflict," *International Security* (Summer 2001), 106; and Robert H. Scales, "Adaptive Enemies: Achieving Victory by Avoiding Defeat," *Joint Forces Quarterly* (Autumn/Winter 1999–2000), 7 and 13.

50. Max Boot, "The Lessons of a Quagmire," *The New York Times*, 16 November 2003; David M. Toczek, *The Battle of Ap Bac, Vietnam: They Did Everything but Learn From it* (Westport: Greenwood Press, 2001), 25; and Thomas Donnelly and Vance Serchuk, "Fighting a Global Counterinsurgency," *National Security Outlook*, American Enterprise Institute Online, 2.

51. *PROVN*, 2–4.

52. *PROVN*, 4.

53. *PROVN*, 8–9.

54. *PROVN*, this information partly comes from the charts on pages 11–12 of the study. For these objectives, see pages 15–23 of *PROVN*. The "Chieu Hoi," or "Open

Arms," Program was a psychological operation in Vietnam with two objectives: to induce Viet Cong defections and to increase the solidarity of South Vietnam's citizens in support of the government.

55. Bernard B. Fall, "The Theory and Practice of Insurgency and Counterinsurgency," *Naval War College Review* (Winter 1998), online version, 4–9; Commander in Chief Far East, *Lessons of the War in Indochina, Volume 2*, trans. V. J. Croizat, Memorandum RM-5271-PR (Santa Monica, CA: RAND Corporation, 1967), 110–111 and 113.

56. Tuchman, 300.

57. Cited in Rowan Scarborough, "Metrics Help Guide Pentagon," *Washington Times*, 5 April 2005, 3.

58. Bikram Singh, "Touchstones of Military Leadership Engaged in Asymmetric Warfare," unpublished research paper, U.S. Army War College, Carlisle Barracks. PA, March 2004, 12–14, 20.

59. Duffy W. White, "Beneficial or Buzzword: Can Operational Commanders Use Measures of Effectiveness During Counterinsurgencies?" unpublished paper, U.S. Naval War College, Newport, RI, May 2004, 13–15.

60. Center for Strategic and International Studies (CSIS) and the Association of the U.S. Army (AUSA), *Task Framework*, Post-Conflict Reconstruction, A joint project of the CSIS and AUSA, Washington, DC, May 2002, 3.

61. Christian Lowe, "DOD Seeks Benchmarks for War on Terror," *Defense News*, 14 March 2005, 4; Center for Emerging Threats and Opportunities (CETO), *CETO Quick Look: Dealing with the Civilian Population in Post-Saddam Iraq*, 6 February 2003, 7; Joseph Anderson, "Military Operational Measures of Effectiveness for Peacekeeping Operations," *Military Review* 36 (September–October 2001), 37 and 42–44; and Robert H. Kellog, "Evaluating Psychological Operations: Planning Measures of Effectiveness," *Special Warfare* (May 2004), online, 2.

62. Larry Cable, "Reinventing the Round Wheel: Insurgency, Counterinsurgency, and Peacekeeping Post Cold War," *Small Wars and Insurgencies* 4 (Autumn 1993), 231.

63. Peter Paret and John W. Shy, *Guerrillas in the 1960's* (New York: Frederick A. Praeger Publishers, 1962), 73–74.

64. Brooks, "U.S. Marines, Miskitos and the Hunt for Sandino," 330–31 and 341–42; Clarke, 207; and Keith F. Kopets, "The Combined Action Program: Vietnam," *Military Review* (July–August 2002), 78–79.

65. Cited in Matt Kelley, "U.S. Intelligence Effort Lacking in Specialists," *San Diego Union-Tribune*, 22 November 2003, 1.

66. For an insightful discussion of CJTF-HOA, see Robert D. Kaplan, *Imperial Grunts: The American Military on the Ground* (New York: Random House, 2005), 6, 171, 273–305.

67. For a complete explanation of legitimacy and the credible capacity to coerce, see Larry Cable, "Reinventing the Round Wheel: Insurgency, Counter-Insurgency, and Peacekeeping Post Cold War." *Small Wars and Insurgencies* 4 (Autumn 1993): 228–62.

Bibliography

Aboul-Enein, Youssef H. and Sherifa Zuhur. *Islamic Rulings on Warfare*. Carlisle, PA: U.S. Army War College Strategic Studies Institute, 2004.

Adams, Thomas K. "Military Doctrine and the Organization Culture of the U.S. Army." Ph.D. dissertation, Syracuse University, 1990.

Alexander, John B. "The Evolution of Conflict Through 2020: Demands on Personnel, Machines, and Equipment." Unpublished Joint Special Operations University Paper prepared for the Conference on "The Changing Nature of Warfare" in support of the "Global Trends 2020" Project of the U.S. National Intelligence Council, May 2004, 1.

Alexander, Martin S. and J. F. V. Keiger. "France and the Algerian War: Strategy, Operations and Diplomacy." *Journal of Strategic Studies* (June 2002): 1–33.

Alexiev, Alex. *The War in Afghanistan: Soviet Strategy and the State of the Resistance*. Santa Monica, CA: RAND Corporation, 1984.

Allison, Graham T. *Essence of Decision: Explaining the Cuban Missile Crisis*. Boston: Little, Brown, and Company, 1971.

Alvis, Michael W. "Understanding the Role of Casualties in U.S. Peace Operations." *Landpower Essay Series No. 99-1*. Arlington, VA: Association of the U.S. Army, January 1999.

Ambrose, Stephen F. *Upton and the Army*. Baton Rouge, LA: Louisiana State University Press, 1964.

Anderson, Joseph. "Military Operational Measures of Effectiveness for Peacekeeping Operations." *Military Review* (September–October 2001): 37–44.

Applegate, Melissa. *Preparing for Asymmetry: As Seen Through the Lens of Joint Vision 2020*. Carlisle Barracks, PA: Strategic Studies Institute, September 2001, 15.

Army Doctrine Publication, Volume 1, Operations. London: HMSO, June 1994: 105–9.

Army Field Manual, Volume V, Operations Other Than War. London: HMSO, 1995.

Arreguin-Toft, Ivan. "How the Weak Win Wars: A Theory of Asymmetric Conflict." *International Security* (Summer 2001): 106.

Aspaturian, Vernon V. "Soviet Foreign Policy," in *Foreign Policy in World Politics*, 7th ed., ed. Roy C. Macridis. Englewood Cliffs, NJ: Prentice Hall, 1989.

Atkinson, Rick. *The Long Gray Line*. Boston, MA: Houghton Mifflin Company, 1989.

————. *Crusade: The Untold Story of the Persian Gulf War*. New York: Houghton Mifflin Company, 1993.

————. "The Raid That Went Wrong." *Washington Post*, 30 January 1994, A1.

————. "Night of a Thousand Casualties," *Washington Post*, 31 January 1994.

Avant, Deborah D. *Political Institutions and Military Change: Lessons From Peripheral Wars*. Ithaca, NY: Cornell University Press, 1994.

Barnett, Correlli. *Britain and Her Army: 1509–1970*. New York: William Morrow and Company, 1970.

Barnett, Thomas P. M. "The Pentagon's New Map." *Esquire* (March 2003).

Baumann, Robert F. *Russian-Soviet Unconventional Wars in the Caucasus, Central Asia, and Afghanistan*, Leavenworth Paper Number 20. Fort Leavenworth, KS: Combat Studies Institute, 1993.

BDM Corporation. *A Study of the Strategic Lessons in Vietnam, Volume III Results of the War*. Washington, DC: Defense Technical Information Center, 1981.

Beckett, Ian. "The Study of Counter-Insurgency: A British Perspective." *Small Wars and Insurgencies* (April 1990): 47–53.

Beckett, Ian and John Pimlott, eds. *Armed Forces and Modern Counter-Insurgency*. New York: St. Martin's Press, Inc., 1985.

Bell, J. Bowyer. "Revolts Against the Crown: The British Response to Imperial Insurgency." *Parameters* 4 (1974): 31–46.

Bernard, Cheryl. "Five Pillars of Democracy: How the West Can Promote an Islamic Transformation." *RAND Review* (Spring 2004): 10–11.

Birtle, Andrew J. *U.S. Counterinsurgency and Contingency Operations Doctrine 1860–1941*. Washington, DC: U.S. Army Center of Military History, 1998.

Blank, Stephen J. *Afghanistan and Beyond: Reflections on the Future of Warfare*. Carlisle Barracks, PA: Strategic Studies Institute, 1993.

Bolger, Daniel P. "The Ghosts of Omdurman." *Parameters* (Autumn 1991): 28–39.

————. *Savage Peace: Americans at War in the 1990s*. Novato, CA: Presidio Press, 1995.

Boot, Max. *Savage Wars of Peace: Small Wars and the Rise of American Power*. New York: Basic Books, 2003.

————. "A Century of Small Wars Shows They Can be Won." *New York Times Week in Review*, 6 July 2003.

————. "The Lessons of a Quagmire." *New York Times*, 16 November 2003.

Booth, Ken. *Strategy and Ethnocentrism*. New York: Holmes and Meier Publishers, Inc., 1979.

————. "The Concept of Strategic Culture Affirmed," in *Strategic Power USA/USSR*, ed. Carl G. Jacobsen. New York: St. Martin's Press, 1990.

de Borchgrave, Arnaud. "Al Qaeda's Privileged Sanctuary." *Washington Times*, 20 June 2002, 19.

————. "Iran's Strategy." *Washington Times*, 18 August 2005.

Borer, Douglas A. *Superpowers Defeated: Vietnam and Afghanistan Compared*. London: Frank Cass, 1999.

Bowden, Mark. *Black Hawk Down*. New York: Penguin Books, 1999.

Brady, Michael J. "The Army and the Strategic Military Legacy of Vietnam." Master's Thesis. U.S. Army Command and General Staff College, 1990.

Braestrup, Peter, ed. *Vietnam as History.* Washington, DC: University Press of America, 1984.

Brewington, Brooks R. "Combined Action Platoons: A Strategy for Peace Enforcement." Unpublished Paper. Quantico, VA: USMC Command and Staff College, 1996.

Brodie, Bernard. *War and Politics.* New York: Macmillan Publishing Company, 1973.

Brooks, David C. "U.S. Marines, Miskitos and the Hunt for Sandino: The Rio Coco Patrol in 1928." *Journal of Latin American Studies* (May 1989): 311–38.

Brooks, David C. "U.S. Marines and Miskito Indians: The Rio Coco Patrol of 1928." *Marine Corps Gazette* (November 1996): 67–68.

Bruton, James K., Jr. "Counterinsurgency in Rhodesia." *Military Review* (March 1979): 26–39.

Brunot, Patrick and Viatcheslav Avioutski. *La Tchétchenie.* Paris: Presses Universitaires de France, 1998.

Builder, Carl. *The Masks of War: American Military Styles in Strategy and Analysis.* Baltimore, MD: Johns Hopkins University Press, 1989.

Bulloch, Gavin. "The Development of Doctrine for Counterinsurgency—The British Experience." *The British Army Review* (December 1995): 21–24.

———. "Military Doctrine and Counter-Insurgency: A British Perspective." *Parameters* (Summer 1996): 4–16.

Burger, Kim. "U.S. Joint Ops Urban Warfare Training 'Insufficient.'" *Jane's Defence Weekly.* 2 October 2002, World Wide Web Early Bird.

Burk, James, ed. *The Adaptive Military: Armed Forces in a Turbulent World,* 2nd ed. New Brunswick, NJ: Transaction Publishers, 1998.

Burroughs, Peter. "An Unreformed Army," in *The Oxford History of the British Army,* eds. David Chandler and Ian Beckett. New York: Oxford University Press, 1996.

Cable, Larry. "Reinventing the Round Wheel: Insurgency, Counter-Insurgency, and Peacekeeping Post Cold War." *Small Wars and Insurgencies* (Autumn 1993): 228–62.

Callwell, Charles C. E. *Small Wars: Their Principles and Practice.* London: His Majesty's Stationary Office, 1896.

Campbell, Kenneth J. "Once Burned, Twice Cautious: Explaining the Weinberger-Powell Doctrine," *Armed Forces and Society* (Spring 1998): 357–74.

Capra, Fritjof. *The Web of Life.* New York: Anchor Books, 1996.

Cassidy, Robert M. "Why Great Powers Fight Small Wars Badly." *Military Review* (September/October 2002): 41–53.

———. *Russia in Afghanistan and Chechnya: Military Strategic Culture and the Paradoxes of Asymmetric Conflict.* Carlisle, PA: Strategic Studies Institute, 2003.

———. "Back to the Street Without Joy: Counterinsurgency Lessons From Vietnam and Other Small Wars." *Parameters* (Summer 2004): 73–83.

———. *Peacekeeping in the Abyss: British and American Doctrine and Practice after the Cold War.* Westport, CT: Praeger, 2004.

Catton, Bruce. *A Stillness at Appomatox.* New York: Washington Square Press, 1953.

Celestan, Gregory J. *Wounded Bear: The Ongoing Russian Military Operation in Chechnya.* Fort Leavenworth, KS: Foreign Military Studies Office, hereafter, FMSO, 1996.

Center for Strategic and International Studies (CSIS) and the Association of the U.S. Army (AUSA). *Task Framework.* Post-Conflict Reconstruction. A Joint Project of the CSIS and AUSA. Washington, DC, May 2002.

Chandler, David and Ian Beckett, eds. *The Oxford History of the British Army.* New York: Oxford University Press, 1996.

Chapman, Anne W., et al. *Prepare the Army for War: A Historical Overview of the Army Training and Doctrine Command, 1973–1998.* Fort Monroe, VA: U.S. Army TRADOC Military History Office, 1998.

Chauprade, Aymeric. *Introduction à l'analyse Géopolitique.* Paris: Ellipses, 1999.

Cheney, Dick. *Defense Strategy for the 1990s: The Regional Defense Strategy.* Washington, DC: GPO, January 1993.

Childs, John. "The Restoration Army, 1660–1702," in *The Oxford History of the British Army,* eds. David Chandler and Ian Beckett. New York: Oxford University Press, 1996.

Chivers, C. J. and Steven Lee Myers. "Chechen Rebels Mainly Driven by Nationalism." *The New York Times,* 12 September 2004.

Churchill, Winston S. *The River War.* London: Prion, 1997.

Clarke, Jeffrey J. *Advice and Support: The Final Years.* Washington: U.S. Army Center of Military History, 1988.

Clarke, Walter and Robert Gosende. "The Political Component: The Missing Vital Element in U.S. Intervention Planning." *Parameters* (Autumn 1996): 35–51.

Clayton, Anthony. *The End of Empire: The Experience of Britain, France, and the Soviet Union/Russia Compared.* Occasional Number 17. Camberley, UK: Strategic and Combat Studies Institute, 1996.

Cline, Lawrence E. *Pseudo Operations and Counterinsurgency: Lessons From Other Countries.* Carlisle, PA: Strategic Studies Institute, 2005.

Cohen, Elliot A. "Constraints on America's Conduct of Small Wars." *International Security* (Fall 1984): 151–81.

———. *Making Do With Less, or Coping With Upton's Ghost.* Carlisle, PA: U.S. Army War College Strategic Studies Institute, May 1995.

Cole, Barbara. *The Elite: The Story of the Rhodesian Special Air Service.* Transkei, South Africa: Three Knights, 1985.

Coll, Steven and Susan B. Glasser. "The Web as Weapon." *Washington Post,* 9 August 2005.

Collins, Joseph W. "The Soviet-Afghan War: The First Four Years." *Parameters* (Summer 1984): 50–51.

Commander in Chief Far East, French Armed Forces. *Lessons of the War in Indochina, Volume 2,* trans. V. J. Croizat. Memorandum RM-5271-PR. Santa Monica, CA: RAND Corporation, 1967.

Cooper, Bert H., Jr. "Malaya (1948–1960)," in *History of Revolutionary Warfare, Volume IV.* eds. H. M. Hannon, R. S. Ballagh and J. A. Cope. West Point, NY: U.S. Military Academy Department of History, 1984.

Coppola, Francis Ford. *Gardens of Stone.* Produced by Columbia TriStar Home Video, 1987. Videocassette.

Cordesman, Anthony. "The West Is Mired in a Losing Battle." *London Financial Times,* 22 July 2004.

———. "An Effective U.S. Strategy for Iraq." Testimony to the Senate Foreign Relations Committee, 2 February 2005. Online. *Fifth Column Magazine.*

Crowe, William J., Jr. "What I've Learned." *Washingtonian* (November 1989): 109, in Christopher M. Gacek. *The Logic of Force: The Dilemma of Limited Force in American Foreign Policy.* New York: Columbia University Press, 1994.

Dauber, Cori. "Poisoning the Well: The Weinberger Doctrine and Public Argument Over Military Intervention." Unpublished manuscript, UNC Chapel Hill, 1998.

Davis, Vincent, ed. *Civil-Military Relations and the Not-Quite Wars of the Present and Future*. Carlisle, PA: Strategic Studies Institute, 1996.

Decker, George H. "Doctrine," *Army* (February 1961): 60–61.

Delbruck, Hans. *The Barbarian Invasions*, trans. Walter J. Renfroe, Jr. Lincoln: University of Nebraska Press, 1980.

Department of History. *Officer's Professional Reading Guide*. West Point, NY: U.S. Military Academy, 1996.

Dewar, James, et al. *Army Culture and Planning in a Time of Great Change*. Santa Monica, CA: RAND Corporation, 1996.

Dewar, Michael. *Brushfire Wars: Minor Campaigns of the British Army Since 1945*. London: Robert Hale, 1990.

Donnelly, Thomas and Vance Serchuk. "Fighting a Global Counterinsurgency." *National Security Outlook*, American Enterprise Institute Online, 2.

Doughty, Robert A. *The Evolution of U.S. Army Tactical Doctrine, 1946–76*. Leavenworth Paper No. 1. Ft Leavenworth, KS: U.S. Army CGSC, 1979.

Downie, Richard Duncan. *Learning from Conflict: The U.S. Military in Vietnam, El Salvador, and the Drug War*. Westport, CT: Praeger, 1998.

Dunlop, John B. *Russia Confronts Chechnya: Roots of a Separatist Conflict*. Cambridge, UK: Cambridge University Press, 1998.

Dunn, Peter M. "The American Army: The Vietnam War, 1965–1973," in *Armed Forces and Modern Counter-Insurgency*, eds. Ian Beckett and John Pimlott. New York: St. Martin's Press, Inc., 1985.

Edwards, Sean J. A. *Mars Unmasked: The Changing Face of Urban Operations*. Santa Monica, CA: RAND Corporation, 2000.

Eikenberry, Karl W. "Take No Casualties." *Parameters* (Summer 1996): 109–18.

Erickson, John. "The Development of Soviet Military Doctrine," in *The Origins of Contemporary Doctrine*, ed. John Gooch. Occasional Number 30. Camberley, UK: Strategic and Combat Studies Institute, 1997.

Expedit, Bernard. "Les Sovietiques en Afghanistan," in *Strategies de la Guerilla: Guerres Revolutionaires et Contre-Insurrections*, ed. Gerard Chaliand. Paris: Gallimard, 1984.

Fall, Bernard B. *Street Without Joy*. New York: Schocken Books, 1961.

———. "The Theory and Practice of Insurgency and Counterinsurgency." *Naval War College Review* (Winter 1998). Online version.

Farrell, Theo. "Sliding into War: The Somalia Syndrome and the U.S. Army Peace Operations Doctrine." *International Peacekeeping* (Summer 1995): 194–214.

———. "Making Sense of Doctrine," in *Doctrine and Military Effectiveness*, eds. Michael Duffy, Thee Farrell and Geoffrey Sloan. Exeter, England: Britannia Royal Naval College, 1997.

Fautua, David T. "The Long Pull Army: NSC 68, the Korean War, and the Creation of the Cold War U.S. Army." *The Journal of Military History* (January 1997): 93–120.

Finch, Raymond. *Why the Russian Military Failed in Chechnya*. Fort Leavenworth, KS: FMSO, 1997.

Fitton, Robert A. *Leadership Quotations from the Military Tradition*. Boulder, CO: Westview Press, 1993.

FM 100-23, Peace Operations. Washington, DC: U.S. Army, 1994.

FM 3-07, Stability Operations and Support Operations. Washington, DC: U.S. Army, 2003.

FM Interim (FMI) 3-07.22, Counterinsurgency Operations. Washington, DC: U.S. Army, 2004.

Foster, Edward. *NATO's Military in the Age of Crisis Management.* London: Royal United Services Institute for Defence Studies, 1995.

Forster, Anthony. Interview by author, 19 December 1993, Manchester, England.

French, David. *The British Way in Warfare: 1688–2000.* London: Unwin-Hyman, 1990.

Frontinus. *Strategems and Aqueducts of Rome,* trans. Charles E. Bennett. Cambridge, MA: Harvard University Press, 1997.

Gacek, Christopher M. *The Logic of Force: The Dilemma of Limited Force in American Foreign Policy.* New York: Columbia University Press, 1994.

Gale, Stephen. "Terrorism 2005: Overcoming the Failure of Imagination." Foreign Policy Research Institute. E-Notes. 16 August 2005.

Garnett, Sherman W. "Russia and Its Borderlands: A Geography of Violence." *Parameters* (Spring 1997): 6–7.

Gates, David. "The Transformation of the Army 1783–1815," in *The Oxford History of the British Army,* eds. David Chandler and Ian Beckett. New York: Oxford University Press, 1996.

Geertz, Clifford. *The Interpretation of Cultures.* New York: Basic Books, 1973.

Gentry, James. "Military Force in an Age of National Cowardice." *Washington Quarterly* (Autumn 1998): 179–91.

Grau, Lester W. *Changing Russian Tactics: The Aftermath of the Battle of Grozny,* Strategic Forum Number 38. Washington, DC: INSS, 1995.

———. *The Bear Went Over the Mountain: Soviet Combat Tactics in Afghanistan.* Washington, DC: NDU Press, 1996.

———. *Bashing the Laser Range Finder With a Rock.* Fort Leavenworth, KS: FMSO, 1997.

———. "Technology and the Second Chechen Campaign: Not All New and Not That Much," in *The Second Chechen War,* ed. Anne Aldis. Occasional Number 40. London: SCSI, 2000.

Gray, Colin S. "National Style in Strategy: The American Example." *International Security* (Fall 1981): 21–47.

———. "Strategic Culture as Context: The First Generation of Theory Strikes Back." *Review of International Studies* 25 (1999): 49–69.

Gray, David L. "New Age Military Progressives: U.S. Army Officer Professionalism in the Information Age," in *Army Transformation: A View From the Army War College,* ed. Williamson Murray. Carlisle, PA: Strategic Studies Institute, July 2001.

Greene, T. N., ed. *The Guerrilla and How to Fight Him.* Washington, DC: Praeger, 1962.

Griffith, Samuel B., II. "Guerrilla, Part I." *Marine Corps Gazette* (July 1950): 43.

Guelton, Frédéric. "The French Army Centre for Training and Preparation in Counter-Guerrilla Warfare (CIPCG) at Arzew." *Journal of Strategic Studies* (June 2002): 35–54.

Gwynn, Charles W. *Imperial Policing.* London: Macmillan and Company, 1934.

Gwynne Jones, Alun. "Training and Doctrine in the British Army Since 1945," in *The Theory and Practice of War,* ed. Michael Howard. New York: Praeger, 1966.

Hackett, John Winthrop. *The Profession of Arms.* London: The Times Publishing House, 1962.

Halperin, Morton H. *Bureaucratic Politics and Foreign Policy.* Washington, DC: The Brookings Institution, 1974.

Hammes, Thomas X. "4th Generation Warfare: Our Enemies Play to Their Strengths." *Armed Forces Journal* (November 2004): 42.

Handel, Michael. *Masters of War: Sun Tzu, Clausewitz, and Jomini.* Portland, OR: Frank Cass and Co. Ltd., 1992.

Hashim, Ahmed S. "The World According to Osama Bin Laden." *Naval War College Review* (Autumn 2001), online archives, 4.

Haswell, Jock. *The British Army: A Concise History.* London: Book Club Associates, 1977.

Hauner, Milan. *The Soviet War in Afghanistan: Patterns of Russian Imperialism.* Philadelphia, PA: University Press of America, 1991.

Head, William and Earl H. Tilford Jr., eds. *The Eagle in the Desert.* Westport, CT: Praeger, 1996.

Hedges, Stephen P. "Military Voices Say Blame Isn't All on Civilians." *Chicago Tribune*, 15 August 2004.

Herbert, Paul H. *"Deciding What Has to Be Done": General William E. Depuy and the 1976 Edition of FM 100-5, Operations.* Leavenworth Paper No. 16. Fort Leavenworth, KS: Combat Studies Institute, U.S. Army CGSC, 1988.

Highland, Grant R. "New Century, Old Problems: The Global Insurgency Within Islam and the Nature of the Terror War." *Essays 2003.* Washington, DC: NDU Press, 2003.

Hoffman, Bruce. *Al Qaeda, Trends in Terrorism and Future Potentialities: An Assessment.* Santa Monica, CA: RAND Corporation, 2003.

———. "Redefining Counterterrorism: The Terrorist Leader as CEO." *RAND Review* (Spring 2004): 15.

Hoffman, Bruce, Jennifer Taw and David Arnold. *Lessons for Contemporary Counterinsurgencies: The Rhodesian Experience.* Santa Monica, CA: RAND Corporation, 1991.

Hoffman, F. G. *Decisive Force: The New American Way of War.* Westport, CT: Praeger, 1996.

Horne, Alistair. *A Savage War of Peace.* London: Macmillan London Limited, 1977.

Howard, Michael, ed. *The Theory and Practice of War.* New York: Praeger, 1966.

———. *The Continental Commitment.* Bristol, Great Britain: Western Printing Services Ltd., 1972.

———. *War in European History.* New York: Oxford University Press, 1977.

———. "The Forgotten Dimensions of Strategy." *Foreign Affairs* (Summer 1979): 975–86.

Huntington, Samuel P. *The Soldier and the State: The Theory and Politics of Civil-Military Relations.* Cambridge, MA: The Belknap Press, 1957.

———. "The Evolution of U.S. National Strategy," in *U.S. National Security Strategy for the 1990s*, eds. Daniel J. Kaufman, David S. Clark and Kevin P. Sheehan. Baltimore, MD: Johns Hopkins University Press, 1991.

Ignatieff, Michael. "The Challenges of American Imperial Power." *Naval War College Review* (Spring 2003): 53–54.

Jacobsen, Carl, ed. *Strategic Power USA/USSR.* New York: St Martin's Press, 1990.

Janowitz, Morris. *The Professional Soldier.* New York: The Free Press, 1960.

Jeffrey, Keith. "Colonial Warfare 1900–39," in *Warfare in the Twentieth Century: Theory and Practice*, eds. Colin McInnes and G. D. Sheffield. Winchester, MA: Unwin Hyman, Inc., 1988.

Jenkins, Brian M. *The Unchangeable War.* RM-6278-2-ARPA. Santa Monica, CA: RAND Corporation, 1970.

———. *Countering al Qaeda: An Appreciation of the Situation and Suggestions for Strategy.* Santa Monica, CA: RAND Corporation, 2002.

———. "Redefining the Enemy: The World Has Changed, but Our Mindset Has Not," *RAND Review* (Spring 2004): 16.

Joes, Anthony James. *America and Guerrilla Warfare.* Lexington, KY: University Press of Kentucky, 2000.

Joffe, Joseph. Unpublished presentation at the Conference on Religion and Terrorism. Harvard University. 21 November 2002.

Johnston, Alistair. "Thinking About Strategic Culture." *International Security* 19 (Spring 1995): 32–64.

———. *Cultural Realism: Strategic Culture and Grand Strategy in Chinese History.* Princeton, NJ: Princeton University Press, 1995.

Jones, David R. "Soviet Strategic Culture," in *Strategic Power USA/USSR*, ed. Carl G. Jacobsen. New York: St. Martin's Press, 1990.

Kafkalas, Peter N. "The Light Infantry Divisions and Low Intensity Conflict: Are They Losing Sight of Each Other?" *Military Review* (January 1986): 18–27.

Kaplan, Robert D. *Imperial Grunts: The American Military on the Ground.* New York: Random House, 2005.

Kaufman, Daniel J., David S. Clark and Kevin P. Sheehan, eds. *U.S. National Security Strategy for the 1990s.* Baltimore, MD: Johns Hopkins University Press, 1991.

Keegan, John. A *History of Warfare.* New York: Vintage Books, 1993.

Kelley, Francis J. *U.S. Army Special Forces 1961–1971.* Washington, DC: Department of the Army, 2004.

Kellog, Robert H. "Evaluating Psychological Operations: Planning Measures of Effectiveness." *Special Warfare* (May 2004), Online.

Kennan, George F. "The Sources of Soviet Conduct." *Foreign Affairs* (Summer 1987): 855–56.

Kennedy, Paul. *The Rise and Fall of the Great Powers.* New York: Random House, 1987.

Keohane, Robert O., ed. *NeoRealism and Its Critics.* New York: Columbia University Press, 1986.

Kier, Elizabeth. "Culture and Military Doctrine: France Between the Wars." *International Security* (Spring 1995): 65–93.

Kilcullen, David. "Countering Global Insurgency." Unpublished paper, Canberra, Australia, November 2004.

King, Gary, Robert O. Keohane and Sidney Verba. *Designing Social Inquiry.* Princeton, NJ: Princeton University Press, 1994.

Kissinger, Henry. "American Strategic Doctrine and Diplomacy," in *The Theory and Practice of War*, ed. Michael Howard. New York: Praeger, 1966.

———. "The Vietnam Negotiations." *Foreign Affairs* (January 1969): 211–34.

———. *Diplomacy.* New York: Simon and Schuster, 1994.

———. Landon Lecture. Kansas State University, 29 April 1996.

Klein, Bradley S. "Hegemony and Strategic Culture: American Power Projection and Alliance Defence Politics." *Review of International Studies* (1988): 133–48.

Klein, Yitzhak. "A Theory of Strategic Culture." *Comparative Strategy* (1991): 3–23.

Knezys, Stasys and Romanas Sedlickas. *The War in Chechnya.* College Station, TX: Texas University Press, 1999.

Knorr, Klaus, ed. *Power, Strategy, and Security: A World Politics Reader*. Princeton, NJ: Princeton University Press, 1983.

Kopets, Keith F. "The Combined Action Program: Vietnam." *Military Review* (July–August 2002): 78–79.

Krepinevich, Andrew F. *The Army and Vietnam*. Baltimore, MD: Johns Hopkins University Press, 1986.

Kupperman, Robert H., and Associates, Inc., *Low Intensity Conflict, Vol. 1, Main Report*. AD-A 137260. Fort Monroe, VA: U.S. Army Training and Doctrine Command, 1983.

Larsen, Eric V. *Casualties and Consensus: The Historical Role of Casualties in Domestic Support for U.S. Military Operations*. Santa Monica, CA: RAND Corporation, 1996.

Lee, Emanoel. *To the Bitter End*. New York: Viking Penguin Inc., 1985.

Legro, Jeffrey W. "Military Culture and Inadvertent Escalation in World War II." *International Security* (Spring 1994): 108–42.

———. "Culture and Preferences in the International Cooperation Two-Step." *American Political Science Review* (March 1996): 118–38.

Lewis, Bernard. "License to Kill: Osama bin Laden's Declaration of Jihad," *Foreign Affairs* (November–December 1998): 15.

———. "The Revolt of Islam." *The New Yorker*, 19 November 2001, Online Archives, 3.

Liddell Hart, B. H. *The British Way in Warfare*. New York: The Macmillan Company, 1933.

———. *When Britain Goes to War: Adaptability and Mobility*. London: Faber and Faber Limited, 1935.

———. *Strategy*, 2nd ed. New York: Praeger, 1967.

Lieven, Anatol. *Chechnya: Tombstone of Russian Power*. New Haven, CT: Yale University Press, 1999.

Lind, William S., et al. "The Changing Face of War: Into the Fourth Generation." Abridged. *Marine Corps Gazette* (October 1989): 25–26.

Litwak, Robert S. "The Soviet Union in Afghanistan," in *Foreign Military Intervention: The Dynamics of Protracted Conflict*, eds. Aeriel E. Levite, Bruce W. Jentleson, and Larry Berman. New York: Columbia University Press, 1992.

Locher, James R., 3rd. "The Goldwater-Nichols Act: Ten Years Later." *Joint Forces Quarterly* (Autumn 1996): 10–17.

Lohman, Charles M. and Robert I. MacPherson. "War Since 1945 Seminar, Rhodesia: Tactical Victory, Strategic Defeat, Synopsis." Quantico, VA: Marine Corps Command and Staff College, Marine Corps Development and Education Command, 7 June 1983.

Lord, Carnes. "American Strategic Culture." *Comparative Strategy* (Fall 1985): 269–91.

Lowe, Christian. "DOD Seeks Benchmarks for War on Terror." *Defense News*, 14 March 2005.

Luttwak, Edward N. "Toward Post-Heroic Warfare." *Foreign Affairs* (May/June 1995): 116.

Macgregor, Douglas A. *Breaking the Phalanx: A New Design for Landpower in the 21st Century*. Westport, CT: Praeger, 1997.

Mack, Andrew. *The Concept of Power and Its Uses in Explaining Asymmetric Conflict*. London: Richardson Institute for Conflict and Peace Research, 1974.

Mack, Andrew. "Why Big Nations Lose Small Wars," in *Power, Strategy, and Security: A World Politics Reader*, ed. Klaus Knorr. Princeton, NJ: Princeton University Press, 1983.

Mackinder, Halford. "The Geographical Pivot of History." *The Geographical Journal* (1904): 423–36.

Mackinlay, John. "Improving Multifunctional Forces." *Survival* (Autumn 1994): 149–73.

———. "War Lords." *RUSI Journal* (April 1998): 24–32.

———. Telephone interview by author, 16 March 2000, West Point, NY.

———. Telephone interview by author, 17 March 2000, West Point, NY.

———. *Globalization and Insurgency.* Adelphi Paper 352. London: The International Institute for Strategic Studies, 2002.

———. *Defeating Complex Insurgency,* Whitehall Paper 64. London: RUSI, 2005.

Mackinlay, John and Jarat Chopra. *A Draft Concept of Second Generation Multinational Operations 1993.* Providence, RI: Thomas J. Watson Institute for International Studies, 1993.

Mackinlay, John and Randolph Kent. "Complex Emergencies Doctrine: The British Are Still the Best." *The RUSI Journal* (April 1997): 39–44.

Macmillan, Alan. "Strategic Culture and National Ways in Warfare: The British Case." *RUSI Journal* (October 1995): 33–38.

Mariano, Stephen J. "Peacekeepers Attend the Never Again School." Master's Thesis, U.S. Naval Postgraduate School, 1995.

Matloff, Maurice. "The American Approach to War: 1919–1945," in *The Theory and Practice of War,* ed. Michael Howard. New York: Praeger, 1966.

———. "Allied Strategy in Europe, 1939–1945," in *Makers of Modern Strategy,* ed. Peter Paret. Princeton, NJ: Princeton University Press, 1986.

McInnes, Colin. *Hot War, Cold War: The British Army's Way in Warfare 1945–1995.* Washington, DC: Brassey's, 1996.

McInnes, Colin and G. D. Sheffield, eds. *Warfare in the Twentieth Century: Theory and Practice.* Winchester, MA: Unwin Hyman, Inc., 1988.

McIntosh, Scott E. "Leading With the Chin: Using Svechin to Analyze the Soviet Incursion Into Afghanistan, 1979–1989." *The Journal of Slavic Military Studies* (June 1995): 420.

McMichael, Scott R. "The Soviet Army, Counter-Insurgency, and the Afghan War," *Parameters* (December 1989): 21–22.

McNamara, Robert S. *In Retrospect: The Tragedy and Lessons of Vietnam.* New York: Times Books, 1995.

Metz, Steven. "Insurgency and Counterinsurgency in Iraq." *The Washington Quarterly* (Winter 2003–2004): 28.

Metz, Steven and Raymond Millen. *Insurgency and Counterinsurgency in the 21st Century: Reconceptualizing Threat and Response.* Carlisle, PA: U.S. Army Strategic Studies Institute, 2004.

Mileham, Patrick. "Ethos: British Army Officership 1962–1992." *The Occasional Number 19.* Camberley, England: Strategic and Combat Studies Institute, 1996.

Mockaitis, Thomas R. *British Counterinsurgency, 1919–60.* New York: St. Martin's Press, 1990.

———. "A New Era of Counter-Insurgency." *The RUSI Journal* (Spring 1991): 73–78.

———. "Low-Intensity Conflict: The British Experience." *Conflict Quarterly* (Winter 1993): 7–16.

Moorcraft, Paul. "Can Al Qaeda Be Defeated?" *Armed Forces Journal* (July 2004): 30–33.

Moore, Robin. *Rhodesia*. New York: Condor, 1977.

Morris, Michael F. "Al Qaeda as Insurgency." Unpublished paper. Carlisle, PA: U.S. Army War College, March 2005.

Moskos, Charles C., John Allen Williams and David R. Segal, eds. *The Postmodern Military*. New York: Oxford University Press, 2000.

Motley, James B. "U.S. Unconventional Conflict Policy and Strategy." *Military Review* (January 1990): 2–16.

Murray, Williamson, ed. *Army Transformation: A View From the Army War College*. Carlisle, PA: Strategic Studies Institute, July 2001.

Murray, Williamson and Allan R. Millett, eds. *Military Innovation in the Interwar Period*. New York: Cambridge University Press, 1996.

Nagl, John. "Learning to Eat Soup With a Knife: British and American Counterinsurgency Learning During the Malayan Emergency and the Vietnam War." Unpublished Ph.D. dissertation, Oxford University, 1997.

———. "Learning to Eat Soup With a Knife." *World Affairs* (Spring 1999): 193–99.

Newman, Richard J. "Vietnam's Forgotten Lessons." *U.S. News and World Report*, 1 May 2000.

Odom, William E. and Robert Dujarric. *Commonwealth or Empire?* Indianapolis: Hudson Institute, 1995.

Olsen, Howard and John Davis. *Training U.S. Army Officers for Peace Operations*. Special Report. Washington, DC: United States Institute of Peace, 1999.

Paret, Peter. *French Revolutionary Warfare From Indochina to Algeria*. New York: Praeger, 1964.

———, ed. *Makers of Modern Strategy*. Princeton, NJ: Princeton University Press, 1986.

Paret, Peter and John W. Shy. *Guerrillas in the 1960's*. New York: Frederick A. Praeger Publishers, 1962.

Pelli, Frank. "Insurgency, Counterinsurgency, and the Marines in Vietnam." Unpublished paper. Quantico, VA: USMC Command and Staff College, 1990.

Peters, Ralph. "The New Warrior Class." *Parameters* (Summer 1994): 16.

———. "The Future of Armored Warfare." *Parameters* (Autumn 1997): 50–59.

Petraeus, David H. "Lessons of History and Lessons of Vietnam." *Parameters* (Autumn 1986): 43–53.

Pfaltzgraff, Robert L. and Richard H. Shultz, Jr., eds. *The United States Army: Challenges and Missions for the 1990s*. Lexington, MA: Lexington Books, 1991.

Pimlott, John. "The British Army: The Dhofar Campaign, 1970–1975," in *Armed Forces and Modern Counter-Insurgency*, eds. Ian F. W. Beckett and John Pimlott. New York: St. Martin's Press, Inc., 1985.

Pintner, Walter. "Russian Military Thought: The Western Model and the Shadow of Suvorov," in *Makers of Modern Stategy*, ed. Peter Paret. Princeton, NJ: Princeton University Press, 1986.

Pipes, Richard. "Is Russia Still an Enemy?" *Foreign Affairs* (September/October 1997): 68.

Porch, Douglas. *The French Foreign Legion*. New York: HarperCollins Publishers, 1991.

Posen, Barry R. *The Sources of Military Doctrine: France, Britain, and Germany Between the World Wars*. Ithaca, NY: Cornell University Press, 1984.

Powell, Colin. *My American Journey*. New York: Random House, 1995.

Pye, Lucien W. and Sydney Verba, eds. *Political Culture and Political Development*. Princeton, NJ: Princeton University Press, 1965.

Record, Jeffrey. *Beyond Military Reform: American Defense Dilemmas.* New York: Pergamon-Brassey's, 1988.

Reid-Daly, Ron. *Selous Scouts, Top Secret War.* Galago, RSA, 1982.

Reid-Daly, R. F. *Pamwe Chete: The Legend of the Selous Scouts.* Weltevreden Park, South Africa: Covos-Day Books, 1999.

Rice, Condoleezza. "The Making of Soviet Strategy," in *Makers of Modern Stategy,* ed. Peter Paret. Princeton, NJ: Princeton University Press, 1986.

Romer, Jean-Christophe. Lecture, French Joint Defense College, 22 January 2001.

Romjue, John L. *American Army Doctrine for the Post-Cold War.* Fort Monroe, VA: U.S. Army Training and Doctrine Command Military History Office, 1997.

―――. *The Army of Excellence: The Development of the 1980s Army.* Fort Monroe, VA: U.S. Army Training and Doctrine Command, Military History Office, 1997.

Rosen, Stephen P. *Winning the Next War: Innovation and the Modern Military.* Ithaca: Cornell University Press, 1991.

―――. "Military Effectiveness: Why Society Matters." *International Security* (Spring 1995): 5–31.

Roy, Ian. "Towards the Standing Army, 1485–1660," in *The Oxford History of the British Army.* eds. David Chandler and Ian Beckett. New York: Oxford University Press, 1996.

Roy, Olivier. *The Lessons of the Soviet/Afghan War.* Adelphi Paper 259. London: International Institute for Strategic Studies, 1991.

Sapolsky, Harvey M. "On the Theory of Military Innovation." *Breakthroughs* (Spring 2000): 35–39.

Sapolsky, Harvey M. and Jeremy Shapiro. "Casualties, Technology, and America's Future Wars." *Parameters* (Summer 1996): 119–27.

Sarkesian, Sam C. *America's Forgotten Wars: The Counterrevolutionary Past and Lessons for the Future.* Westport, CT: Greenwood Press, 1984.

―――. "The Myth of U.S. Capability in Unconventional Conflicts." *Military Review* (September 1988): 2–17.

Scales, Robert H. "Adaptive Enemies: Achieving Victory by Avoiding Defeat." *Joint Forces Quarterly* (Autumn/Winter 1999–2000): 7–13.

Scarborough, Rowan. "Metrics Help Guide Pentagon." *Washington Times,* 5 April 2005.

Schein, Edgar. "Organizational Culture." *American Psychologist* (February 1990): 109–19.

Schneider, James J. *The Structure of Strategic Revolution.* Novato, CA: Presidio Press, 1994.

Segal, David R. and Dana P. Eyre. "The U.S. Army in Peace Operations at the Dawn of the Twenty-First Century." Unpublished report (draft) prepared for the U.S. Army Research Institute for the Behavioral and Social Sciences, 1994.

Shultz, Richard H., Jr. "Doctrine and Forces for Low Intensity Conflict," in *The United States Army: Challenges and Missions for the 1990s,* eds. Robert L. Pfaltzgraff and Richard H. Shultz, Jr. Lexington, MA: Lexington Books, 1991.

―――. *The Secret War Against Hanoi.* New York: HarperCollins Publishers, 1999.

Shultz, Richard H., Douglas Farah and Itamara V. Lochard. *Armed Groups: A Tier—One Security Priority.* INSS Occasional Paper 57. USAF Academy, CO: Institute for National Security Studies, 2004.

Shy, John. "The American Military Experience: History and Learning." *Journal of Interdisciplinary History* (Winter 1971): 205–28.

Shy, John and Thomas W. Collier. "Revolutionary War," in *Makers of Modern Strategy*, ed. Peter Paret. Princeton, NJ: Princeton University Press, 1986.

Simkins, Peter. "The Four Armies 1914–1918," in *The Oxford History of the British Army*, eds. David Chandler and Ian Beckett. New York: Oxford University Press, 1996.

Singh, Bikram. "Touchstones of Military Leadership Engaged in Asymmetric Warfare." Unpublished thesis. Carlisle Barracks, PA: U.S. Army War College, March 2004.

Smith, James M. "USAF Culture and Cohesion: Building an Air Force and Space Force for the 21st Century." *INSS Occasional Paper 19*. Colorado Springs, CO: U.S. Air Force INSS, 1996.

Smith, Richard. "The Requirement for the United Nations to Develop an Internationally Recognized Doctrine for the Use of Force in Intra-State Conflict." *Occasional Paper Number 10*. Camberley, England: Strategic and Combat Studies Institute, 1994.

Snider, Don M. "U.S. Civil-Military Relations and Operations Other Than War." In *Civil-Military Relations and the Not-Quite Wars of the Present and Future*, ed. Vincent Davis. Carlisle Barracks, PA: Strategic Studies Institute, 1996.

———. "An Uninformed Debate on Military Culture." *Orbis* (Winter 1999): 1–16.

———. "Postmodern Soldiers." *World Policy Journal* (Spring 2000): 47–54.

Snider, Don M., John A. Nagl and Tony Pfaff. *Army Professionalism, the Military Ethic, and Officers in the 21st Century*. Carlisle, PA: U.S. Army War College Strategic Studies Institute, December 1999.

Snow, Donald M. *The Shape of the Future*, 2nd ed. New York: M. E. Sharpe, 1995.

Snyder, Jack. *The Soviet Strategic Culture: Implications for Limited Nuclear Operations*. Santa Monica, CA: RAND Corporation, 1977.

———. "The Concept of Strategic Culture: Caveat Emptor," in *Strategic Power USA/USSR*, ed. Carl G. Jacobsen. New York: St Martin's Press, 1990.

Sorley, Lewis. *A Better War*. New York: Harcourt Brace & Company, 1999.

Spiers, Edward. "The Late Victorian Army," in *The Oxford History of the British Army*, eds. David Chandler and Ian Beckett. New York: Oxford University Press, 1996.

Stevenson, Charles A. "The Evolving Clinton Doctrine on the Use of Force." *Armed Forces and Society* 22 (Summer 1996): 511–25.

Stoessinger, John G. *Why Nations Go to War*, 5th ed. New York: St. Martin's Press, 1990.

Strachan, Hew. "The British Way in Warfare," in *The Oxford History of the British Army*. eds. David Chandler and Ian Beckett. New York: Oxford University Press, 1996.

———. *The Politics of the British Army*. New York: Clarendon Press, 1997.

Strawson, John. "The Thirty Years Peace," in *The Oxford History of the British Army*, eds. David Chandler and Ian Beckett. New York: Oxford University Press, 1996.

Stroup, Theodore G., Jr. "Leadership and Organizational Culture: Actions Speak Louder Than Words." *Military Review* (January–February 1996): 44–49.

Summers, Harry G., Jr. *On Strategy: A Critical Analysis of the Vietnam War*. Novato, CA: Presidio Press, 1982.

Taber, Robert and Bard O'Neill. *The War of the Flea: Guerrilla Warfare in Theory and Practice*. New York: Lyle Stuart, Inc., 1965.

Tho, Tran Dinh. *Pacification*. Washington, DC: U.S. Army Center of Military History, 1997.

Thomas, Timothy. *The Caucasus Conflict and Russian Security: The Russian Armed Forces Confront Chechnya, Part III*. Fort Leavenworth, KS: FMSO, 1997.

————. "The Battle of Grozny: Deadly Classroom for Urban Combat." *Parameters* (Summer 1999): 87–102.

Thompson, Loren B., ed. *Low-Intensity Conflict: The Pattern of Warfare in the Modern World*. Lexington, MA: Lexington Books, 1989.

Thompson, Robert. "Emergency in Malaya," in *War in Peace; Conventional and Guerrilla Warfare since 1945*, ed. Sir Robert Thompson. New York: Harmony Books, 1982.

Toczek, David M. *The Battle of Ap Bac, Vietnam: They Did Everything but Learn From It*. Westport: Greenwood Press, 2001.

Travers, Tim. "The Army and the Challenge of War 1914–1918," in *The Oxford History of the British Army*, eds. David Chandler and Ian Beckett. New York: Oxford University Press, 1996.

Trevis, Major Anthony, British Army. Interview by author, 14 April 2000, West Point, NY.

Tse-Tung, Mao. *On Protracted War*. Peking: Foreign Language Press, 1967, 9–10.

————. *On Guerrilla Warfare*, trans. Samuel B. Griffith, II. Champaign, IL: University of Illinois Press, 2000.

Tsygankov, Andrei P. "Hardline Eurasianism and Russia's Contending Geopolitical Perspectives." *Eastern European Quarterly* 32 (Fall 1998): 317–20.

Tuchman, Barbara. *The March of Folly: From Troy to Vietnam*. New York: Ballantine Books, 1984.

Tucker, David. "Fighting Barbarians." *Parameters* (Summer 1998): 69.

Turabian, Kate L. *A Manual for Writers*, 5 th ed. Chicago: University of Chicago Press, 1987.

Tzu, Sun. *The Art of War*, trans. Samuel B. Griffith. New York: Oxford University Press, 1982.

U.S. Army. *A Program for the Pacification and Long-Term Development of South Vietnam*. Washington, DC: Department of the Army, 1966.

U.S. Marine Corps Center for Emerging Threats and Opportunities (CETO). *CETO Quick Look: Dealing With the Civilian Population in Post-Saddam Iraq*. 6 February 2003.

U.S. Marine Corps. *Small Wars Manual*. Washington, DC: Government Printing Office, 1940.

U.S. Marine Corps Combat Development Command. *Small Wars*, Draft. Quantico, VA: U.S. Marines Corps, 2004.

Utley, Harold H. "An Introduction to the Tactics and Techniques of Small Wars." *The Marine Corps Gazette* (August 1933): 45–46

Utley, Robert M. *Frontiersmen in Blue*. New York: Macmillan Company, 1967.

————. *Frontier Regulars: The United States Army and the Indian, 1866–1890*. New York: Macmillan Publishing Co., Inc., 1973.

————. "The Contribution of the Frontier to the American Military Tradition." *The Harmon Memorial Lecture Series Number 19*. Colorado Springs, CO: U.S. Air Force Academy, 1977.

Van Dyke, Carl. "Kabul to Grozny: A Critique of Soviet (Russian) Counter-Insurgency Doctrine." *The Journal of Slavic Military Studies* (December 1996): 690–91.

Van Riper, Paul and Robert H. Scales. "Preparing for Warfare in the 21st Century." *Parameters* 27 (Autumn 1997): 4–14.

Verrier, Anthony. *An Army for the Sixties*. London: Secker and Warburg, 1966.

Vetock, Dennis J. *Lessons Learned: A History of U.S. Army Lesson Learning*. Carlisle Barracks, PA: U.S. Army Military History Institute, 1988.

Vlahos, Michael. "The End of America's Postwar Ethos." *Foreign Affairs* (Summer 1988): 1091–1107.

———. *Terror's Mask: The Insurgency Within Islam*. Laurel, MD: Johns Hopkins University Press, 2001.

von Bismarck, Otto. Cited in Griffith, Colonel Samuel B. II. "Guerrilla, Part I." *Marine Corps Gazette* (July 1950): 43.

Waddell, Ricky Lynn. "The Army and Peacetime Low Intensity Conflict 1961–1993: The Process of Peripheral and Fundamental Military Change." Ph.D. dissertation, Columbia University, 1994.

Ware, Michael. "Inside Iran's Secret War for Iraq." *Time*, 22 August 2005.

Weigley, Russell F. *Towards an American Army: Military Thought From Washington to Marshall*. New York: Columbia University Press, 1962.

———. *History of the United States Army*. New York: Macmillan Publishing Company, Inc., 1967.

———. *The American Way of War: A History of United States Military Strategy and Policy*. Bloomington, IN: Indiana University Press, 1973.

———. *Eisenhower's Lieutenants, Volume I*. Baltimore: Johns Hopkins University Press, 1981.

———. *History of the United States Army*. Bloomington, IN: Indiana University Press, 1984.

———. "Reflections on Lessons From Vietnam," in *Vietnam as History*, ed. Peter Braestrup. Washington, DC: University Press of America, 1984.

———. "American Strategy From Its Beginnings Through the First World War," in *Makers of Modern Strategy*, ed. Peter Paret. Princeton, NJ: Princeton University Press, 1986.

Weinberger, Casper. "The Uses of Military Power." News Release 609-84. Washington, DC: Office of the Assistant Secretary of Defense for Public Affairs, November 1984.

Wells, Gordon M. *The Center of Gravity Fad: Consequence of the Absence of an Overarching American Theory of* War. Land Power Essay Number 01-01. Arlington, VA: AUSA Institute of Land Warfare, March 2001.

Weyand, Fred C. and Harry G. Summers, Jr. "Vietnam Myths and American Realities." *CDRS CALL*. Ft. Leavenworth, KS: U.S. Army CGSC, July–August 1976.

White, Duffy W. "Beneficial or Buzzword: Can Operational Commanders Use Measures of Effectiveness During Counterinsurgencies." Unpublished thesis. Newport, RI: U.S. Naval War College, May 2004.

Wilkie, Edith B. and Beth C. DeGrasse. *A Force for Peace: U.S. Commanders' Views of the Military's Role in Peace Operations*. Washington, DC: Peace Through Law Education Fund, 1999.

Willmott, H. P. "Mau Mau Terror," in *War in Peace: Conventional and Guerrilla Warfare since 1945*, ed. Sir Robert Thompson. New York: Harmony Books, 1982.

Wilson, John B. *Maneuver and Firepower: The Evolution of Divisions and Separate Brigades*. Washington, DC: U.S. Army Center of Military History, 1998.

Winton, Harold R. *To Change an Army*. Lawrence, KS: University Press of Kansas, 1988.

Worley, D. Robert. *Waging Ancient War: Limits on Preemptive Force*. Carlisle, PA: U.S. Army Strategic Studies Institute, 2003.

Yardley, Michael and Dennis Sewell. *A New Model Army*. London: W. H. Allen and Co., 1989.

Index

will (domestic cohesion), 21, 27–28
Wilson, John, 124
Wood, Leonard, 123
World War II (WWII), 44, 100–101, 111–12, 153
World War I (WWI), 79, 110–11, 113

Yeltsin, Boris, 61
Yermelov, Aleksey Petrrovich, 60, 61
Yom Kippur War, 102

Zarqawi, Abu Masab, 2, 13
zero-deaths syndrome, 29
Zimbabwe African National Union (ZANLA), 142
Zimbabwe African People's Union (ZAPU), 142
Zimbabwe People's Revolutionary Army (ZIPRA), 142
zones of peace and turmoil, 17